PROBLEM SOLUTIONS MANUAL
for the text

Economic Evaluation and Investment Decision Methods

Tenth Edition, 2000

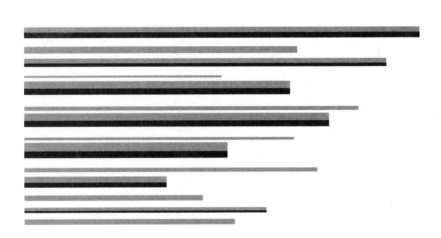

FRANKLIN J. STERMOLE
PROFESSOR EMERITUS, COLORADO SCHOOL OF MINES
CHAIRMAN, INVESTMENT EVALUATIONS CORPORATION

JOHN M. STERMOLE
INSTRUCTOR, COLORADO SCHOOL OF MINES
ADJUNCT PROFESSOR, UNIVERSITY OF DENVER COLLEGE OF LAW
PRESIDENT, INVESTMENT EVALUATIONS CORPORATION

INVESTMENT EVALUATIONS CORPORATION
3070 South Newcombe Way
Lakewood, Colorado 80227

This publication is designed to provide accurate and authoritative information in regard to the subject matter covered. It is sold with the understanding that neither the authors nor the publisher is engaged in rendering legal, accounting, tax, futures/securities trading, or other professional services. If legal advice or other expert assistance is required, the services of a competent professional person should be sought.

From a Declaration of Principles jointly adopted by a Committee of the American Bar Association and a Committee of Publishers.

Trademarks:

Microsoft Excel is a registered trademark of Microsoft Corporation.
HP10B, HP12C, HP17BII are registered trademarks of Hewlett Packard Company.
EVA is a registered trademark of G. Bennett Stewart III.

CHAPTER 2 PROBLEM SOLUTIONS

2-1 Solution: All Values in Millions

```
P=?     -       -    ................   - $70
_____
0       1       2    ...............  19  20 years
```

Calculating P given F:

$$P = 70(P/F_{7.0\%,20}) = \$18.088$$
(0.2584)

Calculating A Given F: *Calculating A Given P:*

$$A = 70(A/F_{7.0\%,20}) = \$1.707$$ $$A = 18.088(A/P_{7.0\%,20}) = \$1.707$$
(0.02439)   (0.09439)

Textbook Problem 2-1 Using Excel Functions

Calculating a Present Value "P" from Single Future Value.
Use the **PV** Wizard Function located in the **Insert** menu under *fx* **Function...**

Remember unlike most financial calculators, you must use the appropriate period "i" value in decimal form or label as a percentage!

Description of Calculation	Eq./ Result	Equation Form
Time 0 present value of $70,000,000 from the end of year 20	($18,089,330)	=PV(0.07,20,0,70000000)
Or, time 0 present value of $70,000,000 from the end of year 20	($18,089,330)	=PV(7%,20,0,70000000)
Or, calculating the present value "P" in a present worth equation:	$18,089,330	=70000000*(1/1.07^20)

By entering the values as a positive the displayed result is negative. You must have an investment (negative cash flow) to generate positive cash flow or before-tax revenue.

Unlike the textbook Single Payment Present Worth Factor, the PV function in most spreadsheets can serve as a combination of a P/F and P/A factor. Parameter order includes the discount rate, number of compounding periods, the amount of any uniform payment realized in each compounding period, "A" and, or a single future value, "F" realized during the final period as is the case in this problem.

2-2 Solution:

P=?	$15,000	$15,000	$15,000
0	1	2	3

Present Value:

$$P = 15,000 \overset{0.8696}{(P/F_{15\%,1})} + 15,000 \overset{0.7561}{(P/F_{15\%,2})} + 15,000 \overset{0.6575}{(P/F_{15\%,3})} = \$34,248$$

$$Or, \quad P = 15,000 \overset{2.2832}{(P/A_{15\%,3})} = \$34,248$$

Future Value:

$$F = 15,000 \overset{1.3225}{(F/P_{15\%,2})} + 15,000 \overset{1.1500}{(F/P_{15\%,1})} + 15,000 = \$52,088$$

$$Or, \quad F = 15,000 \overset{3.4725}{(F/A_{15\%,3})} = \$52,088$$

$$Or, \quad F = 34,248 \overset{1.5209}{(F/P_{15\%,3})} = \$52,088$$

Textbook Problem 2-2

Calculating a Present Value "P" from Several Future Values or a Uniform Series.
Use the **PV** and **FV** Wizard Functions located in the **Insert** menu under *fx* **Function...**

Description of Calculation	Eq./ Result	Equation Form
Time zero accumulation of the future values of $15,000 from the end of years	($34,248)	=PV(0.15,3,15000,0)
Or, time zero present value of $15,000 from the end of years 1, 2 & 3	($34,248)	=PV(0.15,1,0,15000)+PV(0.15,2,0,15000)+PV(0.15,3,0,15000)
Or, calculating the present value "P" using an P/A factor	$34,248	=15000*(1.15^3-1)/(0.15*(1.15^3))
End of year three accumulated future value of $15,000 from the end of years	($52,088)	=FV(0.15,3,15000,0)
Or, End of year three accumulated future value of $15,000 from the end of ye	($52,088)	=FV(0.15,2,0,15000)+FV(0.15,1,0,15000)-15000
Or, calculating the future value "F" using an F/A factor	$52,088	=15000*((1.15^3)-1)/0.15

2-3 Solution:

```
P=?     –        –     $15,000 $15,000 $15,000    –        –
                                                              F=?
0       1        2        3       4       5        6        7
```

$$P = 15,000\,(P/A_{15\%,3})\,(P/F_{15\%,2}) = \$25,895$$

with factors 2.2832 and 0.7561

$$F = 15,000\,(F/A_{15\%,3})\,(F/P_{15\%,2}) = \$68,886$$

with factors 3.4725 and 1.3225

$$F = 25,895\,(F/P_{15\%,7}) = \$68,881$$

with factor 2.6600

And,

$$P = 68,886\,(P/F_{15\%,7}) = \$25,894$$

with factor 0.3759

The differences in answers are due to factor round-off error.

Textbook Problem 2-3

Calculating Present and Future Values from a Uniform Series.
Use the PV and FV Wizard Function located in the Insert menu under fx Function...

> Calculating the present value from another present value is sometimes referred to as "nesting" a function inside of another function, or, creating a "nested" equation as follows:

Description of Calculation	Eq./ Result	Equation Form
Time zero accumulation of the future values of $15,000 from the end of years 3, 4 & 5	($25,897)	=-PV(0.15,2,0,PV(0.15,3,15000,0))
Or, time zero present value of $15,000 from the end of years 3, 4 & 5	($25,897)	=PV(0.15,1,0,15000)+PV(0.15,2,0,15000)+PV(0.15,3,0,15
Or, calculating the present value "P" using a P/A and P/F factor	$25,897	=15000*(1.15^3-1)/(0.15*(1.15^3))*(1/1.15)^2
End of year seven accumulated future value of $15,000 from the end of years 3, 4 & 5.	($68,886)	=-FV(0.15,2,0,FV(0.15,3,15000,0))
Or, End of year seven accumulated future value of $15,000 from the end of years 3, 4	($68,886)	=FV(0.15,4,0,15000)+FV(0.15,3,0,15000)+FV(0.15,2,0,150
Or, calculating the future value "F" using an F/A and F/P factor	$68,886	=15000*((1.15^3-1)/0.15)*(1.15)^2

2-4 Solution:

Case A, Solving for Annual Payments

$15,000   A=?   A=?   A=?   A=?
_____

   0   1   2   3   4 years

$$A = 15{,}000\,(A/P_{15\%,4}) \overset{0.35027}{=} \$5{,}254 \text{ per year}$$

Case B, Solving for Monthly Payments

$15,000   A=? A=? A=? . . . . . . A=?
_____

   0   1   2   3 . . . . . . 48 months

Period "i" = 15.0% per year / 12 months per year = 1.25% / month.

$$A = 15{,}000\,(A/P_{1.25\%,48}) \overset{0.02783}{=} \$417.46 \text{ per month}$$

Textbook Problem 2-4

Calculating a Uniform Series of Values "A" From a Present Value "P"
Use the **PMT** Wizard Function located in the **Insert** menu under *fx* **F**unction...

Annual Payments, Years 1-4

Description of Calculation	Eq./ Result	Equation Form
Solving for A in years one through four for a known present value is equivalent to determining the necessary mortgage payments on a four year loan with annual payments.	($5,254)	=PMT(0.15,4,15000)
Or, calculating the uniform series "A" using a Capital Recovery "A/P" Factor:	$5,254	=15000*((0.15*(1.15^4))/((1.15^4)-1))

Monthly Payments, Months 1-48

Description of Calculation	Eq./ Result	Equation Form
Solving for A in months one through fourty eight is the same procedure based on the appropriate period interest rate and compounding periods.	($417.46)	=PMT(0.15/12,48,15000)
Or, calculating the uniform series "A" using a Capital Recovery "A/P" Factor:	$417.46	=15000*((0.0125*(1.0125^48))/((1.0125^48)-1)

2-5 Solution: Values in Thousands

-	-	-	....	-	$30	$30	$30	$30
0	1	2	....	17	18	19	20	21

Case A, Calculating "P" at the End of Year 17, Given "A"

$$P = 30\overset{3.1699}{(P/A_{10.0\%,4})} = \$95.097$$

Case B, Calculating "P" at Time Zero, Given "F" or "A"

$$P = 30\overset{3.1699}{(P/A_{10.0\%,4})}\overset{0.1978}{(P/F_{10.0\%,17})} = \$18.810$$

Or, by taking the uniform series forward first:

$$P = 30\overset{4.6410}{(F/A_{10.0\%,4})}\overset{0.1351}{(P/F_{10.0\%,21})} = \$18.810$$

Case C, Calculating A in Years 1-17.

$$A_{1-17} = 18.810\overset{0.12466}{(A/P_{10\%,17})} = \$2.345$$

	A	B	C	D	E	F
1	**Textbook Problem 2-5**			*Sign convention is important to*		
2				*determine the appropriate*		
3				*present value, or investment required*		
4	Calculating a Present Value "P" and a Uniform Series "A" from Four Future Values			*today @ 10% per year to cover the*		
5	Use the **PV** and **PMT** Wizard Functions located in the Insert menu under *fx* Function...			*anticipated costs of college*		
6						
7						
8	**Calculating the Present Value Today of the Estimated Annual Cost of College**					
9	**Description of Calculation**	**Eq./ Result**		**Equation Form**		
10	End of year 17 present value of $30,000 from the end of years 18, 19, 20 & 2	($95,096)		=PV(0.1,4,30000,0)		
11	Time zero present value of end of year 17 present value (Cell B10).	($18,814)		=PV(0.1,17,0,-B10)		
12						
13	Or, time 0 present value in one equation	($18,814)		=PV(0.1,17,0,-PV(0.1,4,30000,0))		
14						
15	Calculating the equivalent annual payments in years 1-17 requires	($2,345)		=PMT(0.1,17,-B13)		
16	utilizing the PMT function, based on the time zero present value.					

2-6 Solution:

Loan A - Nominal Flat Interest Rate of 6.5%

    Down Payment = $20,000(0.20) = $4,000
    Total Interest Paid (Eq 2-14) = $16,000(0.065)(3 years) = $3,120

Loan Cost = $16,000 principal + $3,120 interest = $19,120

    Nominal 6.5% Flat Interest, Loan Payment Per Month
    A = $19,120 / 36 = $531.11

Loan B - Nominal Interest Rate of 9.0% Compounded Monthly

    Down Payment = $20,000(0.20) = $4,000

    Nominal 9.0% Compound Interest, Loan Payment Per Month
    Period Interest Rate = 0.090 / 12 = 0.0075 or 0.75% per month.

$$A = 16,000 \overset{0.03180}{(A/P_{0.75\%,36})} = \$508.80 \quad \text{(Lowest Monthly Cost)}$$

A comparison of the monthly loan payments concludes the least cost
approach is to select Loan Alternative B. Comparing the alternatives
by calculating the present cost for each follows:

Loan A: C=$4,000   C=$532.11 .... C=$532.11
           _____
            0   1   36

                                       31.00928
PW Cost @ 10.0% per month = 4,000 + 532.11(P/A_{0.83\%,36}) = $20,500

Loan B: C=$4,000   C=$508.80 .... C=$508.80
           _____
            0   1   36

                                       31.00928
PW Cost @ 10.0% per month = 4,000 + 508.80(P/A_{0.83\%,36}) = $19,778

*The lowest present worth cost is Loan Option B. This analysis
suggests that it is better to buy with the "B" scenario. Further, for
an investor with other interest opportunities at 10.0% compounded
monthly, it would make slightly better economic sense to buy with cash
than with the "A" alternative, but the Loan B scenario is the best.*

2-7 Solution:

$1,000 -   - $2,000   -   -   F=?
_____
    0   1 9   10   11..... 19   20 semi-annual periods

The nominal interest rate of 6% compounded semi-annually gives
semi-annual period interest, $i = 6\%/2 = 3\%$

$$\overset{1.8061}{\phantom{F = 1,000(F/P_{3,20})}} \quad \overset{1.3439}{}$$

$$F = 1{,}000(F/P_{3,20}) + 2{,}000(F/P_{3,10}) = \$4{,}494$$

For annual periods, use an effective interest rate/year:

$$E = (1+0.03)^2 - 1 = 0.0609$$

$$F = 1{,}000(F/P_{6.09\%,10}) + 2{,}000(F/P_{6.09\%,5}) = \$4{,}494$$

2-8 Solution:

            A=$500   A=$500 . . .   A=$500
P = ? _____
       0   1   2 . . . . 20 semi-annual periods

$i = 4\%$ per semi-annual period for a nominal interest rate of
8% compounded semi-annually.

$$\overset{13.5903}{\phantom{P = 500(P/A_{4\%,20})}}$$

$$P = 500(P/A_{4\%,20}) = \$6{,}795$$

2-9 Solution:

P=$5,000   A   A .... A
_____ F=$10,000
    0   1   2 6

$$\overset{0.20336}{\phantom{A = 5,000(A/P_{6,6})}} \quad \overset{0.14336}{}$$

$$A = 5{,}000(A/P_{6,6}) + 10{,}000(A/F_{6,6}) = \$2{,}450$$

$$\overset{0.7050}{} \quad \overset{0.20336}{}$$

$$A = [5{,}000 + 10{,}000(P/F_{6,6})](A/P_{6,6}) = \$2{,}450$$

$$\overset{1.4185}{} \quad \overset{0.14336}{}$$

$$A = [5{,}000(F/P_{6,6}) + 10{,}000](A/F_{6,6}) = \$2{,}450$$

2-10 Solution:

P=$3,000   A .... A
━━
  0   1 .... 36 months

Nominal interest rate "r" is 12.0% compounded monthly, therefore, the period interest rate "i" = 12.0%/12 months, or 1.0% per month.

$(A/P_{1.0\%,36})$ = $0.01(1.01)^{36} / ((1.01)^{36} - 1) = 0.03321$

$$A = 3,000(A/P_{1.0\%,36}) = \$99.63$$

with 0.03321 shown above.

2-11 Solution:

-       A   A .... A
━━ F = $10,000
0   1   2 .... 20 quarterly periods

i = 1.5% per period

$A/F_{1.0\%,20} = 0.04542$
$A/F_{2.0\%,20} = 0.04116$

Interpolating: $(0.04542 - 0.04116)/2 = 0.00213$

$(A/F_{1.5\%,20}) = 0.04542 - 0.00213 = 0.04329$

$$A = 10,000(A/F_{1.5\%,20}) = \$432.90$$

with 0.04329 shown above.

Mathematically, without interpolation:

$A/F_{1.5\%,20} = 0.015/(1.015)^{20} - 1 = 0.043246$

$A = 10,000(0.043246) = \$432.46$ (correct result)

The difference between $432.90 and $432.46 is interpolation error

2-12 Solution:

```
P=?      $1,000     $1,000 . . . . . $1,000
_____
0          1          2 . . . . . . .  10 years
0    1     2     3     4 . . . . . . .  20 semi-annual periods
```

r=8% compounded semi-annually, so i=4% per semi-annual period.

$$A = 1{,}000\,\overset{0.49020}{(A/F_{4\%,2})} = \$490.20$$

An equivalent time diagram:

```
P=?    490.2    490.2    490.2    490.2 . . . . $490.2
_____
0        1        2        3        4 . . . . . . 20
```

$$P = 490.2\,\overset{13.5903}{(P/A_{4\%,20})} = \$6{,}661.97$$

Or, find the effective interest rate, E, per year:

$$P = 1{,}000\,(P/A_{E\%,10})$$
$$E = (1 + 0.04)^2 - 1 = 0.0816 = 8.16\%$$

Explicitly solving for the factor given E = 8.16% yields:

$$P/A_{8.16\%,10} = \frac{(1.0816)^{10}-1}{0.0816(1.0816)^{10}} = 6.66192$$

$$P = 1{,}000(6.66192) = \$6{,}661.92 \text{ difference above due to round-off}$$

Or, by treating each cash flow as a unique future value "F,"

$$\text{Alternately, } P=1{,}000[\overset{0.9246}{P/F_{4,2}} + \overset{0.8548}{P/F_{4,4}} + \overset{0.7903}{P/F_{4,6}} + \ldots + \overset{0.4564}{P/F_{4,20}}]= \$6{,}662$$

2-13 Solution:

$3,000	$6,000	$7,000	$7,000	$4,000
0	1	2	3	4

$$P = 3{,}000 + 6{,}000 \overset{0.8929}{(P/F_{12,1})} + 7{,}000 \overset{0.7972}{(P/F_{12,2})} + 7{,}000 \overset{0.7118}{(P/F_{12,3})}$$

$$+ 4{,}000 \overset{0.6355}{(P/F_{12,4})} = \$21{,}462$$

Or,

$$P = 3{,}000 + 6{,}000 \overset{0.8929}{(P/F_{12,1})} + 7{,}000 \overset{1.6901}{(P/A_{12,2})} \overset{0.8929}{(P/F_{12,1})}$$

$$+ 4{,}000 \overset{0.6355}{(P/F_{12,4})} = \$21{,}462$$

$$F = 3{,}000 \overset{1.5735}{(F/P_{12,4})} + 6{,}000 \overset{1.4049}{(F/P_{12,3})} + 7{,}000 \overset{1.2544}{(F/P_{12,2})}$$

$$+ 7{,}000 \overset{1.1200}{(F/P_{12,1})} + 4{,}000 = \$33{,}770$$

Note: $7{,}000(F/P_{12,2}) + 7{,}000(F/P_{12,1}) = 7{,}000(F/A_{12,2})(F/P_{12,1})$

$$A = 21{,}462 \overset{0.32923}{(A/P_{12,4})} = \$7{,}066 = 33{,}770 \overset{0.20923}{(A/F_{12,4})}$$

2-14 Solution:

P=?	$1,000	$1,000	. . . .	$1,000
0	1	2 20		F=?

$$F = 1{,}000 \overset{57.2750}{(F/A_{10,20})} = \$57{,}275$$

$$P = 1{,}000 \overset{8.5136}{(P/A_{10,20})} = \$8{,}514$$

Or, $P = 57{,}275 \overset{0.1486}{(P/F_{10,20})} = \$8{,}511$ *difference due to round-off*

2-15 Solution:

$2,000 $1,000 $1,000 .... $1,000

```
_____
0               1               2 ................. 5 years
```

A) *Calculate the Future Value "F" of the Payments Assuming a
   nominal interest rate of 20% compounded annually, so
   effective interest is also 20%.*

$$\overset{2.4883}{} \qquad \overset{7.4418}{}$$

$$F = 2,000(F/P_{20\%,5}) + 1,000(F/A_{20\%,5}) = \$12,419$$

B) *Calculate the Future Value Based on Semi-Annual Compounding:*

Period i = 20%/2 = 10% per semi-annual period

Effective Interest Rate, $E = (1.1)^2 - 1 = 0.21$ or, 21.0%

$$\overset{2.5937}{} \qquad \overset{7.58925}{}$$

$$F = 2,000(F/P_{21\%,5}) + 1,000(F/A_{21\%,5}) = \$12,777$$

C) *Equivalent Semi-Annual Payments for Semi-Annual Compounding:*

```
-            A=F(A/F10%,2) ... A
_____
                                     F=$1,000
0            1               2
```

i = 10%   (semi-annual compound interest)

$A = 1,000(A/F_{10\%,2}) = \$476.19$

$2,000 $476.19 $476.19 .... $476.19

```
_____
                                                          F=?
0          1           2 .................... 10
           (10 semi-annual periods in 5 years)
```

$$\overset{2.5937}{} \qquad\qquad \overset{15.9374}{}$$

$$F = 2,000(F/P_{10\%,10}) + 476.19(F/A_{10\%,10}) = \$12,776$$

2-16 Solution:

$(1.05)^4 - 1 = 1.2155 - 1 = 0.2155$

Effective interest rate: E = 21.55%

2-17 Solution: **Effective annual interest rate is 20% or 0.20.**

$$(1 + i)^4 - 1 = 0.20$$
$$(1 + i)^4 = 1.20$$
$$i = (1.20)^{0.25} - 1 = 0.0466 \quad \text{or, } 4.66\% \text{ per quarterly period}$$
Nominal rate $r = (4.66\%/\text{period})(4 \text{ periods}) = 18.64\%$

2-18 Solution:

```
       --      $1,000      $1,000 .............. 1,000
 A)  ─────────────────────────────────────────────── F=?
       0          1          2 . . . . . . . . . 40 years
```

$i = 15\%$ per year

$$\overset{1779.0903}{F = 1,000(F/A_{15\%,40})} = \$1,779,090$$

```
       --      $1,000      $1,100   gradient + $100/yr ...
 B)  ─────────────────────────────────────────────── F=?
       0          1          2 .................. 40 years
```

$$\overset{6.5168 \qquad\qquad 1779.0903}{F = (1,000 + 100(A/G_{15\%,40}))(F/A_{15\%,40})} = \$2,938,488$$

The A\G Factor gives the following time diagram with an equivalent uniform series of values in years 1-40:

$$\overset{6.5168}{A = 1,000 + 100(A/G_{15,40})} = \$1,651.68, \text{ giving the following:}$$

```
       --     $1,651.68   $1,651.68 ........... $1,651.68
 B)  ─────────────────────────────────────────────── F=?
       0          1          2 ................. 40 years
```

$$\overset{1779.0903}{F = 1,651.68(F/A_{15,40})} = \$2,938,488$$

$$\overset{0.003733}{\text{C)} \quad P = 1,779,090(P/F_{15,40})} = \$6,642$$

$$\overset{6.6418}{Or, \quad P = 1,000(P/A_{15,40})} = \$6,642$$

2-19 Solution:

BTCF	-8,000	-2,000	-3,000	-2,500
Years	0	1	2	3
Months	0	12	24	36

A) Monthly Compounding Periods,

Nominal i = 12.0%
Period i = 12.0% / 12 months = 1.0% per month

$$PWC = -8,000 \underset{0.8874}{-2,000(P/F_{1\%,12})} \underset{0.7876}{-3,000(P/F_{1\%,24})} \underset{0.6989}{-2,500(P/F_{1\%,36})}$$

= -13,885

B) Annual Compounding Periods

Nominal i = 12.0%
Period i = 12.0% / 12 months = 1.0% per month
Effective Interest Rate Using Eq 2-9; $(1+i)^m - 1$
$(1+.01)^{12} - 1 = 0.126825$ or 12.68%

$$PWC = -8,000 \underset{0.8874}{-2,000(P/F_{12.68\%,1})} \underset{0.7876}{-3,000(P/F_{12.68\%,3})}$$

$$\underset{0.6989}{-2,500(P/F_{12.68\%,4})}$$

= -13,885

2-20 Solution:

P=? $6,000 $6,000 $8,000 $8,000 $10,000 $10,000
```
0        1 ...... 5      6 ....... 9      10 ........ 15
```

$$P = 6{,}000 \overset{3.7908}{(P/A_{10,5})} + 8{,}000 \overset{3.1699}{(P/A_{10,4})} \overset{0.6209}{(P/F_{10,5})}$$

$$+ \ 10{,}000 \overset{4.3553}{(P/A_{10,6})} \overset{0.4241}{(P/F_{10,9})} = \$56{,}961$$

$56,961 is less than $70,000, so accept the offer of $70,000 now to maximize profit.

Alternately:

$$P = 6{,}000 \overset{3.7908}{(P/A_{10,5})} + 8{,}000 (\overset{5.7590}{(P/A_{10,9})} - \overset{3.7908}{(P/A_{10,5})})$$

$$+ \ 10{,}000 (\overset{7.6061}{(P/A_{10,15})} - \overset{5.7590}{(P/A_{10,9})}) = \$56{,}961$$

Or,

$$P = 10{,}000 \overset{7.6061}{(P/A_{10,15})} - 2{,}000 \overset{5.759}{(P/A_{10,9})} - 2{,}000 \overset{3.7908}{(P/A_{10,5})} = \$56{,}961$$

Another alternate solution looks at comparing future values:

$$F = 70{,}000 \overset{4.1772}{(F/P_{10,15})} = \$292{,}404$$

$$F = 6{,}000 \overset{6.1051}{(F/A_{10,5})} \overset{2.5937}{(F/P_{10,10})} + 8{,}000 \overset{4.6410}{(F/A_{10,4})} \overset{1.7716}{(F/P_{10,6})}$$

$$+ \ 10{,}000 \overset{7.7156}{(F/A_{10,6})} = \$237{,}941$$

To maximize future value, accept $70,000 now.

2-21 Solution:

$$\overset{0.13147}{\text{Equivalent Annual Payments, A} = 56,961(A/P_{10,15})} = \$7,488$$

Alternate Solution:

$$\overset{0.03147}{A = 237,969(A/F_{10,15})} = \$7,488$$

2-22 Equivalent Annual Cost Solution:

		← Gradient Series →		
$11,000	$500	$550	$600 .... $950	
				Salvage=$2,000
0	1	2	3 10	

$$\overset{0.14903}{A = 11,000(A/P_{8,10})} + 500 + \overset{3.8713}{50(A/G_{8,10})} - \overset{0.06903}{2,000(A/F_{8,10})}$$

$$A = 1,639 + 500 + 194 - 138 = \$2,195 \text{ per year}$$

2-23 Solution:

-	-	- .... -	$100	$100 ..... $100
0	1	2 30	31	32 48

A) Monthly - Discrete Interest, Discrete Dollars:

A nominal interest rate "r" of 15.0%, compounded monthly yields the following period interest rate, "i":

$$i = 0.15/12 = 0.0125 = 1.25\%$$

$$(P/A_{i,n}) = [(1+i)^n-1]/i(1+i)^n \quad \text{so,} \quad (P/A_{1.25\%,18}) = 16.0295$$

$$(P/F_{i,n}) = 1/(1+i)^n \quad \text{so,} \quad (P/F_{1.25\%,30}) = 0.6889$$

$$\overset{16.0295}{P = 100(P/A_{1.25\%,18})} \overset{0.6889}{(P/F_{1.25\%,30})} = \$1,104$$

2-23 Solution: *Continued*

B) *Yearly - Discrete Interest, Discrete Dollars:*

-	-	-	$1,200	$600
0	1	2	3	4

$$\begin{array}{cc} 0.6575 & 0.5718 \end{array}$$
$$P = 1,200(P/F_{15,3}) + 600(P/F_{15,4}) = \boxed{\$1,132}$$

The value $1,132 is a common result, but incorrect when compared with the monthly timing scenario described in Case A! The present value should be based on the annual effective discrete interest rate for a 15% nominal interest rate compounded monthly. Use Eq. 2-9 (developed in Section 2.3 of the textbook) to calculate the effective interest rate "E" as follows:

$$E = (1.0125)^{12} - 1 = 0.16075 \text{ or } 16.07\%$$

$$\begin{array}{cc} 0.6395 & 0.55096 \end{array}$$
$$P = 1,200(P/F_{16.07\%,3}) + 600(P/F_{16.07\%,4}) = \$1,098$$

Close to the $1,104 result from Case A, the $6 difference is due to the approximation of annual values for monthly payments.

C) *Yearly - Effective Continuous Interest, Discrete Dollars:*

The continuous interest rate (r) that is equivalent to the effective discrete interest rate of 16.07% is calculated using Eq. 2-10:

$$E = e^r - 1 = 0.1607, \text{ re-arranging gives } e^r = 1.1607$$

$$r = \ln(1.1607) = 0.1490 \text{ or } 14.9\%$$

$$\begin{array}{cc} 0.6395 & 0.5510 \end{array}$$
$$P = 1,200(P/F_{14.9\%,3}) + 600(P/F_{14.9\%,4}) = \$1,098$$

This result is identical to the Case B result.

Appendix B is continuous interest with discrete dollar values:

e = the natural log base
r = 14.9% or, 0.149
n = 3 and 4 respectively

For a continuous interest rate and discrete $, $P/F_{r,n} = 1/e^{rn}$

2-23 Solution: *Continued*

   D) *Yearly - Continuous Interest, Continuous Flowing Dollars:*

```
  -          -          ← $1,200 →← $600 →
  _____
  0          1          2          3          4
```

Working with the same continuous interest calculated in Case C, assume the dollars are realized uniformly over years 3 and 4 as illustrated on the time diagram. Appendix C gives:

$$P/F^*_{r,n} = [(e^r-1)/r]/e^{rn}$$

$$= (e^r-1)/(re^{rn})$$

$$
\overset{0.6896}{} \qquad\qquad \overset{0.5942}{}
$$
$$P = 1,200(P/F^*_{14.9\%,3}) + 600(P/F^*_{14.9\%,4}) = \$1,184$$

2-24 Solution:

```
 P=?    $600      $700 .. gradient ..$1,200  $1,200  $1,200  $1,200
 _____
                                                                    F=?
  0      1         2 ............... 7        8       9       10
```

$$
\overset{2.5515}{} \quad \overset{4.5638}{} \qquad\qquad \overset{2.4018}{} \quad \overset{0.4523}{}
$$
A) $P = [600+100(A/G_{12,7})](P/A_{12,7})+1,200(P/A_{12,3})(P/F_{12,7}) = \$5,206$

$$
\overset{2.1720}{} \quad \overset{4.1114}{} \qquad\qquad \overset{3.0373}{} \quad \overset{0.5066}{}
$$
Or, $P = [600+100(A/G_{12,6})](P/A_{12,6})+1,200(P/A_{12,4})(P/F_{12,6}) = \$5,206$

$$
\overset{3.1058}{}
$$
B) $F = 5,206(F/P_{12,10}) = \$16,169$

$$
\overset{2.5515}{} \quad \overset{10.0890}{} \quad \overset{1.4049}{} \qquad\quad \overset{3.3744}{}
$$
Or, $F = [600+100(A/G_{12,7})](F/A_{12,7})(F/P_{12,3})+1,200(F/A_{12,3}) = \$16,169$

2-25 Solution:

```
                   - ............. -        $5,000 ............. $5,000
      P=?   _____
            0         1 .......... 4        5 ................... 14
```

$$
\overset{6.4177}{} \quad \overset{0.7084}{}
$$
$$P = 5,000(P/A_{9,10})(P/F_{9,4}) = \$22,731$$

If the payments start at the end of year 1 instead of at the end of year 5, the time zero cost is: $5,000(P/A_{9,10}) = \$32,090$

2-26 Solution:

$16,000	A=?	A=?	A=? . . . . A=?

```
0        1        2        3  . . . . . . . . . . . 36
```

A) 10% annual add-on interest:

Uniform Monthly Principal = 16,000/36 = $444.44
Uniform Monthly Interest = 16,000(0.10)/(12) = $133.33
Uniform End-of month add-on payments = 444.44 + 133.33 = $577.78

B) 10% annual percentage rate compounded monthly:

Using the mathematical definition of $A/P_{i,n}$ where i = 10%/12:

i = 0.10/12 = 0.00833 per month,   n = 36 months

$$A/P_{i,n} = i(1+i)^n/[(1+i)^n-1]$$
$$= 0.00833(1.00833)^{36}/[(1.00833)^{36}-1] = 0.032267$$

$$\overset{0.032267}{\text{End-of-month payments} = 16,000(A/P_{0.833\%,36})} = \$516.27$$

2-27 Solution:

APR of 11.5% compounded monthly is a period interest rate "i" of
0.115/12 = 0.009583 or 0.9583% per month.

End of Month Payments (A_{End}):

$$A_{End} = 15,000(\overset{0.026094}{A/P_{0.9583\%,48}}) = \$391.42 \text{ per month.}$$

Beginning of Month Payments (A_{Beg}):

$$A_{Beg} = 391.32(\overset{0.9905}{P/F_{0.9583\%,1}}) = \$387.61$$

An alternate beginning-of-month solution:

$$\$15,000 = A + A(\overset{37.6979}{P/A_{0.9583\%,47}})$$

$$\$15,000 = A(1 + 37.6979)   A = \$387.62$$

2-28 Solution:

```
C=$1,500      OC=$400            OC=$500            OC=$600
 ──────────────────────────────────────────────────────── L=$300
   0             1                  2                  3
```

Present Worth Cost at 15%:

$$\begin{array}{ccc} 0.8696 & 0.7561 & 0.6575 \end{array}$$
$$P = 1,500 + 400(P/F_{15,1}) + 500(P/F_{15,2}) + (600-300)(P/F_{15,3})$$
$$= \$2,423$$

Or,

$$\begin{array}{ccc} 0.9071 & 2.2832 & 0.6575 \end{array}$$
$$P = 1,500 + [400 + 100(A/G_{15,3})](P/A_{15,3}) - 300(P/F_{15,3})$$

$$P = 1,500 + 1,120 - 197 = \$2,423$$

Future Worth Cost at 15%:

$$\begin{array}{ccc} 1.5209 & 1.3225 & 1.1500 \end{array}$$
$$F = 1,500(F/P_{15,3}) + 400(F/P_{15,2}) + 500(F/P_{15,1}) + (600-300)$$
$$= \$3,685$$

Or,

$$\begin{array}{ccc} 1.5209 & 0.9071 & 3.4725 \end{array}$$
$$F = 1,500(F/P_{15,3}) + [400 + 100(A/G_{15,3})](F/A_{15,3}) - 300$$

$$F = 2,281 + 1,704 - 300 = \$3,685$$

Or,

$$1.5209$$
$$F = 2,423(F/P_{15,3}) = \$3,685$$

Equivalent Annual Cost at 15%:

$$0.43798$$
$$A = 2,423(A/P_{15,3}) = \$1,061$$

Or,

$$0.28798$$
$$A = 3,685(A/F_{15,3}) = \$1,061$$

2-29 Solution:

A) $\leftarrow$\$300$\rightarrow$ $\leftarrow$\$400$\rightarrow$ $\leftarrow$\$400$\rightarrow$ $\leftarrow$\$400$\rightarrow$ $\leftarrow$\$500$\rightarrow$
_____

0   1   2   3   4   5

From Appendix C: $P/F^*_{r,n} = [(e^r-1)/r](1/e^{rn})$

$P/A^*_{r,n} = [(e^{rn}-1)/r](1/e^{rn})$

From Appendix B: $P/F_{r,n} = 1/e^{rn}$

$$\begin{array}{cccc} 0.9563 & 0.8740 & 0.7988 & 0.7300 \end{array}$$
$P = 300(P/F^*_{9,1}) + 400(P/F^*_{9,2}) + 400(P/F^*_{9,3}) + 400(P/F^*_{9,4})$

$$0.6672$$
$+ 500(P/F^*_{9,5}) = \$1,582$

Or,

$$\begin{array}{cccc} 0.9563 & 2.6291 \quad 0.9139 & & 0.6672 \end{array}$$
$P = 300(P/F^*_{9,1}) + 400(P/A^*_{9,3})(P/F_{9,1}) + 500(P/F^*_{9,5})$

$= \$1,582$

Note that since $400(P/A^*_{9\%,3})$ is a discrete year 1 sum, the continuous interest single payment present worth factor $(P/F_{9\%,1})$ from Appendix B, is needed to bring the year 1 sum to time 0. The continuous interest, continuous flow of money factor $(P/F^*_{9\%,1})$ is NOT valid for this calculation.

Continuously Flowing Yearly Payments:

From Appendix C: $A/P^*_{r,n} = re^{rn}/(e^{rn}-1)$

$$0.24836$$
$A = 1,582(A/P^*_{9,5}) = \$393$

$$1.5683$$
$F = 1,581.61(F/P_{9,5}) = 1,582(e^{0.09(5)}) = \$2,480.46$

2-29 Solution: *Continued*

B)

		(150+200)	(200+200)	(200+200)	(200+250)	
←$150→		←$350→	←$400→	←$400→	←$450→	←$250→

0	1	2	3	4	5	6

From Eq 2-10: Effective discrete interest rate "E" = 0.09 = $e^r - 1$

r = ln(1.09) = 0.0862 or 8.62%

$$P = 150(P/F^*_{8.62,1}) + 350(P/F^*_{8.62,2}) + 400(P/F^*_{8.62,3}) + 400(P/F^*_{8.62,4})$$
(0.9581, 0.8790, 0.8064, 0.7398)

$$+450(P/F^*_{8.62,5}) + 250(P/F^*_{8.62,6}) = \$1,530.91$$
(0.6787, 0.6226)

This result is very similar to the $1,529 discrete compounding, discrete value result from text Example 2-8.

$$A = 1,530.91(A/P^*_{8.62,5}) = \$376.89$$
(0.24619)

$$F = 1,530.91(F/P_{8.62,5})$$
(1.5388)

Or, $F = 1,530.91(e^{0.0862(5)}) = \$2,355.76$

C)

–	$300	$400	$400	$400	$500

0	0.5	1.5	2.5	3.5	4.5

Effective discrete interest rate given a 9.0% continuous rate:

E = $e^r - 1$ = $e^{0.09} - 1$ = 0.0942 = 9.42%

$$P = 300(P/F_{9.42,0.5}) + 400(P/A_{9.42,3})(P/F_{9.42,0.5}) + 500(P/F_{9.42,4.5})$$
(0.9560, 2.5125, 0.9560, 0.6669)

P = $1,581.03

This result is nearly equal to the result in (A).

2-30 Solution:

A)   *End of Period Values*

		$120	$120	$120
P=?	—			
	0	1	2	3 years

$$\overset{0.8929}{P = 120(P/F_{12,1})} + \overset{0.7972}{120(P/F_{12,2})} + \overset{0.7118}{120(P/F_{12,3})} = \$288.23$$

$$\overset{2.4018}{P = 120(P/A_{12,3})} = \$288.22$$

B)   *Beginning of Period Values*

$120	$120	$120	
P=?			—
0	1	2	3 years

$$\overset{1.6901}{P = 120 + 120(P/A_{12,2})} = \$322.81$$

$$Or, \quad \overset{2.4018 \quad 1.1200}{P = 120(P/A_{12,3})(F/P_{12,1})} = \$322.81$$

C)   *Mid-Period Values*

$-	$120	$120	$120	$-
P=?				
0	0.5	1.5	2.5	3 years

$$\overset{0.94491}{P = 120(P/F_{12,0.5})} + \overset{0.84367}{120(P/F_{12,1.5})} + \overset{0.75328}{120(P/F_{12,2.5})} = \$305.02$$

$$\Downarrow \qquad\qquad \Downarrow \qquad\qquad \Downarrow$$

$$P = 120[1/(1+.12)]^{0.5} + 120[1/(1+.12)]^{1.5} + 120[1/(1+.12)]^{2.5}$$

D)   *End of Period Timing Variation to Match Mid-Period Timing*

$60	$120	$120	$60
P=?			
0	1	2	3 years

$$\overset{1.6901 \qquad\qquad 0.71178}{P = 60 + 120\ (P/A_{12,2}) + 60(P/F_{12,3})} = \$305.52$$

2-31 Solution:

Annual Revenue = $2,400,000 per year, computed as follows:

$$10{,}000{,}000 \text{ watts } X \ \frac{1\,kw}{1{,}000 \text{ watts}} \ X \ 6{,}000 \text{ hrs/yr } X \ \$.04/kwh$$

A) End of Period Values (000's)

```
        -       $2,400 ..................... $2,400
P=?   ─────────────────────────────────────────────
        0          1 ......................... 10
```

$$P = 2{,}400 \overset{6.1446}{(P/A_{10,10})} = \$14{,}747$$

B) Beginning of Period Values (000's)

```
    $2,400    $2,400 ............... $2,400     -
P=?  ─────────────────────────────────────────────
        0          1 .................... 9     10
```

$$P = 2{,}400 + 2{,}400 \overset{5.7590}{(P/A_{10,9})} = \$16{,}222$$

$$Or, \quad P = 2{,}400 \overset{6.1446}{(P/A_{10,10})} \overset{1.1000}{(F/P_{10,1})} = \$16{,}222$$

Timing issues only effect the placement of dollars on the time diagram. Once established, the discounting methodology is applied to the corresponding values. Obviously the beginning of period approach moves dollars closer to the present without any discounting so one should expect a greater present value if everything else is held constant. However, many analysts argue that there is no single check realized at the beginning or end of a period, but a series of dollars flowing through the period. To approximate this, you might consider treating the cash flows as mid-period values, which is the Case C solution to this problem.

2-31 Solution: *Continued*

C)   *Mid-Period Values (000's)*

```
     -   $2,400   $2,400 ............ $2,400      -
P=?  ─────────────────────────────────────────────
     0    0.5      1.5 .............. 9.5     10
```

$$P = 2,400(P/F_{10,0.5}) + 2,400(P/F_{10,1.5}) + \,.\,.\, + 2,400(P/F_{10,9.5})$$

with values 0.95346, 0.86678, 0.40436 above the respective terms, and

$$[1/(1.1)]^{0.5} \qquad [1/(1.1)]^{1.5} \qquad [1/(1.1)]^{9.5}$$

P = $15,467

Or, $P = 2,400(P/A_{10,10})(F/P_{10,0.5}) = \$15,467$

with values 6.1446 and 1.04881 above the respective terms.

As one might expect, the case C mid-period result is halfway between the case A and case B results.

D)   *End of Period Timing Variation to Approximate Mid-Period Discounting (000's)*

```
    $1,200        $2,400 .............. $2,400    $1,200
P=? ─────────────────────────────────────────────────
    0              1 ................... 9         10
```

$$P = 1,200 + 2,400(P/A_{10,9}) + 1,200(P/F_{10,10}) = \$15,484$$

with values 5.5790 and 0.3855 above the respective terms.

This case D result very closely approximates the Case C Mid-Period approach.

Consistency in timing methodology is really the key. Properly allocated dollars should yield similar present, future or annual values for the relevant discounting methodology.

2-32 Solution: All Values in Thousands

Payments	P=?	1,100	1,100	1,100	700	700
	0	1	2	3	4	5

Annual
Interest   6.5%   6.5%   7.0%   7.5%   7.5%

To determine the present value of the loan, each payment must be discounted at the corresponding interest rate for each compounding period, (years). This will require the mathematical definition for the factors found in Chapter 2, or at the beginning of Appendix A.

$$P = 1,100 \underset{1.8206}{(P/A_{6.5\%,2})} + 1,100 \underset{0.93458}{(P/F_{7.0\%,1})} \underset{0.88166}{(P/F_{6.5\%,2})}$$

$$+ 700 \underset{1.7956}{(P/A_{7.5\%,2})} \underset{0.93458}{(P/F_{7.0\%,1})} \underset{0.88166}{(P/F_{6.5\%,2})} = \$3,944.72$$

Year	Loan Balance	Payment	Interest Rate	Accrued Interest	Principal	Loan Balance
1	3,944.72	1,100.00	6.5%	256.41	843.59	3,101.13
2	3,101.13	1,100.00	6.5%	201.57	898.43	2,202.70
3	2,202.70	1,100.00	7.0%	154.19	945.81	1,256.89
4	1,256.89	700.00	7.5%	94.27	605.73	651.15
5	651.15	700.00	7.5%	48.85	651.15	0.00

Although $3,944.72 represents the current loan balance, it does not necessarily represent the market value of the loan. Such a value would depend on current and forecasted market interest rates and the returns demanded by other investors at that time for perceived risk.

Textbook Problem 2-32

Calculating Present Value or Loan Balance.
Remember you must use the appropriate period "i" value.

Calculating the Current Loan Balance (Values in 000's)   **Loan Amortization Schedule**

or,

Year	Loan Payment	Interest Rate	Present Value	Present Value
0	$ -	0.00%	0	0
1	$ 1,100.00	6.50%	$1,032.86	$1,032.86
2	$ 1,100.00	6.50%	$969.83	$969.83
3	$ 1,100.00	7.00%	$906.38	$906.38
4	$ 700.00	7.50%	$536.55	$536.55
5	$ 700.00	7.50%	$499.11	$499.11
			$ 3,944.73	$ 3,944.73

Year	Beginning Balance	Payment	Interest	Principal	Ending Balance
0	$ 3,944.73	$ -	$ -	$ -	$ 3,944.73
1	$ 3,944.73	$ 1,100.00	$ 256.41	$ 843.59	$ 3,101.13
2	$ 3,101.13	$ 1,100.00	$ 201.57	$ 898.43	$ 2,202.71
3	$ 2,202.71	$ 1,100.00	$ 154.19	$ 945.81	$ 1,256.90
4	$ 1,256.90	$ 700.00	$ 94.27	$ 605.73	$ 651.16
5	$ 651.16	$ 700.00	$ 48.84	$ 651.16	$ -

The first "Present Value" column determines the present value using using the mathematical definitions for a P/Fi,n factor.

The second "Present Value" column utilizes the "PV" function. Note in the later years in this column, to determine the present value of the payments, the calculation "nests" several "PV" functions to properly account for the time value of money considerations.

CHAPTER 3 PROBLEM SOLUTIONS

3-1 Purchase New vs Repair Existing Equipment

Purchase New Equipment:

Cost of New	-$240				
Operating Costs	-$20	-$40	-$50	-$30	
					$100
	0	1	2	3	

Repair Existing Equipment:

Repair Cost	-$50			
Operating Costs	-$20	-$140	-$140	-$70
	0	1	2	3

PW Cost Purchase New:

$$\underset{0.8696}{} \quad \underset{0.7561}{} \quad \underset{0.6575}{}$$

$$-260 - 40(P/F_{15,1}) - 50(P/F_{15,2}) + 70(P/F_{15,3}) = -\$287$$

PW Cost Repair Existing:

$$\underset{0.8696}{} \quad \underset{0.7561}{} \quad \underset{0.6575}{}$$

$$-70 - 140(P/F_{15,1}) - 140(P/F_{15,2}) - 70(P/F_{15,3}) = -\$344$$

Select Purchase New with the least negative present worth cost.

Incremental Analysis, Purchase-Repair:

-$190	$100	$90	$140
0	1	2	3

Incremental NPV $= -190 + 100(P/F_{15,1}) + 90(P/F_{15,2}) + 140(P/F_{15,3})$
$\qquad\qquad = +\$57.0 > 0$, *So accept the purchase option.*

Or, PWC Purchase - PWC Repair $= -287 - -344 = +\$57.0$

Incremental ROR $= 31.4\%$ is the "i" that makes incremental NPV equal 0.
$\qquad\qquad 31.4\% > 15.0\%$ *so accept the purchase option.*

3-2 Solution:

P=? $3,000 ..... $3,000 $5,000 ..... $5,000 $6,000 ... $6,000

```
0     1 ......... 5        6 .......... 13        14 ....... 16
```

$$P = 3,000 \overset{3.9927}{(P/A_{8,5})} + 5,000 \overset{5.7466}{(P/A_{8,8})} \overset{0.6806}{(P/F_{8,5})} + 6,000 \overset{2.577}{(P/A_{8,3})} \overset{0.3677}{(P/F_{8,13})}$$

P = 11,978 + 19,556 + 5,685 = $37,219 at time zero.

Value at the end of the 3rd year = $(37,219) \overset{1.2597}{(F/P_{8,3})}$ = $46,885

Alternate Solution, Value at year 3:

$$[6,000 \overset{8.8514}{(P/A_{8,16})} - 1,000 \overset{7.9038}{(P/A_{8,13})} - 2,000 \overset{3.9927}{(P/A_{8,5})}] \overset{1.2597}{(F/P_{8,3})} = \$46,885$$

3-3 Solution:

Machine A

```
                              -10,000
  -50,000    -5,000    -5,000 ..  -5,000    -5,000 ..  -5,000
 ──────────────────────────────────────────────────────── 10,000
    0          1         2 ...... 5          6 ....... 10
```

$$PWC_A = -50,000 - 5,000 \overset{6.1446}{(P/A_{10,10})} - 10,000 \overset{0.6209}{(P/F_{10,5})} + 10,000 \overset{0.3855}{(P/F_{10,10})}$$

$$= -83,077 \text{ least cost approach.}$$

Machine B

```
 -40,000        -8,000      -8,500 ........ grad=-500 ... -12,500
 ─────────────────────────────────────────────────────────────
    0             1          2 ......................... 10
```

$$PWC_B = -40,000 - (8,000 + 500 \overset{3.7255}{(A/G_{10,10})}) \overset{6.1446}{(P/A_{10,10})} = -100,603$$

Select Machine A to minimize cost of service.

3-4 Solution: *Profit Per Year: $25,000 - $15,000 = $10,000*

```
 -$120,000      $10,000        $10,000 .............. $10,000
                                                            $70,000
 ───────────────────────────────────────────────────
     0              1              2 ................. 15
```

PW Eq: $0 = -120,000 + 10,000(P/A_{i,15}) + 70,000(P/F_{i,15})$

For projects with lives of 10 years or more start trial and error using an i value equal to (average profit)/(initial investment), or, 10/120 = 8.33%, or approximately 8.0%.

@ i = 8%:   10,000(8.559) + 70,000(0.3152) = $107,654
@ i = 7%:   10,000(9.108) + 70,000(0.3624) = $116,448
@ i = 6%:   10,000(9.712) + 70,000(0.4173) = $126,331

$$i = 6.0\% + 1.0\% \left(\frac{126,331 - 120,000}{126,331 - 116,448} \right) = 6.64\%$$

3-5 Solution:

Purchase:

```
                   -1,400                         -1,400
                     -700                           -700
   -250,000        -1,900 ................... -1,900
   -250,000        -4,000 ................... -4,000
   ─────────────────────────────────────────────  Sale Value = L
      0              1 ....................... 10
```

Rent:

```
      -           -18,000 ................. -18,000
   ─────────────────────────────────────────────
      0              1 ....................... 10
```

This breakeven analysis is based on equating the PW Cost of Purchasing with the PW Cost of Renting and solving for the breakeven salvage, designated as "L." Note that this analysis is before-tax and assumes a cash acquisition. These parameters have the potential to impact the breakeven value due to the tax deductibility of interest on borrowed money and property taxes as would the timing of the rental payments.

PW Cost of Purchase = PW Cost of Renting

$$
\overset{6.7101}{-250,000 - 4,000(P/A_{8,10})} + \overset{0.4632}{L(P/F_{8,10})} = \overset{6.7101}{-18,000(P/A_{8,10})}
$$

-250,000 - 26,840 + 0.4632L = -120,782   Breakeven L = $336,913

Escalation rate in home value is analologous to rate of return:

$0 = -250,000 + 336,913(P/F_{i,10})$ i = Escalation Rate = 3.03% / Yr

3-6 Solution:

```
-$800          $40 . . . . . . . . . . . . . . . $40
                                                      $1,000
     0           1 . . . . . . . . . . . . . . . . 40  semi-annual periods
```

Present Worth Equation: $0 = -800 + 40(P/A_{i,40}) + 1,000(P/F_{i,40})$

By trial and error, $i = 5.197\%$ semi-annual period ROR by calculator.

The Nominal or Annual Bond ROR, commonly referred to as "Yield to Maturity," is 5.197% x 2 = 10.394% compounded semi-annually.

If the bond is callable in 8 years (16 semi-annual periods):

```
C=?            $40 . . . . . . . . . $40
                                            $1,000
     0           1 . . . . . . . . . . 16  semi-annual periods to call date
```

Present Worth Cost Equation:

$$C = 40(P/A_{3,16}) + 1,000(P/F_{3,16}) = \$1,125.64$$

An investor can pay $1,125.64 for this old bond to realize a 6% ROR compounded semi-annually to the call date on this bond investment.

3-7 Solution:

```
C=?            $40 . . . . . . . . . . . $40
                                              $1,000
     0           1 . . . . . . . . . . . 40  semi-annual periods to maturity
```

Present Worth Equation:

$$\begin{array}{cc} 17.159 & 0.1420 \end{array}$$
$$C = 40(P/A_{5,40}) + 1,000(P/F_{5,40}) = \$828.36$$

3-8 Solution:

```
-50,000        -2,000        -2,000 . . . . . .      -2,000
━━━━━━━━━━━━━━━━━━━━━━━━━━━━━━━━━━━━━━━━━━━━━━━━━━━━━  130,000
   0             1             2 . . . . . . . . . .  10
```

Present Worth Equation:

$50,000 = -2,000(P/A_{i,10}) + 130,000(P/F_{i,10})$

$i = 7\%:\quad -2,000(7.0236) + 130,000(0.5083) = \$52,032$

$i = 8\%:\quad -2,000(6.7101) + 130,000(0.4632) = \$46,796$

$i = 7\% + 1\%\left(\dfrac{52,032 - 50,000}{52,032 - 46,796}\right) = 7.39\% > 7.0\%$ bank interest,

The investment in the land is slightly better, but the two alternatives are very close to being economically a breakeven.

Alternate future worth analysis confirms this — the following analysis considers the FV if the money were deposited in the bank account instead of into the land:

$$
\begin{array}{cc}
1.9672 & 13.8164 \\
\end{array}
$$

$50,000(F/P_{7,10}) + 2,000(F/A_{7,10}) = \$125,993 < \$130,000$, select "land."

3-9 Solution:

```
                      C=$100
C=$60      I=$40      I=$40      I=$40      I=$70 . . .  I=$70
━━━━━━━━━━━━━━━━━━━━━━━━━━━━━━━━━━━━━━━━━━━━━━━━━━━━━━━━━━━━━━━
  0          1          2          3         4 . . . . . 10
```

Year 0 Present Worth Equation:

$60 = -100(P/F_{i,2}) + 40(P/A_{i,3}) + 70(P/A_{i,7})(P/F_{i,3})$

Trial and Error:

$i=40\% = -100(0.5102) + 40(1.589) + 70(2.263)(0.3644) = +\$70.26$

$i=50\% = -100(0.4444) + 40(1.407) + 70(1.883)(0.2963) = +\$50.90$

$i = ROR = 40\% + (50\%-40\%)\left(\dfrac{70.26 - 60.00}{70.26 - 50.90}\right) = 45.3\%$

3-10 Solution: *Values Are In Thousands, Income Sign Convention*

Lease Option:

-500	-500	-500	-750	-750	-750	-750	0
0	1	2	3	4	5	6	7

Purchase Option:

-2,000	0	0	0	-600	0	0	0
0	1	2	3	4	5	6	7

$$\text{PC}_{\text{Lease}} = -500 - 500 \underset{1.5278}{(P/A_{20},2)} - 750 \underset{2.5887}{(P/A_{20},4)} \underset{0.6944}{(P/F_{20},2)} = -2,612$$

$$\text{PC}_{\text{Purchase}} = -2,000 - 600 \underset{0.4823}{(P/F_{20},4)} = -2,289 \quad \textit{Least Cost Alternative}$$

Note that using the "replacement-in-kind" assumption for the lease at the end of year 3 would make the year 3, 4, 5 and 6 lease costs -$500 instead of -$750, making the present worth cost of leasing -$2,162 instead of -$2,612. This would make leasing look economically better than purchasing which is not correct if you really expect the year 3 through 6 lease costs will actually be -$750.

Incremental Analysis (Purchase — Lease):

-1,500	500	500	750	150	750	750	—
0	1	2	3	4	5	6	7

Present Worth Equation (Note, Savings are Analogous to Income):

$$0 = -1,500 + 500(P/A_i,2) + 750(P/F_i,3) + 150(P/F_i,4)$$

$$+ 750(P/A_i,2)(P/F_i,4)$$

i = Incremental ROR = 28.0% > 20.0%, *so, accept purchase*

$$\text{NPV @ 20\%} = -1,500 + 500 \underset{1.5278}{(P/A_{20},2)} + 750 \underset{0.5787}{(P/F_{20},3)} + 150 \underset{0.4823}{(P/F_{20},4)}$$

$$+ 750 \underset{1.5278}{(P/A_{20},2)} \underset{0.4823}{(P/F_{20},4)} = +323 > 0 \; \textit{Accept Purchase}$$

or, PWC Purchase — PWC Lease = -2,289 - -2,612 = +323

3-11 Solution: *All Values in Thousands*

Project Before-tax Cash Flows

-100	-200	90 90	240
0	1	2 9	10

A) Discrete Interest, Discrete Dollar Values
Present Worth Equation:

$$0 = -100 - 200(P/F_{i,1}) + 90(P/A_{i,8})(P/F_{i,1}) + 240(P/F_{i,10})$$

Approximate i = 90 / (100+200) = 0.30 or 30%

i=30% = -100-200(0.7692)+90(2.9247)(0.7692)+240(0.0725) = -\$33.96
i=25% = -100-200(0.8000)+90(3.3289)(0.8000)+240(0.1074) = +\$5.45

i = ROR = 25% + (30%-25%)[(5.45-0)/(5.45+33.96)] = 25.69%

Due to interpolation error, the 25.69% result is a little high. The true interpolation error-free ROR is 25.60% which is most easily obtained using an iterative routine from a spreadsheet or financial calculator.

Cumulative Cash Position Diagram; ROR i = 25.6%

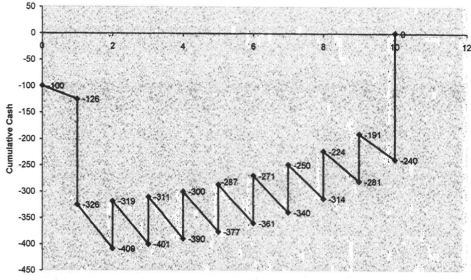

Project Life, (Years)

Calculator Keystrokes for the Rate of Return (ROR) and Net Present Value (NPV) in Problem 3-11 A.

HP 10B

equals gold/green key

	[ ] [CLEARALL]		
1	[P/YR]		
100	[+/-]	[CFj]	
200	[+/-]	[CFj]	
90	[CFj]		
8	[Nj]		
240	[CFj]		
	[IRR/YR]	= 25.6%	
15	[I/YR]		
	[NPV]	= $136.6	

HP 12C

	[f]	[REG]		
	[f]	[FIN]		
100	[CHS]	[g]	[CF₀]	
200	[CHS]	[g]	[CFj]	
90	[g]	[CFj]		
8	[g]	[Nj]		
240	[g]	[CFj]		
	[f]	[IRR]	= 25.6%	
15	[i]			
	[f]	[NPV]	= $136.6	

HP 17BII

[FIN]				
[CFLO]				
FLOW(0)=?	100		[INPUT]	
FLOW(1)=?	200	[+/-]	[INPUT]	
TIMES(1)=1	1		[INPUT]	
FLOW(2)=?	90		[INPUT]	
TIMES(2)=1	8		[INPUT]	
FLOW(3)=?	240		[INPUT]	
TIMES(3)=1	1		[INPUT]	
[EXIT]				
[CALC]				
[IRR%]	=25.6%			
15	[I%]	[NPV]	= $136.6	

Texas Instruments BAII Plus

[CF]					
[2nd]	[CLRWork]	[2nd]	[CLRTVM]		
[2nd]	[P/Y]	1	[ENTER]		
[CF]	100	[+/-]	[ENTER]	[→]	
CO1	200	[+/-]	[ENTER]	[→]	
		FO1:	1	[ENTER]	[→]
CO2	90	[ENTER]	[→]		
		FO2:	8	[ENTER]	[→]
CO3	240	[ENTER]	[→]		
		FO3:	1	[ENTER]	
[IRR]	[CPT]	= 25.6%			
[NPV]	I =	15	[ENTER]	[→]	[CPT] $136.59

Problem 3-11 Solution Continued:

B) *Continuous Interest, Discrete Dollar Values (Appendix B)*

$0 = -100 - 200(P/F_{r,1}) + 90(P/A_{r,8})(P/F_{r,1}) + 240(P/F_{r,10})$

$r = ROR = 23.01\%$

C) *Continuous Interest, Continuous Flowing Dollars (Appendix C & B)*

Year 0 cost flows from time 0 to the end of year 1.

← -100 →	← -200 →	← 90 →	. . . .	← 90 →	← 150 →
0	1	2	3 . . .	10	11	12

Present Worth Equation:

$0 = -100(P/F^*_{r,1}) - 200(P/F^*_{r,2}) + 90(P/A^*_{r,9})(P/F_{r,2}) + 150(P/F^*_{r,12})$

$r = ROR = 22.76\%$

First note that there is no discrete time zero value in this solution. All cash flows are assumed to flow continuously during each compounding period. Since the salvage could not be continuously realized as the project cash is generated, the salvage has been pushed to year 12. Second, you should note that $P/F_{r,2}$ is a continuous interest discrete value factor from Appendix B. It is used because the $P/A^*_{r,9}$ converts the income stream of $90 to a discrete sum at the beginning of year 3 (the end of year 2).

D) *Continuous Interest, Continuous Flowing Dollars*

Year 0 cost is treated as a discrete sum at time zero while all other values are assumed to flow continuously through each period.

-100 ←	-200 →	← 90 →	. . . . . .	← 90 →	← 150 →
0	1	2 9		10	11

Present Worth Equation:

$0 = -100 - 200(P/F^*_{r,1}) + 90(P/A^*_{r,9})(P/F_{r,1}) + 150(P/F^*_{r,11})$

Note that $P/F_{r,1}$ is a continuous interest, discrete value factor. It is used because $P/A^*_{r,9}$ converts the income stream of $90 to a discrete sum at the beginning of year 2 (the end of year 1).

$r = ROR = 23.73\%$

Problem 3-11 Solution Continued:

E) Mid-Period Discrete Dollars, Discrete Compounding Interest

	C=$100	C=$200	I=$90	I=$90	I=$240
Years	0	1	2	9	10
Discount Periods	0	0.5	1.5	8.5	9.5

PW Eq: $0 = -100 - 200(P/F_{i,0.5}) + 90(P/F_{i,1.5}) + \cdots$

$\qquad + 90(P/F_{i,8.5}) + 240(P/F_{i,9.5})$

Or, $\quad 0 = -100 - 200(P/F_{i,0.5}) + 90(P/A_{i,8})(P/F_{i,0.5}) + 240(P/F_{i,9.5})$

$\qquad$ i = 27.1% by interpolation between 25% and 30%

An alternate method for calculating mid-period discrete ROR using a financial calculator is to take the mid-period discrete diagram based on annual periods and convert it to a semi-annual period diagram as follows:

-100 -200	0	90	0	90	0	90	0	240	0
0 1	2	3	4	5 16	17	18	19	20 semi-annual

Using a spreadsheet or financial calculator that will handle twenty uneven cash flows or more, the semi-annual period i = 12.66%.

Now, using text Equation 2-9, $E = (1+i)^n - 1$ to convert the semi-annual period ROR, i, to the equivalent effective interest rate per year, $E = (1 + 0.1266)^2 - 1 = 0.2693$ or 26.93%. The difference in this result and the 27.1% result initially calculated with the time value of money factors is due to interpolation error. The 26.93% result is the correct annual ROR. This is reproduced below in spreadsheet form:

	A	B	C	D	E	F	G	H	I
1	Problem 3-11, Case E - Mid-Period Approach to ROR:								
2									
3	Semi-Annual Periods		Cash Flow		**Rate of Return Using the IRR Function**				
4	0		-100		=IRR(C4:C24) =		12.66%		
5	1		-200		*This is the semi-annual period i value*				
6	2		0						
7	3		90		=((1+G4)^2)-1		26.93%		
8	4		0		Using Equation 2-9 the period i value				
9	5		90		is converted to an effective interest				
10	6		0		rate per year.				
11	7		90						
12	8		0		=G4*2		25.33%		
13	9		90		Taking the period i times the number of				
14	10		0		compounding periods per year gives the				
15	11		90		equivalent nominal interest rate, i, com-				
16	12		0		pounded semi-annually.				
17	13		90						
18	14		0						
19	15		90						
20	16		0						
21	17		90						
22	18		0						
23	19		240						
24	20		0						
25									

3-12 Solution: *All Values in Thousands*

Purchase Option:

Cost of Truck	-$240			$100 Salvage
Operating Costs	-$20	-$40	-$50	-$30
	-$260	-$40	-$50	$70

0	1	2	3

Lease Option:

Operating Costs	-$10	-$20	-$20	-$10
Lease Payments	-$60	-$120	-$120	-$60
	-$70	-$140	-$140	-$70

0	1	2	3

PW Cost Purchase:

$$-260 - 40(P/F_{15,1}) - 50(P/F_{15,2}) + 70(P/F_{15,3}) = -\$286.6$$

with factors 0.8696, 0.7561, 0.6575

PW Cost Lease:

$$-70 - 140(P/F_{15,1}) - 140(P/F_{15,2}) - 70(P/F_{15,3}) = -\$343.6$$

with factors 0.8696, 0.7561, 0.6575

Select Purchasing with the least negative present worth cost.

Incremental Analysis, Purchase-Lease:

-$190	$100	$90	$140
0	1	2	3

Incremental NPV = $-190 + 100(P/F_{15,1}) + 90(P/F_{15,2}) + 140(P/F_{15,3})$
= $+\$57.0 > 0$, *So accept the purchase option.*

Incremental ROR = 31.4% is the "i" that makes incremental NPV equal 0.
  31.4% > 15.0% *so accept the purchase option.*

Incremental PVR = 57.0 / 190 = 0.30 > 0, *so, accept purchase.*

3-13 Solution Based on Income Sign Convention:

Purchase:

```
  -        -120,000  ...................................  -120,000
        _____
     0         1      ...................................     5
```

Produce Internally:

```
                                     -10,000
  -40,000    -100,000    -100,000    -100,000    -100,000    -100,000
        _____
     0          1           2           3           4           5
```

Incremental Timeline; (Produce Internally - Purchase)

```
                                     -10,000
  -40,000     20,000      20,000      20,000      20,000      20,000
        _____
     0          1           2           3           4           5
```

A) ROR, NPV, and PVR Analysis:

$$40,000 = 20,000(P/A_{i,5}) - 10,000(P/F_{i,3})$$

$i = 35.47\% > 30\%$ *produce internally.*

$$\overset{2.4356}{NPV = 20,000(P/A_{30,5})} - \overset{0.4552}{10,000(P/F_{30,3})} - 40,000 = +\$4,160 > 0$$

Positive NPV indicates sufficient savings to produce internally.

$PVR = 4,168/40,000 = 0.1042 > 0$ *so accept internal production.*

B) PW Cost Analysis:

Present Worth Cost of Purchase:

$$\overset{2.4356}{-120,000(P/A_{30,5})} = -\$292,272$$

Present Worth Cost Producing Internally:

$$-40,000 - \overset{2.4356}{100,000(P/A_{30,5})} - \overset{0.4552}{10,000(P/F_{30,3})} = -\$288,112 \text{ Least Cost}$$

PWC Produce - PWC Purchase = NPV; $-288,112 - -292,272 = +\$4,160$

3-14 Solution (Dollar values per share of stock):

Stock Investment: F_1 = Year 10 Stock Sale Value

```
   -30           2 ....... 2        4 ......... 4
  ─────────────────────────────────────────────────  F₁ = 93
    0            1 ....... 5        6 ........ 10
```

Present Worth Equation:

$$0 = -30 + 2(P/A_i,5) + 4(P/A_i,5)(P/F_i,5) + 93(P/F_i,10)$$

By trial and error, i = ROR = 17.75%

Dividend Re-investment at 8% Per Year,
F_2 = Accrued Year 10 Dividend Value:

```
    -          -2 ..... -2        -4 ...... -4
  ─────────────────────────────────────────────────  F₂ = 40.71
    0           1 ....... 5        6 ....... 10
```

$$5.8666 \quad 1.4693 \quad\quad 5.8666$$

Where: $F_2 = 2(F/A_{8\%},5)(F/P_{8\%},5) + 4(F/A_{8\%},5) = \$40.71$

Stock Investment and Dividend Re-investment Combined:

```
   -30          - .............................. -
  ─────────────────────────────────────────────────  F₁ + F₂ = 133.71
    0            1 ......................... 10
```

Present Worth Equation:

$$0 = -30 + 133.71(P/F_i,10)$$

By trial and error, i = Growth ROR = 16.12%

3-15 Solution:

(A) Initial Investment:

```
-250,000        100,000 ............ 100,000
                                            150,000
    0               1 ................. 5
```

   PW Eq: 0 = -250,000 + 100,000(P/A$_{i,5}$) + 150,000(P/F$_{i,5}$)

         i = ROR$_A$ = 36.1%

(B) Re-investment of Profits:

```
                                  -150,000
   -          -100,000 .........  -100,000    2,000,000

   0              1 ................ 5           6
```

   PW Eq: 0 = -100,000(P/A$_{i,4}$) - 250,000(P/F$_{i,5}$) + 2,000,000(P/F$_{i,6}$)

         i = ROR$_A$ = 45.8%

(A&B) Initial Investment and Re-investment Combined:

```
-250,000           0 ................ 0      2,000,000

   0               1 ................ 5          6
```

Present Worth Equation:

   PW Eq: 0 = -250,000 + 2,000,000(P/F$_{i,6}$)

   @ i = 40% = -250,000 + 2,000,000(0.1328) = 15,621
   @ i = 50% = -250,000 + 2,000,000(0.0878) =-74,417

   By Interpolation, i = 41.73% = Growth ROR

   By Calculator = 41.4%

3-16 Solution: *Let X = Monthly Payment*

Value = $100,000

Payments = X   X   X X   - Sale
                                                        Value=$25,000

          0   1   2 29   30

Present Worth Equation:

$$100{,}000 = X + \overset{25.0658}{X(P/A_{1\%},29)} + \overset{0.7419}{25{,}000(P/F_{1\%},30)}$$

$$X = \frac{100{,}000 - 25{,}000(0.7419)}{1 + 25.0658} = \$3{,}124.88$$

Payment	Month	Beginning Balance	Accrued Interest	Lease Payment	Reduced Principal	Ending Balance
1	0	100,000.00	0	3,124.88	3,124.88	96,875.12
2	1	96,875.12	968.75	3,124.88	2,156.13	94,718.99
3	2	94,718.99	947.19	3,124.88	2,177.69	92,541.30
4	3	92,541.36	925.41	3,124.88	2,199.47	90,341.89

Or, Use a Present Worth Equation to Determine the Lease Principal:

$$\overset{22.7952}{\$3{,}124.88(P/A_{1\%},26)} + \overset{0.7644}{\$25{,}000(P/F_{1\%},27)} = \$90{,}342$$

3-17 Solution:

  -$1,000
  $50,000 A=?   A=? .... A=?

          0   1   2 .... 80 quarters

Period i = 8%/4 = 2%, $A = 50{,}000 \overset{0.02516}{(A/P_{2\%},80)} = \$1{,}258$ per quarter

PW Eq: $50{,}000 - 1{,}000 = 50{,}000 \overset{0.02516}{(A/P_{2\%},80)} (P/A_{i},80)$

        $49{,}000 = 1{,}258(P/A_{i},80)$,   so, $38.9507 = P/A_{i},80$

        i=2%: $P/A_{2},80 = 39.745$
        i=3%: $P/A_{3},80 = 30.201$

Effective Interest Rate Being Paid on the Loan is:

$$i = 2\% + 1\%\left(\frac{39.745 - 38.951}{39.745 - 30.201}\right) = 2.083\% \text{ per quarter or nominal } 8.332\%$$

3-18 Solution: *All Values in Millions*

Development A:

```
                     C=$2.0
                     I=$1.8        I=$1.8                                I=$1.8
      C=$1.0         OC=$0.7       OC=$0.7 ...................... OC=$0.7
```
───
```
      0              1             2 ......................... 10
```

Development B:

```
                                   I=$2.0                                I=$2.0
      C=$1.0         C=$0.9        OC=$0.9 ...................... OC=$0.9
```
───
```
      0              1             2 ......................... 10
```

Incremental Time Line For B - A:

```
      C=0            C=0           I=0 .......................... I=0
```
───
```
      0              1             2 ......................... 10
```

ROR Analysis:

ROR_A PW Eq: $1.0 = 1.1(P/A_{i,10}) - 2.0(P/F_{i,1})$ $i = 45.1\%$

ROR_B PW Eq: $1.0 = [1.1(P/A_{i,9}) - 0.9](P/F_{i,1})$ $i = 45.1\%$

ROR_{B-A} PW Eq: $0 = 0$ *There is no economic difference with A & B.*

NPV Analysis:

$$\overset{5.0188}{NPV_A = 1.1(P/A_{15,10})} - \overset{0.8696}{2.0(P/F_{15,1})} - 1.0 = \$2.782$$

$$\overset{4.7716}{NPV_B = [1.1(P/A_{15,9})} - 0.9]\overset{0.8696}{(P/F_{15,1})} - 1.0 = \$2.782$$

$NPV_{B-A} = 0$, *so A and B are economically equivalent.*

PVR Analysis:

$$PVR_A \text{ Denominator} = 1.0 + [2.0-(1.8-0.7)]\overset{0.8696}{(P/F_{15,1})} = 1.783$$

$$PVR_A = \frac{2.782}{1.783} = 1.56 > 0$$

$$PVR_B \text{ Denominator} = 1.0 + 0.9\overset{0.8696}{(P/F_{15,1})} = 1.783$$

$$PVR_B = \frac{2.782}{1.783} = 1.56 > 0$$

3-18 Solution Continued:

Note that if you do not net the year 1 costs and revenues for A before calculating the present worth cost denominator for PVR$_A$, you do not get the equivalence of A and B shown with both ROR and NPV.

$$\text{Incorrect PVR}_A = \frac{2.782}{1 + 2(P / F_{15,1}} = 1.01$$

3-19 Solution: **All Values in Thousands**

Investment A:

Sunk Costs

C=$100	C=$200	–	I=$120	I=$120	. . . .	I=$120
-2	-1	0	1	2	. . . .	12

Investment B:

		–	C=$350	I=$150	. . . .	I=$150	–	–
-2	-1	0	1	2	. . . . .	10	11	12

$$\text{NPV}_A \text{ @ Time Zero} = 120(\overset{4.4392}{P/A_{20\%},12}) = \$532.7$$

$$\text{NPV}_B \text{ @ Time Zero} = [-350 + 150(\overset{4.0310}{P/A_{20\%},9})](\overset{0.8333}{P/F_{20\%},1}) = \$212.2$$

Cumulative NPV = 532.7 + 212.2 = $744.9

$744.9 is the maximum value of the company @ i* = 20%

Note, the past incurred costs (sunk costs) are not relevant to the analysis decision in this simplified before tax analysis. In a proper after-tax evaluation, only the remaining tax effects from the expenditure should be considered.

3-20 Solution: *Before-tax Cash Flows in 000's*

Year	0	1	2	3	4	5
Revenues		1,612.0	1,378.0	910.0	655.2	487.9
-Royalty Cost		-225.7	-192.9	-127.4	-91.7	-68.3
-Operating Cost		-175.0	-193.0	-212.0	-233.0	-256.0
-Research & Dev.	-750.0	-250.0				
-Equipment		-670.0				
-Patent Rights	-100.0					
Before-Tax CF	-850.0	291.3	992.1	570.6	330.5	163.6

NPV Analysis:

$$\text{NPV @ 15\%} = -850 + 291.3\overset{0.8696}{(P/F_{15,1})} + 992.1\overset{0.7561}{(P/F_{15,2})} + 570.6\overset{0.6575}{(P/F_{15,3})}$$

$$+ 330.5\overset{0.5718}{(P/F_{15,4})} + 163.6\overset{0.4972}{(P/F_{15,5})} = +\$798.9 > 0, \text{ accept}$$

ROR Analysis:

$$\text{PW Eq:} \quad 0 = -850 + 291.3(P/F_{i,1}) + 992.1(P/F_{i,2}) + 570.6(P/F_{i,3})$$

$$+ 330.5(P/F_{i,4}) + 163.6(P/F_{i,5})$$

NPV @ 50% = +$41
NPV @ 70% = -$168   ROR = i = 50% + 20%(41/209) = 53.9% > i*=15%

By Financial Calculator, i = ROR = 53.276% > i* = 15%, accept

Ratio Analysis:

PVR = 798.9/850 = 0.94 > 0   B/C Ratio = PVR + 1 = 1.94 > 1.0

Break-even Uniform Selling Price Per Unit:

Year	0	1	2	3	4	5
Revenues		62X	53X	35X	24X	17X
-Royalties		-8.68X	-7.42X	-4.90X	-3.36X	-2.38X
-Operating Cost		-175.0	-193.0	-212.0	-233.0	-256.0
-Research & Dev.	-750.0	-250.0				
-Equipment Cost		-670.0				
-Patent Rights	-100.0					
Before-Tax CF	-850.0	53.32X	45.58X	30.10X	20.64X	14.62X
		-1,095	-193	-212	-233	-256

$$\text{PW Eq: } 0 = -850 + (53.32X-1,095)\overset{0.8696}{(P/F_{15,1})} + (45.58X-193)\overset{0.7561}{(P/F_{15,2})}$$

$$+ (30.10X-212)\overset{0.6575}{(P/F_{15,3})} + (20.64X-233)\overset{0.5718}{(P/F_{15,4})} + (14.62X-256)\overset{0.4972}{(P/F_{15,5})}$$

0 = -2,348.0 + 119.69X   *Break-even Price, X = $19.62 per unit*

3-21 Solution: *Before-tax Cash Flows in 000's*

Year	0	1	2	3	4	5
Revenues		1,612.0	1,378.0	910.0	655.2	487.9
-Royalty Cost		-225.7	-192.9	-127.4	-91.7	-68.3
-Operating Cost		-175.0	-193.0	-212.0	-233.0	-256.0
-Intangible	-750.0	-250.0				
-Tangible		-670.0				
-Min Rights Acq.	-100.0					
Before-Tax CF	-850.0	291.3	992.1	570.6	330.5	163.6

NPV Analysis:

$$\phantom{NPV @ 15\% = -850 + 291.3(P/F_{15,1})}\;0.8696\;0.7561\;0.6575$$

$$NPV @ 15\% = -850 + 291.3(P/F_{15,1}) + 992.1(P/F_{15,2}) + 570.6(P/F_{15,3})$$

$$\;0.5718\;0.4972$$

$$+ 330.5(P/F_{15,4}) + 163.6(P/F_{15,5}) = +\$798.9 > 0,\ accept$$

ROR Analysis:

PW Eq: $0 = -850 + 291.3(P/F_{i,1}) + 992.1(P/F_{i,2}) + 570.6(P/F_{i,3})$

$$+ 330.5(P/F_{i,4}) + 163.6(P/F_{i,5})$$

NPV @ 50% = +$41

NPV @ 70% = -$168   ROR = i = 50% + 20%(41/209) = 53.9% > i* = 15%

By financial calculator, i = ROR = 53.276% > i* = 15%, accept

PVR Analysis:

PVR = 798.9/850 = 0.94 > 0,   B/C Ratio = PVR + 1 = 1.94 > 1.0

Break-even Uniform Selling Price Per Unit:

Year	0	1	2	3	4	5
Revenues		62X	53X	35X	24X	17X
-Royalties		-8.68X	-7.42X	-4.90X	-3.36X	-2.38X
-Operating Cost		-175.0	-193.0	-212.0	-233.0	-256.0
-Intangible	-750.0	-250.0				
-Tangible		-670.0				
-Min Rights Acq	-100.0					
Before-Tax CF	-850.0	53.32X	45.58X	30.10X	20.64X	14.62X
		-1,095	-193	-212	-233	-256

$$\;0.8696\;0.7561$$

PW Eq: $0 = -850 + (53.32X-1,095)(P/F_{15,1}) + (45.58X-193)(P/F_{15,2})$

$$\;0.6575\phantom{(30.10X-212)(P/F_{15,3}) + (20.6}\;0.5718\phantom{4X-233)(P/F_{15,4}) + (14.6}\;0.4972$$

$$+ (30.10X-212)(P/F_{15,3}) + (20.64X-233)(P/F_{15,4}) + (14.62X-256)(P/F_{15,5})$$

$0 = -2,348.0 + 119.69X$ *Break-even Price, X = $19.62 per bbl*

3-22 Solution: *Before-tax Cash Flows in 000's*

Year	0	1	2	3	4	5
Revenues		1,612.0	1,378.0	910.0	655.2	487.9
-Royalty Cost		-225.7	-192.9	-127.4	-91.7	-68.3
-Operating Cost		-175.0	-193.0	-212.0	-233.0	-256.0
-Development	-750.0	-250.0				
-Mine Equipment		-670.0				
-Min Rights Acq	-100.0					
Before-Tax CF	-850.0	291.3	992.1	570.6	330.5	163.6

NPV Analysis:

$$\text{NPV @ 15\%} = -850 + 291.3\overset{0.8696}{(P/F_{15,1})} + 992.1\overset{0.7561}{(P/F_{15,2})} + 570.6\overset{0.6575}{(P/F_{15,3})}$$

$$+ 330.5\overset{0.5718}{(P/F_{15,4})} + 163.6\overset{0.4972}{(P/F_{15,5})} = +\$798.9 \quad \textbf{accept}$$

ROR Analysis:

$$\text{PW Eq: } 0 = -850 + 291.3(P/F_{i,1}) + 992.1(P/F_{i,2}) + 570.6(P/F_{i,3})$$

$$+ 330.5(P/F_{i,4}) + 163.6(P/F_{i,5})$$

NPV @ 50% = +$41
NPV @ 70% = -$168   ROR = i = 50% + 20%(41/209) = 53.9% > i*=15%

By financial calculator, i = ROR = 53.276% > i* = 15%, **accept**

Ratio Analysis:

PVR = 798.9/850 = 0.94 > 0   B/C Ratio = PVR + 1 = 1.94 > 1.0

Break-even Uniform Selling Price Per Unit:

Year	0	1	2	3	4	5
Revenues		62X	53X	35X	24X	17X
-Royalties		-8.68X	-7.42X	-4.90X	-3.36X	-2.38X
-Operating Cost		-175.0	-193.0	-212.0	-233.0	-256.0
-Mine Dev	-750.0	-250.0				
-Mine Equipment		-670.0				
-Min Rights Acq	-100.0					
Before-Tax CF	-850.0	53.32X	45.58X	30.10X	20.64X	14.62X
		-1,095	-193	-212	-233	-256

$$\text{PW Eq: } 0 = -850 + (53.32X-1,095)\overset{0.8696}{(P/F_{15,1})} + (45.58X-193)\overset{0.7561}{(P/F_{15,2})}$$

$$+ (30.10X-212)\overset{0.6575}{(P/F_{15,3})} + (20.64X-233)\overset{0.5718}{(P/F_{15,4})} + (14.62X-256)\overset{0.4972}{(P/F_{15,5})}$$

$$0 = -2,348.0 + 119.69X \quad \textit{Break-even Price, X = \$19.62 per ton}$$

Excel Solutions to Text Problem 3-20, 3-21 and 3-22

	A	B	C	D	E	F	G	H	I	J
1	Spreadsheet Functions for Rate of Return (IRR or @IRR), Growth ROR (MIRR or @MIRR), and Net Present Value (NPV or @NPV).									
2	In Excel, access functions using the fx button from the main menu bar or, select, Insert, Function... then select the appropriate category.									
3	Evaluation Dates	1/1/01	1/1/02	1/1/03	1/1/04	1/1/05	1/1/06			
4	Year	0	1	2	3	4	5			
5	Production		62	53	35	24	17			
6	Selling Price		$26.00	$26.00	$26.00	$27.30	$28.70			
7	Revenue		1,612	1,378	910	655	488			
8	- Royalties		(226)	(193)	(127)	(92)	(68)			
9	Net Revenue		1,386	1,185	783	563	420			
10	- Operating Costs		(175)	(193)	(212)	(233)	(256)			
11	- Development Costs	(750)	(250)							
12	- Equipment Cost		(670)							
13	- Acquisition Cost	(100)								
14	Before-Tax Cash Flows, BTCF	(850)	291	992	571	330	164			
15	Discounted BTCF, DBTCF	(850)	253	750	375	189	81			
16	Cumulative DBTCF	(850)	(597)	153	529	718	799	(NPV @ Time Zero)		
17										
18		=C14*(1/(1+$B$20))^C4			=SUM($B$15:C15)					
19										
20	Discount Rate, i*	15.00%								
21										
22	Equation Form		Result	Discussion						
23	=NPV($B$20,C14:G14)+B14		$799	*This is the correct solution in either Excel or Lotus!*						
24	@NPV(B20,C14:G14)+B14		$799	*Correct Lotus form of net present value equation.*						
25	=NPV($B$20,B14:G14)		$695	*This is an incorrect, year -1 value with either Excel or Lotus!*						
26				*Note: Do not include time 0 inside the NPV function when calculating a time 0 NPV.*						
27	=XNPV($B$20,B14:G14,B3:G3)		$799	*This "date based" X function is ideal for mid-period discounting!*						
28				*Note: this function does include the time zero value.*						
29										
30	=MIN(B16:G16)		($850.00)	*Maximum Capital Exposure (Denominator for Ratios)*						
31	=G16/ABS(B30)		$0.94	*Present Value Ratio, PVR = (Net Present Value / Maximum Capital Exposure)*						
32	=B31+1		$1.94	*Benefit Cost Ratio, B/C Ratio = PVR +1*						
33	=IRR(B14:G14)		53.3%	*This is regular compound interest rate of return.*						
34	@IRR(0.15,B14..G14)		53.3%	*Lotus form of rate of return equation.*						
35				*Note: When using the IRR function, include time zero in the cash flow range!*						
36	=XIRR(B14:G14,B3:G3)		53.3%	*This "date based" X function is ideal for mid-period discounting!*						
37	=MIRR(B14:G14,$B$20,$B$20)		31.3%	*This is the compound interest "growth rate of return"*						
38				*on investment dollars. It is always based on a single*						
39				*time zero investment growing to a single future sum.*						
40										
41	Present Worth Equation for NPV by Hand = -850 + 291.3(P/F$_{15\%,1}$) + 992.1(P/F$_{15\%,2}$) + 570.6(P/F$_{15\%,3}$) + 330.5(P/F$_{15\%,4}$) + 163.6(P/F$_{15\%,5}$) = 799									
42										
43										

3-23 Solution: *Existing Machine (A):*

```
                    -25,000
     0     -4,500  -5,500  -2,500  -3,000  -3,500  -4,000
    ─────────────────────────────────────────────────────── 7,000
     0       1       2       3       4       5       6
```

Present Worth Cost of Existing Machine (PWC$_A$):

$$\underset{0.8333}{} \qquad\qquad \underset{0.6944}{} \qquad\qquad \underset{0.3349}{}$$

$$PWC_A = -4,500(P/F_{20,1}) - 30,500(P/F_{20,2}) + 7,000(P/F_{20,6})$$

$$\underset{1.274}{} \quad \underset{2.5887}{} \quad \underset{0.6944}{}$$

$$- [2,500 + 500(A/G_{20,4})](P/A_{20,4})(P/F_{20,2}) = -28,224$$

Annual Cost of Existing Machine (AC$_A$):

$$\underset{0.30071}{}$$

$$AC_A: \; -28,224(A/P_{20,6}) = -8,487$$

Replacement Machine (B):

```
 -21,000  -2,000  -2,500  -3,000  -3,500  -4,000  -4,500
 ─────────────────────────────────────────────────────── 4,000
     0       1       2       3       4       5       6
```

Present Worth Cost of Replacement Machine (PWC$_B$):

$$\underset{1.9788}{} \qquad \underset{3.3255}{} \qquad\qquad \underset{0.3349}{}$$

$$-21,000 - [2,000 + 500(A/G_{20,6})](P/A_{20,6}) + 4,000(P/F_{20,6}) = -29,602$$

Annual Cost of Replacement (AC$_B$):

$$\underset{0.30071}{}$$

$$AC_B: \; -29,603(A/P_{20,6}) = -8,902$$

Incremental Analysis (B-A):

```
 -21,000  2,500  28,000   -500    -500    -500   -3,500
 ───────────────────────────────────────────────────────
     0      1       2       3       4       5       6
```

Incremental NPV:

$$\underset{0.8333}{} \qquad\qquad \underset{0.6944}{} \qquad\qquad \underset{2.1065}{} \quad \underset{0.6944}{}$$

$$-21,000 + 2,500(P/F_{20,1}) + 28,000(P/F_{20,2}) - 500(P/A_{20,3})(P/F_{20,2})$$

$$\underset{0.3349}{}$$

$$- 3,500(P/F_{20,6}) = -1,377 \; so, \; reject \; replacement \; machine \; B.$$

or, Incremental NPV = PWC$_B$ - PWC$_A$ = -29,602 - -28,224 = -1,378

3-24 Solution:

The specified discount rates on Treasury Bills are nominal or annual rates, so half of 5% or 2.5% is the discount rate or interest on this six month T-Bill. The interest is paid within 10 days of the T-Bill purchase date, so assume the purchase cost and interest occur at the same time.

```
Int=$250 ⎤                                      Terminal
C=$10,000 ⎦ Net Inv=$9,750                      Value=$10,000
         ──────────────────────────────────────────────────
         0                                      1 six month period
```

Present Worth Equation: $\$9,750 = 10,000(P/F_i,1)$

i = 6 month period interest rate = 2.5641%
So, nominal annual rate of return = 5.13% compounded semi-annually.

3-25 Solution: *All Values in Millions*

```
              -4                        Yr 9 BTCF = 10
   -1.5       -5      4 ........... 4    ⎛  4  ⎞ ←
   ──────────────────────────────────────⎝  6  ⎠
                                              ↓
    0        1      2 ........... 8     9       ↘
```

Present Worth Equation:

$$0 = -1.5 - 9(P/F_i,1) + 4(P/A_i,7)(P/F_i,1) + 10(P/F_i,9)$$

By calculator, i = ROR = 34.6%

Project Growth ROR: Re-investment Income @i* = 15%

```
       -         -        -4 .......... -4   -10
       ──────────────────────────────────────────  F = 60.91
       0        1        2 .......... 8      9
                11.0668     1.15
```

Where: $F = 4(F/A_{15},7)(F/P_{15},1) + 10 = \$60.91$

Initial Investment plus Re-investment Income:

```
   -1.5       -9       -  ............  -    -
   ────────────────────────────────────────── 60.91
    0        1       2 ........... 8      9
```

Growth ROR Present Worth Equation:

$$0 = -1.5 - 9.0(P/F_i,1) + 60.91(P/F_i,9)$$

by calculator = 24.1%

3-25 *Solution Continued:*

NPV Analysis:

$$\overset{0.8696}{-1.5 - 9.0(P/F_{15,1})} + \overset{4.1604}{4.0(P/A_{15,7})}\overset{0.8696}{(P/F_{15,1})} + \overset{0.2843}{10(P/F_{15,9})} = +\$7.99$$

Calculating NPV from the values used to determine growth ROR gives the same NPV result:

$$NPV = -1.5 - \overset{0.8696}{9.0(P/F_{15,1})} + \overset{0.2843}{60.91(P/F_{15,9})} = +\$7.99$$

PVR Calculation:

$$PVR = 7.99 \,/\, [1.5 + \overset{0.8696}{9.0(P/F_{15,1})}] = 0.86$$

3-26 *Solution:*   *All Values in Millions*

C=NPV$_0$	-1.5	-2.0	1.0	1.0	1.0	4.0
0	1	2	3	4 9		10

On a before-tax basis, NPV represents the additional cost that could be incurred at year 0 to receive a 15% rate of return. In this problem, NPV equals the maximum year 0 development cost that can be incurred and still have the project return 15% on invested capital.

Time Zero NPV Analysis at i* of 15%:

$$= \overset{0.8696}{-1.5(P/F_{15,1})} - \overset{0.7561}{2.0(P/F_{15,2})} + \overset{4.1604}{1.0(P/A_{15,7})}\overset{0.7561}{(P/F_{15,2})} + \overset{0.2472}{4.0(P/F_{15,10})}$$
$$= 1.32$$

Time Zero NPV Analysis at i* of 10%:

$$= \overset{0.9091}{-1.5(P/F_{10,1})} - \overset{0.8264}{2.0(P/F_{10,2})} + \overset{4.8684}{1.0(P/A_{10,7})}\overset{0.8264}{(P/F_{10,2})} + \overset{0.3855}{4.0(P/F_{10,10})}$$
$$= 2.55$$

At the lower discount rate of 10% the project NPV increased by more than $1.23 million, nearly doubling the original value. Lower discount rates always lead to increased value from positive revenue streams.

3-27 Solution: *Values in Millions of Dollars, X = Acquisition Cost*

-X	–	–	-2.5	1.5	1.3 grad/yr=-0.2 ...
0	1	2	3	4	5 11

In a before-tax analysis, the year 0 break-even property acquisition cost, X, equals the year 0 NPV for property.

Time 0 NPV Equation:

$$X = -2.5 \overset{0.5787}{(P/F_{20,3})} + [1.5 - 0.2 \overset{2.5756}{(A/G_{20,8})}] \overset{3.8372}{(P/A_{20,8})} \overset{0.5787}{(P/F_{20,3})}$$

X = \$0.72   to break-even with a 20% ROR

This represents the maximum price a buyer could pay to develop the property three years later to get a 20% ROR. The owner should make the same analysis. The minimum sales price for an owner who uses the same analysis numbers would be \$0.740 million. Any amount over that price would make selling economically better than developing from the owner viewpoint.

3-28 Solution, *Summary of Input Data:*

Year	0	1	2	3	4
Intangible Drilling	$250,000				
Tangible Completion	$100,000				
Lease Cost (Sunk)	$0				
Production, Bbl/yr		17,500	9,000	6,500	3,000
Selling Price, $/Bbl		$20.00	$20.00	$21.00	$22.05
Operating Cost, $/Bbl		$4.00	$4.00	$4.00	$4.00
Royalties(12.5% Gross,$/Bbl)		$2.50	$2.50	$2.63	$2.76

Before-Tax Cash Flow Calculations:

Year	0	1	2	3	4
Gross Revenue		350,000	180,000	136,500	66,150
-Royalties		-43,750	-22,500	-17,063	-8,269
Net Revenue Interest		306,250	157,500	119,437	57,881
-Operating Expenses		-70,000	-36,000	-26,000	-12,000
-Capital Costs	-350,000				
Before-Tax CF	-350,000	236,250	121,500	93,437	45,881

Net Present Value:

$$\text{NPV @ 12\%} = -350,000 + 236,250 \underset{0.8929}{(P/F_{12,1})} + 121,500 \underset{0.7972}{(P/F_{12,2})}$$

$$+ 93,437 \underset{0.7118}{(P/F_{12,3})} + 45,881 \underset{0.6355}{(P/F_{12,4})} = 53,474$$

Present Value Ratio, PVR: 53,474 / 350,000 = 0.15

Benefit Cost Ratio: PVR + 1 = 1.15

Rate of Return, ROR, (i value that makes NPV = 0):

$$0 = -350,000 + 236,250(P/F_{i,1}) + 121,500(P/F_{i,2})$$

$$+ 93,437(P/F_{i,3}) + 45,881(P/F_{i,4})$$

i = 25%: -16,607
i = 20%:   7,438

i = ROR = 20% + (25%-20%)(7,438-0)/(7,438+16,607) = 21.55%

3-28 Solution Continued …

Growth ROR Calculation:

$$\overset{1.4049}{F = 236,250(F/P_{12,3})} + \overset{1.2544}{121,500(F/P_{12,2})} + \overset{1.1200}{93,438(F/P_{12,1})} + 45,881$$

$$F = \$634,849$$

Growth ROR Present Worth Equation:

$$0 = -350,000 + 634,849(P/F_{i,4})$$

GROR = i = 16.05%

Break-even Uniform Price per Barrel: Let X = price/barrel each year. Due to royalties, only 87.5% of production is available to generate revenues to pay off the initial investment, and give a 12.0% ROR.

$$0 = -350,000 + \overset{0.8929}{(15,313X-70,000)(P/F_{12,1})} + \overset{0.7972}{(7,875X-36,000)(P/F_{12,2})}$$

$$+ \overset{0.7118}{(5,688X-26,000)(P/F_{12,3})} + \overset{0.6355}{(2,625X-12,000)(P/F_{12,4})}$$

$$25,667X = 467,335$$

Breakeven Uniform Price per Barrel X = $18.21/bbl

3-29 Solution, *5.0% Caried Interest - Backing in for a 25.0% Working Interest & a 21.875% Net Revenue Interest After Payout:*

Year	0	1	2	3	4
Intangible Drilling	$250,000				
Tangible Completion	$100,000				
Lease Cost	$0				
Production, Bbl/yr		17,500	9,000	6,500	3,000
Selling Price,$/Bbl		$20.00	$20.00	$21.00	$22.05
Operating Cost,$/Bbl		$4.00	$4.00	$4.00	$4.00
Royalties(12.5%Gross,$/Bbl)		$2.50	$2.50	$2.63	$2.76

Pay-out Calculation:

When the cumulative value of net revenue (defined here as production times the selling price less royalties and cash operating costs) gives revenue equal to the total dollars invested, the project is at pay-out. In this case, $350,000 has been spent, and the price in years 1 and 2 is constant at $20.00 per barrel. Due to the two royalties, the producer only gets 82.5% of each barrel to pay off the investment. Hence, pay-out in production is calculated as follows:

Yr 1 Pay-out Basis: $350,000-[17,500x($20.00(0.825)-$4.00)]=$131,250
Yr 2 Pay-out Basis: $131,250-[9,000x($20.00(0.825)-$4.00)]=$ 18,750
Yr 3 Pay-out: $ 18,750 = (X bbl)($21.00(0.825)-$4.00)   X = 1,407 bbl

So, in year 3, 1,407 barrels would be subject to the over-riding royalty interest of 5.0%, after which (the reversion point), 5,093 barrels would be subject to the 25.0% working interest and a 21.875% net revenue interest (25.0% adjusted for ¼ of the 12.5% royalty).

Year	0	1	2	3	4
Carried Interest Rev.(5%)		17,500	9,000	1,477	-
+N.R.I.*(21.875% After Reversion)		0	0	23,396	14,470
Total Net Revenue		17,500	9,000	24,873	14,470
-Operating Exp.(25% A.R.**)		0	0	-5,093	-3,000
Before-Tax CF	0	17,500	9,000	19,780	11,470

* Net Revenue Interest, ** After Reversion

NPV Analysis, i = 12%:

$$
\begin{array}{cccc}
0.8929 & 0.7972 & 0.7118 & 0.6355
\end{array}
$$
$$
= 17,500(P/F_{12,1}) + 9,000(P/F_{12,2}) + 19,780(P/F_{12,3}) + 11,470(P/F_{12,4})
$$

=$44,169

PVR and ROR are infinite due to zero investment.

Problem 3-29 *Farmout Before-Tax Cash Flows:*

Year	0	1	2	3	4
Gross Revenue		350,000	180,000	136,500	66,150
-Production Royalty		-43,750	-22,500	-17,063	-8,269
-Overriding Royalty		-17,500	-9,000	-24,873	-11,470
Net Revenue Interest		288,750	148,500	94,564	57,881
-Operating Expenses		-70,000	-36,000	-19,500	-12,000
-Capital Costs	-350,000				
Before-Tax CF	-350,000	218,750	112,500	75,064	45,881
Discounted CF	-350,000	195,322	89,685	53,431	29,157
Cumulative DCF	-350,000	-154,678	-64,993	-11,562	17,595

Net Present Value, NPV @ 12% = 17,595
Rate of Return, ROR, i = 15.2% > 12.0%, acceptable
Present Value Ratio, PVR = 17,595 / 350,000 = 0.05 > 0, acceptable

NPV Profile: Problem 3-29, Royalty vs Farmout

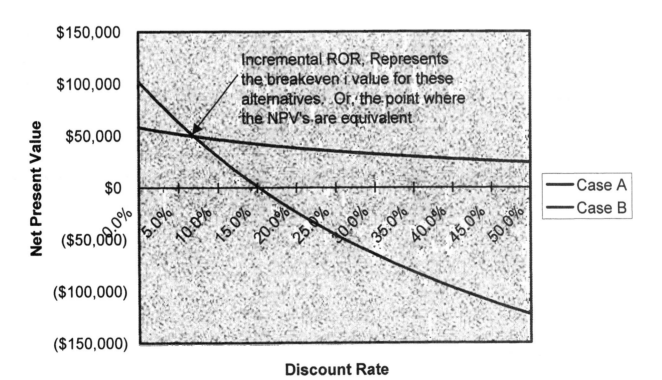

3-30 Solution: *All Values in Thousands*

Period Interest Rate = $\dfrac{\text{Nominal Rate of 12.0\%}}{\text{12 Monthly Compounding Periods}}$ = **1% per month**

Effective Annual Rate, E, = $[(1.01)^{12}-1]$ = 0.1268 or **12.68%**

Purchase Compressor:

Installation=$75
Acquisition =$1,000   –   –   C=$225   –
                                                                                   L=$300

Years	0	1	2	3	4	5
Months	0	12	24	36	48	60

Present Worth Cost Analysis of Purchase Using a Monthly i:
 0.6989 0.5504
$1,075 + 225(P/F_{1,36}) - 300(P/F_{1,60}) = \$1,067.13$

Annual Period Present Worth Cost Analysis of Purchase Using an effective annual interest rate, E:
 0.6989 0.5504
$1,075 + 225(P/F_{12.68\%,3}) - 300(P/F_{12.68\%,5}) = \$1,067.13$ Least Cost
 0.02224
Monthly Cost: $(1-60) = 1,067.13(A/P_{1,60}) = \$23.73$ Least Cost

Lease Compressor:

Installation = $75
Lease Payment = $24 ...... $24 ..... $24 .... $24

| Months | 0 .... | 12 ...... | 24 .... | 59 |

Present Worth Cost Analysis of Leasing:

Using a monthly period interest rate, i:
 44.4046
$99 + 24(P/A_{1,59}) = \$1,164.71$
 0.02224
Monthly Cost: $(1-60) = 1,164.71(A/P_{1,60}) = \$25.90$

Annual Period Present Worth Cost Analysis of Leasing:

75+6(24)=$219	12(24)=$288	12(24)=$288	12(24)=$288	12(24)=$288	6(24)=$144
Year 0	1	2	3	4	5

Using effective annual interest rate, E:
 2.99436 0.5505
$219 + 288(P/A_{12.68,4}) + 144(P/F_{12.68,5}) = \$1,160.64$

3-31 Solution:

A)   10 Year Bond Analysis

Value(P)=?   I=\$800 .... I=\$800

Maturity Value = \$10,000

0   1 .... 10 years

i=8%:   P = \$10,000

              7.360   0.5584

i=6%:   P = 800 $(P/A_{6,10})$ + 10,000 $(P/F_{6,10})$ = \$11,472

              6.144   0.3855

i=10%: P = 800 $(P/A_{10,10})$ + 10,000 $(P/F_{10,10})$ = \$8,770

B) 30 Year Bond Analysis

Value(P)=?   I=\$800 .... I=\$800

Maturity Value = \$10,000

0   1 .... 30 years

i=8%:   P = \$10,000

             13.765   0.1741

i=6%:   P = 800 $(P/A_{6,30})$ + 10,000 $(P/F_{6,30})$ = \$12,753

             9.427   0.05731

i=10%: P = 800 $(P/A_{10,30})$ + 10,000 $(P/F_{10,30})$ = \$8,115

C) 30 Year Zero Coupon Bond

Value(P)=?   –   –

Maturity Value = \$10,000

0   1 .... 30 years

                0.099377

i=8%:   P = 10,000 $(P/F_{8,30})$ = \$994

                0.17411

i=6%:   P = 10,000 $(P/F_{6,30})$ = \$1,741

                0.05731

i=10%: P = 10,000 $(P/F_{10,30})$ = \$573

3-32 Solution:

Current Remediation System:

```
-        -$50,000  -$50,000 . . .  -$50,000  -$50,000  -$50,000
─────────────────────────────────────────────────────────────
0           1         2  . . . . . . 5         6         7
```

                    5.0330
PW Cost: -50,000(P/A$_{9,7}$) = -$251,650

Upgraded Remediation System:

```
-$75,000    -$35,000   -$35,000 . . . . . . -$35,000
────────────────────────────────────────────────────
0            1          2  . . . . . . . . . 5
```

                    3.8897
PW Cost: -75,000 - 35,000(P/A$_{9,5}$) = -$211,140 least cost alternative.

Incremental Analysis (Upgrade - Current):

```
-$75,000     $15,000   $15,000 . . . $15,000   $50,000   $50,000
────────────────────────────────────────────────────────────────
0            1         2   . . . 5            6         7
```

Incremental NPV @ 9.0%:

       1.7591   0.6499   3.8897
50,000(P/A$_{9,2}$)(P/F$_{9,5}$) + 15,000(P/A$_{9,5}$) - 75,000 = $40,510

$40,510 > 0, *so accept the upgrade investment.*

3-33 Solution:

Alternative 1

-$170,000 -$35,000   -$35,000 . . . . -$35,000
                                                          $50,000
───
     0   1   2 5

PW Cost Equation:

$$\begin{array}{cc} 3.8897 & 0.6499 \end{array}$$

$-170{,}000 - 35{,}000(P/A_{9,5}) + 50{,}000(P/F_{9,5}) = -\$273{,}645$ least cost

Alternative 2

   -       -$50,000   -$50,000 . . .-$50,000   -$50,000 . . . -$50,000
───
   0   1   2 5   6 10

$$6.4177$$

PW Cost Equation: $-50{,}000(P/A_{9,10}) = -\$320{,}885$

Incremental Analysis (Alternative 1 - Alternative 2)

-$170,000 $15,000 $15,000 . . $15,000 $65,000 $50,000
───
   0   1   2 4   5   6-10

Incremental NPV @ 9.0%:

$$\begin{array}{cccc} 0.6499 & 3.8897\ 0.6499 & 3.2397 \end{array}$$

$65{,}000(P/F_{9,5}) + 50{,}000(P/A_{9,5})(P/F_{9,5}) + 15{,}000(P/A_{9,4}) - 170{,}000$

$= \$47{,}235$

Or, Looking at the differences in the present worth costs will also give the incremental NPV result as follows:

Incremental NPV = PW Cost$_1$ - PW Cost$_2$

$$= -273{,}645 - -320{,}885 = +47{,}240$$

The difference in the two results is round-off error in the factors.

3-34 Solution:

Nominal Interest Rate = 10.0% Compounded Monthly
Period Interest Rate = 10.0%/12 = 0.833%
Effective Interest Rate, E = $(1.00833)^{12} - 1 = 10.47\%$

Option 1; Catalytic Converter

```
Equipment   -70,000
O & M       - 6,000    -12,000    -12,000    -12,000    -12,000    -6,000
            _____
               0          1          2          3          4          5
```

$$\qquad\qquad\qquad\qquad 3.13788 \qquad\qquad\qquad 0.60782$$

PW Cost$_1$ = $-76,000 - 12,000(P/A_{10.47\%,4}) - 6,000(P/F_{10.47\%,5})$

$\qquad$ = -117,301   select the least cost, Alternative 1

Option 2; Two 1,000 Pound Carbon Canisters

Carbon Replacement: 2 Canisters * 1,000 lbs ea * $4.00/lb = $8,000

Time Zero: Allocate 3 Replacements: 3 * $8,000 = $24,000

Year One: Allocate 6 Replacements: 6 * $8,000 = $48,000

Year Two: Allocate 3 Replacements: 3 * $8,000 = $24,000
             Allocate 2 Replacements: 2 * $8,000 = $16,000 $40,000

Year Three: Allocate 2 Replacements: 2 * $8,000 = $16,000
             Allocate 1 Replacement: 1 * $8,000 = $ 8,000 $24,000

Year Four: Allocate 1 Replacement: 1 * $8,000 = $ 8,000
             Allocate 1/2 Replacement: 0.5 * $8,000 = $ 4,000 $12,000

Year Five: Allocate 1/2 Replacement: 0.5 * $8,000 = $ 4,000

```
Equipment        -15,000
Can. Replace.    -24,000    -48,000    -40,000    -24,000    -12,000    -4,000
                 _____
                    0          1          2          3          4          5
```

$$\qquad\qquad\qquad\qquad 0.90522 \qquad\qquad\qquad 0.81943$$

PW Cost$_2$ = $- 39,000 - 48,000(P/F_{10.47\%,1}) - 40,000(P/F_{10.47\%,2})$

$$\qquad\quad 0.74177 \qquad\qquad\qquad 0.67146 \qquad\qquad\qquad 0.60782$$

$\quad - 24,000(P/F_{10.47\%,3}) - 12,000(P/F_{10.47\%,4}) - 4,000(P/F_{10.47\%,5})$

$\quad$ = -143,519

NPV = PW Cost$_1$ - PW Cost$_2$ -117,301 - -143,519 = 26,218 > 0, Accept 1

CHAPTER 4 PROBLEM SOLUTIONS

4-1 Solution: *All Values in Thousands*

Project A

```
C=$300     I=$450     I=$450 . . . . . . . . .  I=$450
_____
   0          1          2 . . . . . . . . .  . 10
```

Project B

```
C=$900     I=$550     I=$550 . . . . . . . . .  I=$550
_____
   0          1          2 . . . . . . . . .  . 10
```

Project C

```
           I=$750
C=$1,200   C=$800     I=$850 . . . . . . . . .  I=$850
_____
   0          1          2 . . . . . . .  . . . 10
```

ROR Analysis:

"A" PW Eq: $0 = -300 + 450(P/A_{i,10})$ $i = ROR_A = 150\% > i^* = 15\%$, *ok*

"B" PW Eq: $0 = -900 + 550(P/A_{i,10})$ $i = ROR_B = 60.6\% > i^* = 15\%$, *ok*

"C" PW Eq: $0 = -1,200 - 50(P/F_{i,1}) + 850(P/A_{i,9})(P/F_{i,1})$

$$i = ROR_C = 45.7\% > i^* = 15\%, \text{ } ok$$

Incremental Analysis, Project B - Project A

```
C=$600     I=$100     I=$100 . . . . . . . . .  I=$100
_____
   0          1          2 . . . . . . . .  . . 10
```

"B-A" PW Eq: $0 = -600 + 100(P/A_{i,10})$

$$i = ROR_{B-A} = 10.5\% < 15\%, \text{ } so \text{ } reject \text{ } B$$

Incremental Analysis, Project C - Project A

```
C=$900     C=$500     I=$400 . . . . . . . . .  I=$400
_____
   0          1          2 . . . . . . . . . . . 10
```

"C-A" PW Eq: $0 = -900 - 500(P/F_{i,1}) + 400(P/A_{i,9})(P/F_{i,1})$

$$i = ROR_{C-A} = 20.5\% > i^* = 15\%, \text{ } so \text{ } select \text{ } C$$

4-1 *Solution Continued:*

NPV Analysis:

$\text{NPV}_A = -300 + 450(P/A_{15,10}) = +\$1,958$
$\text{NPV}_B = -900 + 550(P/A_{15,10}) = +\$1,860$
$\text{NPV}_C = -1,200 - 50(P/F_{15,1}) + 850(P/A_{15,9})(P/F_{15,1}) = +\$2,283$

Since $\text{NPV}_{B-A} = -98$ *and* $\text{NPV}_{C-A} = +\$325$, *"C" is the economic choice.*

Alternative "C" is the economic choice for $i^*=15\%$ *since* NPV_{C-A} *and* NPV_{C-B} *are both positive. As always, the largest total investment NPV is the economic choice.*

PVR Analysis:

$\text{PVR}_A = 1,958/300 = 6.5 > 0,$ *so satisfactory*
$\text{PVR}_B = 1,860/900 = 2.1 > 0,$ *so satisfactory*
$\text{PVR}_C = 2,283/[1,200+50(P/F_{15,1})] = 1.8 > 0,$ *so satisfactory*

$\text{PVR}_{B-A} = (1,860-1,958)/600 = -0.2 < 0,$ *unsatisfactory, select A over B*
$\text{PVR}_{C-A} = (2,283-1,958)/(900 + 500(P/F_{15,1})) = +0.2 > 0$ *select C over A*

Sensitivity for NPV Analysis at $i^* = 25\%$:

$\text{NPV}_A = -300 + 450(P/A_{25,10}) = +\$1,307$ *Select the maximum NPV.*
$\text{NPV}_B = -900 + 550(P/A_{25,10}) = +\$1,064$
$\text{NPV}_C = -1,200 - 50(P/F_{25,1}) + 850(P/A_{25,9})(P/F_{25,1}) = +\$1,115$

Select A, as indicated graphically using an NPV Profile comparison.

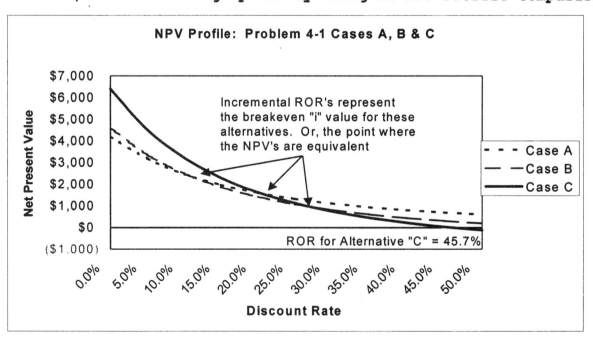

4-2 Solution: *All Vaues in Thousands*

```
  -80           290              290
 -200          -160 . . . . .   -160       -360
 -280           130 . . . . .    130       -360
```
_____

```
  0              1 . . . . . . . 5          6
```

Net Present Value: $-280 + 130(P/A_{i,5}) - 360(P/F_{i,6})$

i	NPV
0%	+ 10.0
5%	+ 14.2
10%	+ 9.6
15%	+ 0.1
20%	- 11.8

15%   + 0.1   *Dual i $\cong$ 15%, the second dual "i" is negative.*

Since NPV @ 20% is -$11.8, reject the project for $i^* = 20\%$.

Escrow Modification Used to Eliminate Cost-Income-Cost

$$\overset{0.3349}{280 + 360(P/F_{20,6})} = 130(P/A_{i,5})$$

$$400.6 = 130(P/A_{i,5})$$

i = PW Cost Modified ROR = 18.6% < $i^* = 20\%$ so reject.

4-3 Solution: Maximize Incremental NPV from Savings

Incremental based on comparison with the current condition, 0 inches.

Incremental Insulation (Inches)	Annual Savings From Insulation	Incremental NPV Analysis Equation	Incremental NPV ($)
0	0	(3.3255)	0.00
1-0	600	$600(P/A_{20,6}) - 1,200 =$	795.30
2-0	800	$800(P/A_{20,6}) - 1,800 =$	860.40*
3-0	900	$900(P/A_{20,6}) - 2,500 =$	492.95
4-0	1,000	$1,000(P/A_{20,6}) - 3,500 =$	-174.80

Select the largest Incremental NPV of +$860.40 at 2 Inches.

Alternate Solution: Minimize Total PW Cost

Insulation (Inches)	PW Cost Calculation	PW Cost ($)
	3.3255	
0	$-1,400 \ (P/A_{20,6}) \qquad\quad =$	-4,655.70
1	$-800 \ (P/A_{20,6}) - 1,200 =$	-3,860.40
2	$-600 \ (P/A_{20,6}) - 1,800 =$	-3,795.30*
3	$-500 \ (P/A_{20,6}) - 2,500 =$	-4,162.80
4	$-400 \ (P/A_{20,6}) - 3,500 =$	-4,830.20

Selecting the least negative option is the economic choice.

Incremental inch-by-inch comparison of mutually exclusive income alternatives (derived from original incremental calculations above).

Incremental Insulation (inches)	Annual Savings From Insulation	Incremental NPV Analysis of Mutually Exclusive Alternatives	Incremental NPV
1-0	600	$600(P/A_{20,6}) - 1,200 =$	795.30
2-1	200	$200(P/A_{20,6}) - \quad 600 =$	65.10*
3-2	100	$100(P/A_{20,6}) - \quad 700 =$	-267.45
4-2	200	$200(P/A_{20,6}) - 1,700 =$	-1035.90

*Selecting 2" of insulation adds $65.10 in value over and above 1"
which had a positive NPV. However, going to three inches generates
-$267.45 less value compared to the 2" level and 4" reduces the value
further. Note that the analysis compares the next level of investment
to the last satisfactory level. The largest level of investment
satisfying both individual and incremental criteria is the economic
choice; 2 inches of insulation.*

4-4 Solution: *All Values in Thousands of Dollars*

This is an income-cost-income analysis situation and involves the Dual ROR problem, as does the cost-income-cost problem.

		C=50	C=50	C=50	C=1,450			
	I=450	I=450	I=450	I=450	I=450	I=450		I=450
-	OC=310	OC=310	OC=310	OC=310	OC=310	OC=310	.....	OC=310

L=300

0	1	2	3	4	5	6 10
BTCF	140	90	90	90	-1,310	140 140+300

$$NPV = 140(P/F_{i,1}) + 90(P/A_{i,3})(P/F_{i,1}) - 1,310(P/F_{i,5})$$

$$+ 140(P/A_{i,5})(P/F_{i,5}) + 300(P/F_{i,10})$$

i	NPV	
0	+ 100.0	
5	- 0.6	4.95%
10	- 37.5	
15	- 43.4	
20	- 35.0	
30	- 5.8	
40	+ 21.9	32.90%
50	+ 42.5	

These are the project dual i values and are not valid for ROR economic decision making.

Although the Dual "i" values are not valid for ROR economic decision-making, the NPV results that were the basis for determining the dual "i" values are valid for economic decision making.

NPV @ $i^* = $ 5% is similar to zero indicating break-even economics.
NPV @ $i^* = $ 15% is negative indicating unsatisfactory economics.
NPV @ $i^* = $ 50% is positive indicating satisfactory economics.

Increasing the minimum ROR to 50% from 15% improves the economics because of the strong rate of reinvestment meaning (as opposed to rate of return meaning) associated with i^* in this income-cost-income analysis.

4-4 Solution Continued:

Escrow Modified ROR Analysis for i* = 5%:

i* = 5%, Modified Year 0 PW Cost = $1,310(P/F_{5,5}) = \$1,026$

$1,026 = 140(P/F_{i,1}) + 90(P/A_{i,3})(P/F_{i,1}) + 140(P/A_{i,5})(P/F_{i,5}) + 300(P/F_{i,10})$

i = Escrow ROR = 5.0%=i* of 5% *Indicates break-even economics.*

Escrow Modified ROR Analysis for i* = 15%:

$$0.49718$$
i* = 15%, Modified Yr 0 PW Cost = $1,310(P/F_{15,5}) = \$651.3$

$651.3 = 140(P/F_{i,1}) + 90(P/A_{i,3})(P/F_{i,1}) + 140(P/A_{i,5})(P/F_{i,5}) + 300(P/F_{i,10})$

i = Escrow ROR = 13.5% < i* = 15%   *Unsatisfactory*

Escrow Modified ROR Analysis for i* = 50%:

$$0.13169$$
i* = 50%, Modified Yr 0 PW Cost = $1,310(P/F_{50,5}) = \$172.5$

$\$172.5 = 140(P/F_{i,1}) + 90(P/A_{i,3})(P/F_{i,1}) + 140(P/A_{i,5})(P/F_{i,5}) + 300(P/F_{i,10})$

i = Escrow Modified ROR = 63.3% > i* = 50% *so satisfactory*

PW Cost Modified ROR analysis and NPV analysis give the same economic conclusion for the different minimum rates of return.

4-5 Solution:

Case A) Net Present Value Analysis

$NPV_1 = 80,000(P/A_{40,6}) - 150,000 = + \$23,440$ *Select the largest, NPV_1*
$NPV_2 = 115,000(P/A_{40,6}) - 230,000 = + \$19,320$

$NPV_2 - NPV_1 = -\$4,120$, *so select NPV_1*

Case B) Break-even Service Life

To determine break-even service, n, set NPV_1=NPV_2 for unknown life, n:
$80,000(P/A_{40,n}) - 150,000 = 115,000(P/A_{40,n}) - 230,000$
$P/A_{40,n} = 2.286$,
break-even service life n=7.34 yrs

For an evaluation life, n, less than 7.34 years, 1 is best.
For evaluation life, n, greater than 7.34 years, 2 is best.

4-6 Solution: *All Values in Dollars*

Alternative A)

```
          C=200              C=230
C=100     I=110    I=110     I=110     I=110 ........ I=110
─────────────────────────────────────────────────────────
   0        1        2         3        4 ........... 8
```

$NPV_A = 110(P/A_{15,8}) - 230(P/F_{15,3}) - 200(P/F_{15,1}) - 100 = +\$68.4$

$PVR_A = 68.4 / [100 + (200-110)(P/F_{15,1})] = +0.38$

The year 3 cost of $230 does not affect the PVR_A denominator because it is offset by the combination of year 2 and 3 income as follows:

$[(-230+110)(P/F_{15,1}) + 110] = +\$5.65$ *which is year 2 net income, not a net cost, resulting from the year 2 and 3 incomes and cost.*

Alternative B)

```
          C=200              C=180
C=100     I=110    I=20      I=110     I=110 ........ I=110
─────────────────────────────────────────────────────────
   0        1        2         3        4 ........... 8
```

$NPV_B = 110(P/A_{15,5})(P/F_{15,3}) - 70(P/F_{15,3}) + 20(P/F_{15,2}) - 90(P/F_{15,1})$

$- 100 = +\$33.3$

$PVR_B = 33.3/\{100+(200-110)(P/F_{15,1})+[(180-110)(P/F_{15,1})-20](P/F_{15,2})\}$

$= 33.3/209.2 = +0.16$

Project "A" with PVR of +0.38 ranks first, project "B" with PVR of +0.16 ranks second.

4-7 Solution:

Annual Worth equations for projects A & B give:

Project A ROR = 40%, Project B ROR = 40%

i) Incremental Analysis for B-A:

```
                              L=150,000                C=100,000
C=50,000        I=20,000 ....... I=20,000   C=40,000   C= 40,000
_____
     0              1 .............  3          4          5
```

$$50,000 = 20,000(P/A_{i,3}) + 150,000(P/F_{i,3}) - 40,000(P/F_{i,4})$$

$$- 140,000(P/F_{i,5})$$

Two values of "i" exist that make the right side of the equation
equal 50,000: i = 12%, and i = 40%.

*No decision can be made from dual "i" values, except to establish the
range of i* values for which the incremental NPV in this problem will
be positive.*

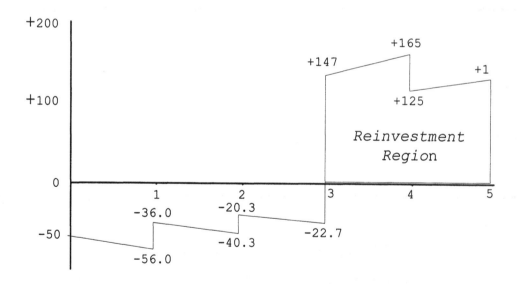

Cumulative Cash Position Diagram for i* = 12%
(Values in 000's)

4-7 Solution Continued:

ii) NPV Analysis:

$$\underset{2.991}{\text{NPV}_A} = 40,000 \underset{2.991}{(P/A_{20,5})} + 100,000 \underset{0.4019}{(P/F_{20,5})} - 100,000 = +\$59,830$$

$$\text{NPV}_B = 60,000 \underset{2.106}{(P/A_{20,3})} + 150,000 \underset{0.5787}{(P/F_{20,3})} - 150,000 = +\$63,165$$

Select project B with the greater NPV.

4-7 iii) Incremental Growth ROR Analysis B-A:

```
                              L=150,000
   C=50,000 I=20,000 I=20,000 I=20,000 C=40,000 C=140,000
   _____
      0       1        2        3        4        5
```

Reinvestment of Income @ 20%

```
                        C=150,000
    -      C=20,000 C=20,000 C=20,000    -        -
   _____    F=320,832
      0       1        2        3        4        5
```

Where $F = [20,000 \underset{3.640}{(F/A_{20,3})} + 150,000] \underset{1.440}{(F/P_{20,2})} = \$320,832$

Alternative B - Alternative A + Income Reinvestment

```
   C=50,000    -        -        -     C=40,000    -
   _____    Net F=180,832
      0       1        2        3        4        5
```

PW Eq: $0 = -50,000 - 40,000(P/F_{i,4}) + 180,832(P/F_{i,5})$

By trial and error, Incremental Growth ROR, i, = 21.5% > i*=20% *indicating satisfactory economics, select B.*

4-7 *Solution Continued:*

iv) *Present Worth Cost Modified Incremental ROR Analysis:*

Present Worth Modified Cost:

$50,000 + 40,000(P/F_{20,4}) + 140,000(P/F_{20,5}) = \$125,560$

C=125,560   I=20,000   I=20,000   I=170,000   -   -
‾‾
       0   1   2   3   4   5

Present Worth Equation: $125,560 = 20,000(P/A_{i,2}) + 170,000(P/F_{i,3})$

By trial and error, i = PW Cost Modified ROR = 21.2% > i*=20%

4-7 v) *Reduce i* to 10% from 20%:*

$$NPV_A = -100 + 40\overset{3.791}{(P/A_{10,5})} + 100\overset{0.6209}{(P/F_{10,5})} = +\$113.7$$

$$NPV_B = -150 + 60\overset{2.487}{(P/A_{10,3})} + 150\overset{0.7513}{(P/F_{10,3})} = +\$111.9$$

Select the greater NPV of \$113,000, alternative A.

4-8 Solution: *All Values in Dollars*

 I=1,000   I=1,000   I=1,000   C=9,000   I=1,000 .... I=1,000
‾‾
    0   1   2   3   4 10

A)   *Net Present Value Analysis:*

$$1,000+1,000\overset{1.528}{(P/A_{20,2})}-9,000\overset{0.5787}{(P/F_{20,3})}+1,000\overset{3.605}{(P/A_{20,7})}\overset{0.5787}{(P/F_{20,3})} = -\$595$$

The -\$595 indicates unsatisfactory economics, so reject the offer.

B)   *PW Cost Modified ROR Analysis:*

Bring the year 3 cost back to year 0 at the minimum ROR:

$$9,000\overset{0.5787}{(P/F_{20,3})} = 1,000 + 1,000(P/A_{i,2}) + 1,000(P/A_{i,7})(P/F_{i,3})$$

Present Worth Cost Modified ROR, i, = 15.9%

15.9% < i of 20%, again indicating unsatisfactory economics, so
                reject the offer.*

4-9 Solution: *All Values in Thousands*

Operation Level A)

```
C=100             Net I=40 .............. Net I=40
─────────────────────────────────────────────────
   0                 1 ...................... 5
```

Operation Level B)

```
C=150             Net I=55 .............. Net I=55
─────────────────────────────────────────────────
   0                 1 ...................... 5
```

NPV Analysis @ $i^* = 20\%$:

$NPV_A = -100 + 40(P/A_{20,5}) = +\$19.6$ *Select A, with the maximum NPV.*

$NPV_B = -150 + 55(P/A_{20,5}) = +\$14.5$

ROR Analysis:

"A" PW Eq: $0 = -100 + 40(P/A_{i,5})$, so $i = ROR_A = 28.6\% > i^* = 20\%$, ok

"B" PW Eq: $0 = -150 + 55(P/A_{i,5})$, so $i = ROR_B = 24.3\% > i^* = 20\%$, ok

Incremental Analysis B-A:

```
C=50              Net I=15 .............. Net I=15
─────────────────────────────────────────────────
   0                 1 ...................... 5
```

"B-A" PW Eq: $0 = -50 + 15(P/A_{i,5})$, so $i = ROR_{B-A} = 15.2\% < i^* = 20\%$

The ROR_{B-A} is less than the minimum ROR of 20%; reject B, select A.

PVR Analysis:

$PVR_A = 19.6/100 = 0.196 > 0$, *satisfactory*

$PVR_B = 14.5/150 = 0.097 > 0$, *satisfactory*

$PVR_{B-A} = (14.5-19.6)/(150-100) = -0.10 < 0$, *unsatisfactory, select A*

Change the Minimum ROR to 12% from 20% over all 5 years:

The total investment and incremental investment ROR results are the same. Comparing them to $i^*=12\%$, however, gives a different economic conclusion, which is to select B.

$NPV_A = -100 + 40(P/A_{12,5}) = +\$44.4$

$NPV_B = -150 + 55(P/A_{12,5}) = +\$48.3$ *Select B, with the greatest NPV.*

Change the Min. ROR to 12% in years 1 & 2, and 20% for years 3, 4 & 5:

$NPV_A = -100 + 40(P/A_{20,3})(P/F_{12,2}) + 40(P/A_{12,2}) = +\$34.75$

$NPV_B = -150 + 55(P/A_{20,3})(P/F_{12,2}) + 55(P/A_{12,2}) = +\$35.28$ breakeven

4-10 Mutually Exclusive Alternatives Solution:

Alternative A

```
    -          I=450        I=450 ............ I=450
    _____
    0           1            2 .............. 10
```

Alternative B

```
  C=800        I=700        I=700 ............ I=700
    _____
    0           1            2 ............. 10
```

Alternative C

```
             I=850
  C=1,300    C=900        I=1,050 ........ I=1,050
    _____
    0           1            2 ............. 10
```

Net Present Value @ i* = 15%:

                5.019
A)   450(P/A$_{15,10}$) = +$2,259

                5.019
B)   700(P/A$_{15,10}$) - 800 = +$2,713

              4.772   0.8696
C) [1,050(P/A$_{15,9}$) - 50](P/F$_{15,1}$) - 1,300 = +$3,014   *Economic Choice*

Since NPV$_{C-B}$ and NPV$_{C-A}$ are positive, "C" with maximum NPV is the economic choice. The mutually exclusive alternative with maximum NPV on total investment always turns out to be the economic choice from incremental NPV analysis.

Present Value Ratio @ i* = 15%:

A)   2,259 / 0 = ∞ > 0, *so acceptable*
B)   2,713 / 800 = +3.39 > 0, *so acceptable*
C)   3,014 /(1,300+50(P/F$_{15,1}$))= 3,014/1,344 = +2.24 > 0, *so acceptable*

B-A) (2,713-2,259)/(800-0)=+0.57 > 0, *so acceptable*

Then, comparing alternative C to alternative B:

C-B) (3,014-2,713)/(500+652.2) = +0.26 > 0, (C is the economic choice)

Since B was preferred to A, there is no real value in comparing C to A. Comparing the next level of incremental investment (C-B), C is preferred to B since the incremental C-B PVR is positive indicating that the additional dollars invested in C over B earn a present worth profit of $0.55 per present worth dollar invested.

4-10 Solution Continued:

Rate of Return Analysis for $i^* = 15.0\%$:

ROR_A: $0 = 450(P/A_i,10)$ $i = \infty\% > i^* = 15\%$

ROR_B: $800 = 700(P/A_i,10)$ $i = 87.34\% > i^* = 15\%$

ROR_C: $1,300 = 1,050(P/A_i,9)(P/F_i,1) - 50(P/F_i,1)$

           $i = 50.9\% > i^* = 15\%$

ROR_{B-A}: $800 = 250(P/A_i,10)$

           $i = 28.8\% > 15\%$, **Accept B over A**

ROR_{C-B}: $500 = \{350(P/A_i,9) - 750\}(P/F_i,1)$

           $i = 21.25\% > i^* = 15\%$ **"C" is the economic choice.**

Changing the Minimum Rate of Return to $i^* = 25\%$:

A) $450(\overset{3.571}{P/A_{25},10}) = +\$1,607$

B) $700(\overset{3.571}{P/A_{25},10}) - 800 = +\$1,700$ **"B" is now the economic choice.**

C) $[1,050(\overset{3.463}{P/A_{25},9}) - 50](\overset{0.800}{P/F_{25},1}) - 1,300 = +\$1,569$

For rate of return analysis, the only incremental alternative generating an incremental rate of return in excess of the new 25.0% minimum rate is (B-A) which indicates selecting alternative "B" is the economic choice, consistent with the NPV results. Incremental C-B is shown below to verify that "B" is preferred to "C." PVR would select "B" also.

ROR_{C-B} $500 = \{350(P/A_i,9) - 750\}(P/F_i,1)$

$i = 21.25\% < i^* = 25\%$ **Accept B with the greater ROR.**

4-10 *Solution Continued:*

Changing the minimum rate of return to 25% for years 1 and 2, then back to 15% for years 3 through 10 causes rate of return to yield inconsistent conclusions, this forces you to a criteria like NPV:

NPV_A = 450(P/A$_{15,8}$)(P/F$_{25,2}$) + 450(P/A$_{25,2}$) = +$1,940

NPV_B = 700(P/A$_{15,8}$)(P/F$_{25,2}$) + 700(P/A$_{25,2}$) - 800 = +$2,218

NPV_C = 1,050(P/A$_{15,8}$)(P/F$_{25,2}$) + 1,050(P/F$_{25,2}$) - 50(P/F$_{25,1}$) - 1,300

       = +$2,347   *Select "C" with the largest NPV.*

Measuring the effect pf changing the minimum ROR with time by using NPV analysis indicates Alternative C as the economic choice. This same result is not achieved by changing the minimum ROR to 25% over the entire evaluation life.   The minimum ROR is a very significant evaluation parameter and must represent other opportunities for investing capital both now and in the future over the evaluation life of projects.   If the minimum ROR is projected to change with time, that change must be built into evaluation calculations as illustrated to achieve valid economic analysis results.

4-11 Solution: *Values in Millions of Dollars*

Alternative A:

C=$32   I=$12   I=$12 .... I=$12
_____
  0   1   2 5

Alternative B:

C=$38   I=$13.5   I=$13.5 .... I=$13.5
_____
  0   1   2 5

Incremental Analysis B-A:

C=$6   I=$1.5   I=$1.5 .... I=$1.5
_____
  0   1   2 5

ROR_A: $0 = -32 + 12(P/A_{i},5)$; $32/12 = (P/A_{i},5) = 2.667$

$i = 25\% + 5\%[(2.689-2.667)/(2.689-2.436)] = 25.43\% > i^*=15\%$, *so ok.*

ROR_B: $0 = -38 + 13.5(P/A_{i},5)$; $38/13.5 = (P/A_{i},5) = 2.815$

$i = 20\% + 5\%[(2.991-2.815)/(2.991-2.689)] = 22.91\% > i^*=15\%$, *so ok.*

ROR_{B-A}: $0 = -6 + 1.5(P/A_{i},5)$; $6/1.5 = (P/A_{i},5) = 4.000$

$i = 7\% + 1\%[(4.100-4.000)/(4.000-3.993)] = 7.93\% < i^*=15\%$ *Reject B,*
                                                                  Select A

$$3.352$$
$NPV_A = -32 + 12(P/A_{15},5) = +\$8.22$ *Select A with largest NPV.*

$NPV_B = -38 + 13.5(P/A_{15},5) = +\$7.25$

$NPV_{B-A} = -6 + 1.5(P/A_{15},5) = -\$0.97 < 0$ *Reject B, Select A.*

4-12 Solution: *All Values in Thousands*

Project A:

```
   C=$240       I=$50 ................................ I=$50
                                                            L=$240
   ────────────────────────────────────────────────────
   0            1 ................................... 5
```

Using Text Equation 3-2, Annual Worth Equation:

$(240 - 240)(A/P_{i,5}) + 240(i) = \$50$

$i = ROR_A = 50/240 = 21\% > i* = 10\%,$ *satisfactory*

Project B:

```
   C=$240       I=$98.5 ............................. I=$98.5
                                                           L=0
   ────────────────────────────────────────────────────
   0            1 ................................... 5
```

Present Worth Equation: $240 = 98.5(P/A_{i,5})$

By trial and error, $i = ROR_B = 30\% > i*=10\%,$ *satisfactory*

Incremental Analysis A-B creates cost followed by revenue:

```
   C=0          I=-$48.5 ............................ I=-$48.5
                                                          L=+$240
   ────────────────────────────────────────────────────
   0            1 ................................... 5
```

Annual Worth Equation: $48.5 = 240(A/F_{i,5})$

$i = ROR = -0.5\% < i*=10\%$ *Reject A, and Select B.*

$NPV_A = 50(P/A_{10,5}) + 240(P/F_{10,5}) - 240 = +\$98.57$

$NPV_B = 98.5(P/A_{10,5}) - 240 = +\$133.41$ *Select B.*

4-13 Solution:

$$\text{NPV}_A = \overset{3.326}{90,000(P/A_{20,6})} - 200,000 = +\$99,340$$

$$\text{NPV}_B = 300,000\overset{2.106}{(P/A_{20,3})} - 500,000 = +\$131,800$$

$$\text{NPV}_C = 120,000\overset{2.991}{(P/A_{20,5})} + 100,000\overset{0.4019}{(P/F_{20,5})} - 300,000 = +\$99,110$$

Maximum Cumulative NPV from $500,000 = \text{NPV}_A + \text{NPV}_C = \$198,450$

$\text{PVR}_A = 0.497$, *1st Choice*
$\text{PVR}_B = 0.264$, *3rd Choice*
$\text{PVR}_C = 0.330$, *2nd Choice*

Growth ROR Analysis Using a 6 Year Evaluation Life:

A) $[90,000\overset{9.930}{(F/A_{20,6})}]P/F_{i,6} = \$200,000$

$893,700(P/F_{i,6}) = \$200,000$

$P/F_{i,6} = 0.2238$; i = Growth ROR = 28.5%, *1st*

B) $[300,000\overset{3.640}{(F/A_{20,3})}\overset{1.728}{(F/P_{20,3})}]P/F_{i,6} = \$500,000$

$1,886,976(P/F_{i,6}) = \$500,000$

$P/F_{i,6} = 0.2650$; i = Growth ROR = 24.8% *3rd*

C) $[120,000\overset{7.442}{(F/A_{20,5})}+100,000]\overset{1.200}{(F/P_{20,1})}P/F_{i,6} = \$300,000$

$1,191,648(P/F_{i,6})=300,000$

$P/F_{i,6}=0.25175$; i = Growth ROR=25.9%, *2nd*

4-14 Solution: *All Values in Thousands*

Alternative A:

```
    C=20         I=12 ................................... I=12
    ─────────────────────────────────────────────────────── L=20
    0            1 ..................................... 12
```

Alternative B:

```
    C=28         I=14 ................................... I=14
    ─────────────────────────────────────────────────────── L=28
    0            1 ..................................... 12
```

ROR Analysis:

"A" PW Eq: $0 = -20 + 12(P/A_{i,12}) + 20(P/F_{i,12})$, $i = ROR_A = 60\% > i^* = 15\%$

"B" PW Eq: $0 = -28 + 14(P/A_{i,12}) + 28(P/F_{i,12})$, $i = ROR_B = 50\% > i^* = 15\%$

Incremental Analysis B-A:

```
    C=8          I=2 .................................... I=2
    ─────────────────────────────────────────────────────── L=8
    0            1 ..................................... 12
```

"B-A" PW Eq: $0 = -8 + 2(P/A_{i,12}) + 8(P/F_{i,12})$

   $i = ROR_{B-A} = 25\% > i^* = 15\%$, *Satisfactory, select alternative B.*

NPV Analysis:

$$
\begin{array}{cc}
6.194 & 0.2567
\end{array}
$$

$NPV_A = -20 + 12(P/A_{15,12}) + 20(P/F_{15,12}) = +\$48.79 > 0$, *Acceptable.*

$NPV_B = -28 + 14(P/A_{15,12}) + 28(P/F_{15,12}) = +\$53.13 > 0$, *Select B.*

Note, the incremental NPV_{B-A} is positive: 53.13-48.79 = \$4.34, indicating that alternative B is the best.

PVR Analysis:

$PVR_A = 48.79/20 = 2.44 > 0$, *Satisfactory.*

$PVR_B = 53.13/28 = 1.90 > 0$, *Satisfactory.*

$PVR_{B-A} = (53.13-48.79)/(28-20) = 0.54 > 0$, *Satisfactory, select B.*

4-14 Continued... Change the minimum ROR to 30% from 15%:

$$\overset{3.190}{} \qquad\qquad \overset{0.0429}{}$$
$$NPV_A = -20 + 12(P/A_{30,12}) + 20(P/F_{30,12}) = +\$19.1 > 0, \; Select \; A.$$

$$NPV_B = -28 + 14(P/A_{30,12}) + 28(P/F_{30,12}) = +\$17.8 > 0$$

Note incremental NPV$_{B-A}$ is negative: 17.8-19.1 = -1.3, indicating that alternative A is the best selection. ROR and PVR give the same conclusion.

4-15 Solution: All Values in Thousands

$$\overset{2.991}{} \qquad\qquad \overset{0.4019}{}$$
$$NPV_A = 150(P/A_{20,5}) + 50(P/F_{20,5}) - 160 = +\$308.75$$

$$\overset{2.589}{} \qquad\qquad \overset{0.4823}{}$$
$$NPV_B = 275(P/A_{20,4}) + 70(P/F_{20,4}) - 320 = +\$425.74$$

$$\overset{2.106}{} \qquad\qquad \overset{0.5787}{}$$
$$NPV_C = 500(P/A_{20,3}) + 100(P/F_{20,3}) - 480 = +\$630.87$$

If A, B, and C are mutually exclusive, select C with the largest NPV.

If A, B, and C are non-mutually exclusive and the budget is $480,000, select A+B to maximize cumulative NPV. Selecting A & B may also be achieved by ranking the projects in descending order of Ratio results, like PVR, as follows. Note ranking does not involve selecting C, even though it has the largest individual NPV. However, in this case, if sufficient funding could be found, all three projects are acceptable compared to other investment opportunities.

$$PVR_A = \frac{308}{160} = 1.93 \qquad PVR_B = \frac{425}{320} = 1.33 \qquad PVR_C = \frac{630}{480} = 1.31$$

If A, B, and C are mutually exclusive, incremental PVR analysis must be made! You do not necessarily want to accept the project with the largest individual PVR.

$$PVR_{B-A} = \frac{426-308}{320-160} = 0.73 > 0, \; so \; select \; B \; over \; A$$

$$PVR_{C-B} = \frac{630-425}{380-320} = 1.28 > 0, \; so, \; select \; C \; over \; B$$

4-16 Solution, i* = 20.0%, Budget = $500 at time zero:

Yr	0	1	2	3	4	5
A)	-200	60	100	-200	300	300
B)	-300	-90	100	200	300	400
C)	-300	250	250	250	250	-600
D)	-300	100	150	-350	400	400

$NPV_A = -200 + 60(P/F_{20,1}) + 100(P/F_{20,2}) - 200(P/F_{20,3})$
$\qquad + 300(P/A_{20,2})(P/F_{20,3}) = +68.9$

$NPV_B = -300 - 90(P/F_{20,1}) + 100 + 100(A/G_{20,4})(P/A_{20,4})(P/F_{20,1})$
$\qquad = +115.6$

$NPV_C = -300 + 250(P/A_{20,4}) - 600(P/F_{20,1}) = +106.1$

$NPV_D = -300 + 100(P/F_{20,1}) + 150(P/F_{20,2}) - 350(P/F_{20,3})$
$\qquad + 400(P/A_{20,2})(P/F_{20,3}) = +38.6$

$PVR_A = 68.9 / 200 = 0.3445$

$PVR_B = 115.6 / \{300 + 90(P/F_{20,1})\} = 115.6 / 375 = 0.3083$

$PVR_C = 106.1 / 300 = 0.3537$

$PVR_D = 38.6 / \{[(350(P/F_{20,1})-150)(P/F_{20,1})-100](P/F_{20,1}) + 300\}$
$\qquad = 38.6 / 315 = 0.1225$

Ranking Order: C, A, B, D
For a $500 Time Zero Budget, Select Alternatives C & A.

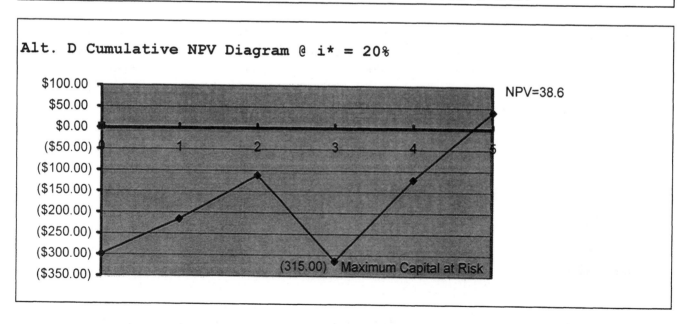

Alt. D Cumulative NPV Diagram @ i* = 20%

4-17 Solution: *Values in Thousands*

Existing Haul Road Alternative A:

Production (tons)	2,000	....	2,000
Profit ($/ton)	$20	....	$20
Net Profit	$40,000	....	$40,000

```
       0            1 .................................... 7
```

$ROR_A = \infty$, *so ok*

$$NPV_A \text{ @ } 15\% = 40,000 \overset{4.1604}{(P/A_{15\%},7)} = \$166,416 > 0, \text{ so ok}$$

Improved Haul Road Alternative B:

Production (tons)	2,500	 2,500	1,500	-
Profit ($/ton)	$20	.... $20	$20	-
Net Profit	$50,000	...... $50,000	$30,000	-
Cost C=$6,000	-	-	-	-

```
       0            1 .......... 5           6          7
```

ROR_B PW Eq: $0 = -6,000 + 50,000(P/A_i,5) + 30,000(P/F_i,6)$

ROR_B, $i = 833\% > i^* = 15\%$, *so ok*

NPV_B @ 15% = $174,578 > 0, *so ok*

Incremental Analysis A-B:

C=$6,000	$10,000	$10,000	-$10,000	-$40,000

```
       0            1 .......... 5           6          7
```

PW Eq: $0 = -6,000 + 10,000(P/A_i,5) - 10,000(P/F_i,6) - 40,000(P/F_i,7)$

Dual "i" values are 3.83% and 163.3%. Neither of the results are valid for economic evaluation purposes because of the combination rate of return and rate of reinvestment meaning included in each. However, the dual solutions do establish the range over which our incremental net present value will be positive.

Using the Escrow Modified ROR Approach:

$$0 = -6,000 - 10,000 \overset{0.4323}{(P/F_{15},6)} - 40,000 \overset{0.3759}{(P/F_{15},7)} + 10,000(P/A_i,5)$$

$$0 = -25,359 + 10,000(P/A_i,5)$$

@15%, NPV = 8,161 > 0, *Accept "B"*
@25%, NPV = 1,534
@30%, NPV = -1,003

ROR = 25%+5%[(1,534-0)/(1,534+1,003)] = 28.0% > 15.0%, *Accept "B"*

4-18 Solution: Values in Thousands of Units or Dollars

Alternative A, Existing Haul Road:

Year	0	1-5	6	7
Production (Tons)		2,000	2,000	2,000
Production (oz)		153	153	153
Revenue ($350/oz gold)x(oz)		53,550	53,550	53,550
-Oper. Costs ($190/oz)x(oz)		-29,070	-29,070	-29,070
Net Revenue		24,480	24,480	24,480
-Capital Costs	-	-	-	-
BTCF	0	24,480	24,480	24,480

PW Eq: $0 = 24,480(P/A_{i,7})$;   *ROR is infinite (no costs).*

$$NPV = 24,480 \overset{4.1604}{(P/A_{15,7})} = \$101,847.$$

Alternative B, Improved Haul Road to Accelerate Production:

Year	0	1-5	6	7
Production (Tons)		2,500	1,500	0
Production (oz)		191.25	114.75	0
Revenue		66,937	40,162	0
-Operating Costs		-36,337	-21,802	0
Net Revenue		30,600	18,360	0
-Capital Costs	-6,000	-	-	-
BTCF	-6,000	30,600	18,360	0

PW Eq: $0 = -6,000 + 30,600(P/A_{i,5}) + 18,360(P/F_{i,6})$; *ROR = 510%*

$$NPV = -6,000 + 30,600 \overset{3.3522}{(P/A_{15,5})} + 18,360 \overset{0.4323}{(P/F_{15,6})} = \$104,514 \ Accept$$

Incremental Analysis B-A:

Year	0	1-5	6	7
Proposed Cash Flow	-6,000	30,600	18,360	0
-Existing Cash Flow	0	24,480	24,480	24,480
Incremental BTCF	-6,000	6,120	-6,120	-24,480

Incremental ROR leads to dual rates, unless cash flows are modified:

$$Mod. \ Yr \ 0 \ Cost: -6,000 - 6,120 \overset{0.4323}{(P/F_{15,6})} - 24,480 \overset{0.3759}{(P/F_{15,7})} = -\$17,848$$

Mod. PW Eq. $= -17,848 + 6,120(P/A_{i,5})$ *ROR = 21.15% > 15%, Accept B*

4-19 Solution: All Values in 000's

```
      -250      115.32      115.32 ................ 115.32
A)   ───────────────────────────────────────────────────── L=0
       0         1           2                       6
```

```
      -250        -           -    ..................   -
B)   ───────────────────────────────────────────────────── L=1,206.7
       0          1           2                       6
```

```
       -       -115.32     -115.32 .............. -115.32
B-A) ───────────────────────────────────────────────────── L=1,206.7
       0          1           2                       6
```

Rate of Return Analysis:

PW Eq$_A$: $0 = -250 + 115.32(P/F_{i,6})$ $i = 30\% > i^* = 15\%$, acceptable
PW Eq$_B$: $0 = -250 + 1,206.7(P/A_{i,6})$ $i = 40\% > i^* = 15\%$, acceptable

PW Eq$_{B-A}$: $0 = -115.32(P/A_{i,6}) + 1,206.7(P/F_{i,6})$

          $i = 22.1\% > i^* = 15\%$, Select "B"

Net Present Value Analysis:
$$\overset{3.7845}{NPV_A = -250 + 115.32(P/A_{15,6})} = 186.4$$

$$\overset{0.4323}{NPV_B = -250 + 1,206.7(P/A_{15,6})} = 271.7 \quad \text{Select "B", Largest NPV}$$

PVR Analysis: PVR$_A$ = 186.4/250 = 0.746
            PVR$_B$ = 271.7/250 = 1.087
            PVR$_{B-A}$ = (271.7-186.4)/115.32(P/A$_{15,5}$)
                 = 0.22 > 0, Select "B"

Growth Rate of Return Analysis, Case A:

```
             -      -115.32    -115.32 ................. -115.32
Reinvest  ───────────────────────────────────────────────────── F=1,009.5
"A" +CF's  0         1          2 .......................... 6
                     Where F = 115.32(F/A15,6) = 1,009.5
```

```
           -250       -          -                          -
A+Reinvest ───────────────────────────────────────────────────── F=1,009.5
            0         1          2 .......................... 6
```

Growth ROR$_A$: $0 = -250 + 1,009.5(P/F_{i,6})$ $i = 26.2\%$

Growth ROR$_B$ is 30% on identical investment, so select B.

FW Profit$_A$ = 1,009.5,   FW Profit$_B$ = 1,206.7   Largest FW Profit is B.

4-20 Solution, All Values in (000's):

Net CF's   -1,470   1,705   897   103   -617   -559   -294
Year   0   1   2   3   4   5   6

Dual "i" values exist for this cost-income-cost situation as follows:

NPV EQ: $0 = -1,470 + 1,705(P/F_{i,1}) + 897(P/F_{i,2}) + 103(P/F_{i,3})$

$$- 617(P/F_{i,4}) - 559(P/F_{i,5}) - 294(P/F_{i,6})$$

Solving the equation above yields dual "i" values of 14.83% and 27.78%. Even though both solutions exceed the minimum rate of return of 12.0%, neither "i" value is valid for economic evaluation purposes because both contain a combination of rate of return and rate of reinvestment meaning. An investor must modify the cost-income-cost cash flow stream to eliminate cost following revenue and obtain cost (negative cash flow) generating revenue (positive cash flow) in order to get valid rate of return meaning in the results.

Present Worth Cost Modification:

                               0.6355   0.5674   0.5066
PW Mod. Cost $= -1,470 - 617(P/F_{12,4}) - 559(P/F_{12,5}) - 294(P/F_{12,6})$
              $= -2,328$

Mod. PW EQ: $0 = -2,328 + 1,705(P/F_{i,1}) + 897(P/F_{i,2}) + 103(P/F_{i,3})$

Modified ROR, i = 11.4% < i* = 12.0% so reject the investment.

Although not asked for, note that the NPV for this project at 12.0% is -17.5 indicating not enough present worth positive cash flow exists to cover all of the years of present worth negative cash flow. This is a slightly unsatisfactory situation leading to rejecting the project.

4-21 Solution, All Values in (000's):

Present Worth Cost Analysis

100,000 Mcf of lost gas at $2.00 per Mcf = $200,000 per year cost.

```
          -      -200,000  -200,000 . . . . . . . -200,000
(1) Present ──────────────────────────────────────────────
          0        1         2   . . . . . . . . .   10
```

$$5.0188$$

PW Cost at 15%: $-200,000(P/A_{15,10}) = -1,003,760$

```
        -1,000,000      -              -  . . . . . . . . .  -
(2) Replace ────────────────────────────────────────────────
          0        1         2   . . . . . . . . .   10
```

PW Cost at 15% = -1,000,000

```
          -400,000   -50,000   -62,000 . . . gradient series
(3) Repair ────────────────────────────────────────────────
          0        1         2   . . . . . . . . .   10
```

$$3.3832 \qquad 5.0188$$

PW Cost at 15% = $-400,000 - [50,000 + 12,000(A/G_{15,10})](P/A_{15,10})$

$\qquad\qquad = -400,000 - 90,598.4(5.0188)$

$\qquad\qquad = -854,695$ Select Repair to Minimize PW Cost.

Incremental Net Present Value Analysis:

```
        -1,000,000 200,000   200,000 . . . . . .  200,000
(2-1) ──────────────────────────────────────────────────
          0        1         2   . . . . . . . . .   10
```

$$5.0188$$

NPV @ 15% $-1,000,000 + 200,000(P/A_{15,10}) = -3,760$ Reject Replace

```
          -400,000  150,000   138,000 . . . . . . .  32,000
(3-1) ──────────────────────────────────────────────────
          0        1         2   . . . . . . . . .   10
```

$$3.3832 \qquad 5.0188$$

NPV @ 15% $-400,000 + [150,000 - 12,000(A/G_{15,10})](P/A_{15,10})$

$\qquad\qquad = +149,065$ Select repair to maximize incremental NPV

CHAPTER 5 PROBLEM SOLUTIONS

5-1 Solution:

Today's Dollar Diagram:

```
                                   R=600
    C=100            C=200         OC=100
    ──────────────────────────────────────
    0                1             2
```

(A) Escalated Dollar Diagram

```
                                              1.210
                                           R=600(F/P₁₀%,₂)=726.0
                                              1.1236
    C=100        C=200(F/P₆%,₁)=212.0    OC=100(F/P₆%,₂)=112.36
    ────────────────────────────────────────────────────────────
    0                1                       2
```

$$\text{NPV} = -100 - 212 \overset{0.8696}{(P/F_{15,1})} + 613.64 \overset{0.7561}{(P/F_{15,2})} = \$179.6$$

(B) Constant Dollar Diagram

```
                    0.9524                        0.9070
    C=100       C=212(P/F₅%,₁)=201.9    I=613.64(P/F₅%,₂)=556.57
    ────────────────────────────────────────────────────────────
    0                1                       2
```

Using Text Eq 5-1:   i*' = (1.15)/(1.05) - 1 = .0952 or 9.52%

$$\text{NPV} = -100 - 201.9 \overset{0.91304}{(P/F_{9.52,1})} + (556.75) \overset{0.83365}{(P/F_{9.52,2})} = \$179.6$$

(C) Today's Dollars Equal Escalated Dollars

This assumes an escalation rate of 0% on costs and revenues each year or that a washout of operating cost and revenue escalation occurs in the revenue producing years.

$$\text{NPV @ 15\%} = -100 - 200 \overset{0.8696}{(P/F_{15,1})} + 500 \overset{0.7561}{(P/F_{15,2})} = \$104.1$$

(D) Today's Dollars Equal Constant Dollars

This assumes both revenues and costs escalate at the rate of inflation. The use of today's dollars makes this a constant dollar analysis requiring the 9.52% constant dollar i* value.

$$\text{NPV @ 9.52\%} = -100 - 200 \overset{0.91304}{(P/F_{9.52,1})} + 500 \overset{0.83365}{(P/F_{9.52,2})} = \$134.2$$

Note also would be feasible to escalate all today's dollars at the forecasted inflation rate of 5.0% and make an escalated dollar analysis @ 15% which would result in the same $134.2 NPV.

5-2 Solution: *All Values in Trillions*

Escalated (Current or Nominal) Dollars:

```
$4.54                                    $4.90
━━━━━━━━━━━━━━━━━━━━━━━━━━━━━━━━━━━━━━━━━━━━━━━━
 1987                                     1988
```

Current (nominal) dollar % gain = $[(4.90-4.54)/4.54](100) = 7.95\%$

Constant (Real) Dollars With 4% Inflation:

```
$4.54                            $4.90(P/F4,1) = $4.71
━━━━━━━━━━━━━━━━━━━━━━━━━━━━━━━━━━━━━━━━━━━━━━━━━━━━━━━
 1987                                     1988
```

Constant (real) dollar % gain: $[(4.71-4.54)/4.54](100) = 3.79\%$

5-3 Solution: *Values in Thousands*

A) Escalated Dollar Analysis

```
                                 I=200(F/P10,2)=$242.0
C0=$50   C1=150(F/P15,1)=$172.5  OC=100(F/P15,2)=$132.2
                                            ━━━━━━━
                                            $109.8
━━━━━━━━━━━━━━━━━━━━━━━━━━━━━━━━━━━━━━━━━━━━━━━━━━━━━━━
  0                   1                       2
```

```
I=200(F/P10,3)=$266.2  I=200(F/P10,4)=$292.8  I=200(F/P10,5)=$322.2
OC=100(F/P15,3)=$152.1 OC=100(F/P15,4)=$174.9 OC=100(F/P15,5)=$201.1
       ━━━━━━                 ━━━━━━                 ━━━━━━
       $114.1                 $117.9                 $121.1
━━━━━━━━━━━━━━━━━━━━━━━━━━━━━━━━━━━━━━━━━━━━━━━━━━━━━━━━━━━━━━━━━━━━
   3                       4                        5
```

PW Eq: $0 = -50 - 172.5(P/F_{i,1}) + 109.8(P/F_{i,2}) + 114.1(P/F_{i,3})$

$$+ 117.9(P/F_{i,4}) + 121.1(P/F_{i,5})$$

ROR $= i = 32.29\%$ *using a financial calculator*

5-3 Solution: *Continued*

B) *Constant Dollar Analysis of Case A*

Net Escalated Dollar Time Diagram From Case A:

-50	-172.5	109.8	114.1	117.9	121.1
0	1	2	3	4	5

Constant Dollar Equivalent Time Diagram for Inflation of 10% per Year:

$$\begin{array}{cccc} & 156.82 & 90.74 & 85.72 \\ C_0{=}50 & C_1{=}172.5(P/F_{10,1}) & 109.8(P/F_{10,2}) & 114.1(P/F_{10,3}) \ldots\ldots \end{array}$$

0	1	2	3 ....

PW Eq: $0 = -50 - 156.82(P/F_{i',1}) + 90.74(P/F_{i',2}) + 85.72(P/F_{i',3})$

$\qquad\qquad + 80.53(P/F_{i',4}) + 75.19(P/F_{i',5})$

Constant Dollar ROR = i' = 20.26%

An alternate solution would be to utilize Equation 5-1 as follows:
$1+i = (1+f)(1+i')$ *and i = 32.29% from Case A and f = 10% as given, so the constant dollar ROR = i' = (1.3229)/(1.10) - 1 = 0.2026 or 20.26%.*

C) *Escalated Dollar Analysis Using the Washout Assumption*

The "washout" assumption assumes that the dollar (not percent) escalation of operating costs is offset by the same dollar escalation of revenue and therefore, profit margins remain uniform at what they would be today.

-50	-172.5	100	100	100	100
0	1	2	3	4	5

PW Eq: $0 = -50 - 172.5(P/F_{i,1}) + 100(P/A_{i,4})(P/F_{i,1})$

Escalated Dollar ROR = i = 25.25%

5-4 Solution:

Escalated and Constant Dollar Selling Price

         Price = $100/Unit   Escalated $ Price = ?
                             ───────────────────────────────────
            Year 0   1   2   3
Escalation Rates |-- 6.0% ---|-- 8.0% ---|-- 10.0% --|

                             1.0600   1.0800   1.1000
Yr 3 Escalated Dollar Price = 100(F/P_{6,1})$ $(F/P_{8,1})$ $(F/P_{10,1})$ = $125.93

                                        Constant $ Price = ?
                             ───────────────────────────────────
            Year 0   1   2   3
 Inflation Rates |-- 5.0% ---|-- 9.0% ---|-- 12.0% --|

                             0.8929   0.7972   0.7118
Yr 3 Constant $ Price = ($125.93)$(P/F_{12,1})$ $(P/F_{9,1})$ $(P/F_{5,1})$ = $98.24

5-5 Solution:

      C=$100,000   Escalated $ Sale Price = X
                    ───
         0   1   2
                                   Constant $ Sale Price = X$(P/F_{10,2})$

Constant $ PW Eq:

$100,000 = X$(P/F_{10,2})$ $(P/F_{25,2})$
     X = $100,000 / [(0.82645)(0.6400)]
     X = $189,062

$1+i = (1+f)(1+i')$ where $f = 0.10$ and $i' = 0.25$ or 25%

Escalated $ Growth Rate = $i = (1+f)(1+i') - 1$

                          $i = (1.10)(1.25) - 1 = 0.375$ or 37.5%

To prove the equivalence of the 37.5% escalated dollar Growth Rate:

Escalated $ PW Eq:

$100,000 = $189,062$(P/F_{37.5,2})$ so proof is complete

5-6 Solution:

	Year 1	Year 2
Escalated \$ Sales	$1,000X(F/P_{10,1})=1,100X$	$1,000X(F/P_{10,2})=1,210X$
Escalated \$ OC	$50,000(F/P_{15,1})=57,500$	$50,000(F/P_{15,2})=66,130$
Escalated Profit	$1,100X - 57,500$	$1,210X - 66,130$
Const. \$ Profit	$(1,100X-57,500)(P/F_{12,1})$	$(1,210X-66,130)(P/F_{12,2})$

Constant Dollar PW Eq: Constant \$ minimum ROR = $i*'$ = 15%

$$100,000 = (1,100X - 57,500)\underset{0.8929}{(P/F_{12,1})}\underset{0.8696}{(P/F_{15,1})}$$

$$+ (1,210X - 66,130)\underset{0.7972}{(P/F_{12,2})}\underset{0.7561}{(P/F_{15,2})}$$

 X = \$116.55 per unit in today's dollar value

Escalated Dollar Solution:

In working with escalated profit, it is necessary to determine the escalated dollar minimum rate of return equivalent to the desired constant dollar figure of 15.0% and given the forecasted inflation rate of 12.0% per year.

$1+i*$ = $(1+f)(1+i*')$, *where* f = 12.0%, $i*'$ = 15.0%,
  $i*$ = 28.8%

$$100,000 = (1,100X - 57,500)(P/F_{28.8,1}) + (1,210X - 66,130)(P/F_{28.8,2})$$

X = \$116.55/unit in today's dollar value.

Escalated \$ year 1 sales price = $116.55(F/P_{10,1})$ = \$128.21/unit

Escalated \$ year 2 sales price = $116.55(F/P_{10,2})$ = \$141.03/unit

Note the equivalence of working with either escalated or constant dollars!

5-7 Solution: *Values in Thousands*

Today's Dollar Time Diagram

			Rev=$150	Rev=$150	Rev=$150
C_{Acq}=?	−	C=$200	OC= $50	OC= $50	OC= $50
0	1	2	3	4	5

Case 1 (Today's Dollars Equal Escalated Dollar Values):

C_{acq} = NPV_{time0}

$$= 100 \underset{2.283}{(P/A_{15\%},3)} \underset{0.7561}{(P/F_{15\%},2)} -200 \underset{0.7561}{(P/F_{15\%},2)} = +\$21.4$$

Case 2: (Today's Dollars Equal Constant Dollar Values):
    For constant dollar NPV analysis, a constant dollar minimum
    rate of return obtained from Equation 5-1 must be used:

Eq. 5-1: $1+i = (1+f)(1+i')$ *or re-arranged,* $i' = [(1+i)/(1+f)] - 1$

Constant $ Minimum ROR $i*' = [(1.15)/(1.07)] - 1 = 0.07477$ *or* 7.477%

C_{Acq} = NPV_{time0} = $100(P/A_{7.47\%},3)(P/F_{7.47\%},2) -200(P/F_{7.47\%},2) = +\$52.1$

The Case 2 solution assumes that the escalation rate for costs and
revenues equals the rate of inflation, as illustrated below:

Escalated Dollar Solution for Case 2 Assumption:

C_{acq}=?	−	C=200$\underset{1.1449}{(F/P_7,2)}$=$228.98	Rev=150$\underset{1.2250}{(F/P_7,3)}$=$183.76
			OC= 50$(F/P_7,3)$=$ 61.25
			Net=$122.51
0	1	2	3

Rev=150$\underset{1.3108}{(F/P_7,4)}$=$196.62	Rev=150$\underset{1.4025}{(F/P_7,5)}$=$210.38
OC= 50$(F/P_7,4)$=$ 65.54	OC= 50$(F/P_7,5)$=$ 70.12
Net=$131.08	Net=$140.26
4	5

$$Escalated\ \$\ NPV = -228.98\underset{0.7561}{(P/F_{15},2)}+122.51\underset{0.6575}{(P/F_{15},3)}+131.08\underset{0.5718}{(P/F_{15},4)}$$

$$+140.26\underset{0.4972}{(P/F_{15},5)} = +\$52.1$$

5-7 Solution: *Case 2 - Constant Dollar Time Diagram:*

$$
\begin{array}{cccc}
& & & 0.81630 \\
& & 0.87344 & \text{Rev}=183.76(P/F_{7,3})=\$150 \\
C_{acq}=? & - & C=228.98(P/F_{7,2})=\$200 & \text{OC}=\ 61.25(P/F_{7,3})=\ \underline{\$50} \\
& & & \text{Net}=\$100
\end{array}
$$

0	1	2	3

$$
\begin{array}{cc}
0.76289 & 0.7129 \\
\text{Rev}=210.38(P/F_{7,5})=\$150 & \text{Rev}=196.62(P/F_{7,4})=\$150 \\
\text{OC}=\ 65.54(P/F_{7,4})=\underline{\$\ 50} & \text{OC}=\ 70.12(P/F_{7,5})=\underline{\$\ 50} \\
\text{Net}=\$100 & \text{Net}=\$100
\end{array}
$$

	4	5	

From Text Eq 5-1, 1+i = (1+f)(1+i')

Constant $ Minimum ROR Equivalent to 15% Escalated $ Minimum ROR

$= i*' = [(1+i*)/(1+f)]-1 = [(1+0.15)/(1+0.07)]-1 = 0.07477$ or 7.477%

$$
\begin{array}{ccc}
& 0.86570 & 0.80548 & 0.74944 \\
\end{array}
$$

Constant $ NPV $= -200(P/F_{7.477,2}) + 100(P/F_{7.477,3}) + 100(P/F_{7.477,4})$

$$
\begin{array}{c}
0.69730 \\
+ 100(P/F_{7.477,5}) = +\$52.1
\end{array}
$$

Case 3) Escalated Dollar Diagram

$$
\begin{array}{cccc}
& & 1.254 & 1.331 \\
& & 200(F/P_{12,2}) & (150-50)(F/P_{10,3}) \\
C_{Acq} & - & C=\$250.8 & \text{Net R}=\$133.1
\end{array}
$$

0	1	2	3

$$
\begin{array}{cc}
1.464 & 1.611 \\
(150-50)(F/P_{10,4}) & (150-50)(F/P_{10,5}) \\
\text{Net R}=\$146.4 & \text{Net R}=\$161.1
\end{array}
$$

	4	5	

$$
\begin{array}{cc}
& 0.6575 & 0.5718 \\
\end{array}
$$

$C_{Acq} = NPV_{\text{time } 0} = 133.1(P/F_{15,3}) + 146.4(P/F_{15,4})$

$$
\begin{array}{cc}
0.4972 & 0.7561 \\
+ 161.1(P/F_{15,5}) - 250.8(P/F_{15,2})
\end{array}
$$

$$= +\$61.69$$

5-7 Solution Continued;

Case 4) Constant Dollar Diagram:

C_{Acq}	—	C'=$250.8X ($P/F_{7,2}$)	Net R'=$133.1X ($P/F_{7,3}$)	Net R'=$146.4 ($P/F_{7,4}$)	Net R'=$161.1X ($P/F_{7,5}$)
0	1	2	3	4	5

Constant Dollar NPV must be made using $i*' = 7.477\%$:

$$C_{Acq} = NPV_{time0} = 133.1(P/F_{7,3})(P/F_{7.477,3}) + 146.4(P/F_{7,4})(P/F_{7.477,4})$$

$$+ 161.1(P/F_{7,5})(P/F_{7.477,5}) - 250.8(P/F_{7,2})(P/F_{7.477,2})$$

$$= +\$61.69, \text{ Identical to Case 3 escalated dollar results.}$$

Case 5 - Washout Assumption (Escalated Dollar Assumption):

Assumes a uniform profit margin in years 3, 4 and 5 of \$100 which is a forecast of the actual dollars to be realized, so costs still escalate, but in revenue producing years, the margin of profit is uniform.

C_{Acq}	—	200($F/P_{12,2}$) C=$250.8	Net R=$100	Net R=$100	Net R=$100
0	1	2	3	4	5

$$C_{Acq} = NPV_{time0} = 100\underset{2.283}{(P/A_{15,3})}\underset{0.7561}{(P/F_{15,2})} - 250.8\underset{0.7561}{(P/F_{15,2})} = -\$17.0$$

5-8 Solution: *Values in Thousands of Dollars*

Break-even Sales Price Analysis

	$R=\$5X$	$R=5X(F/P_{10,1})=\$5.5X$	$R=5X(F/P_{10,1})(F/P_{6,1})=\$5.83X$
C=\$100	OC=\$8	OC=8$(F/P_{15,1})=\$9.2$	OC=8$(F/P_{15,1})(F/P_{8,1})=\$9.94$

```
0              1              2                          3
```

Constant Dollar Present Worth Equation for $i*' = 12\%$:

$0 = -100 + (5X-8)(P/F_{7,1})(P/F_{12,1}) + (5.5X-9.2)(P/F_{7,2})(P/F_{12,2})$

$\quad + (5.83X-9.94)(P/F_{7,3})(P/F_{12,3})$

To work in escalated dollars, calculate $i*$ *equivalent to* $i*'$:

$(1+i) = (1+f)(1+i')$ *so* $i* = \{(1.07)(1.12) - 1\} = 0.1984$ *or* 19.84%

$i* = 19.84\%$ *is equivalent to* $i*' = 12\%$ *for inflation of 7% per year.*

Escalated $ PW Eq for equivalent $i* = 19.84\%$:

$$\overset{0.83445}{} \qquad \overset{0.69630}{}$$

$0 = -100 + (5X-8)(P/F_{19.84,1}) + (5.5X-9.2)(P/F_{19.84,2})$

$$\overset{0.58102}{}$$

$\quad + (5.83X-9.94)(P/F_{19.84,3})$

Both the constant dollar or escalated dollar present worth equation simplify as follows:

$0 = -100 + 11.389X - 18.8569; \quad 118.8569 = 11.389X$

Escalated Dollar Selling Price X = \$10.44 per unit in year 1.

$\quad X = \$10.44$ per unit in year 1.

$\quad X(1.1) = \$11.48$ per unit in year 2

$\quad X(1.1)(1.06) = \$12.17$ per unit in year 3.

5-9 Solution: *All Values in Thousands*

Reclamation Cost, Escrow Fund Analysis:

Let X equal the annual reclamation costs in years 27 through 56:

$$1,000 = X \underset{15.372}{(P/A_{5\%},30)} \underset{0.2812}{(P/F_{5\%},26)}$$

$$1,000 = X(4.3226), \quad therefore, \quad X = \$231.34$$

Since the problem statement indicated that the dollars in escrow today are to be invested in 9.0% U.S. Treasury Bonds, the future reclamation costs need to be discounted at the 9.0% rate in order to determine the dollars to be invested today.

$$231.34 \underset{10.274}{(P/A_{9\%},30)} \underset{0.1064}{(P/F_{9\%},26)} = \$252.89$$

$252,890 is the total amount of 9.0% bonds to be purchased today, to cover anticipated reclamation costs over 30 years, beginning 27 years from today.

5-10 Solution: Today's Dollar Values in Millions

Year	0	1	2	3	4	5
BTCF	-100	-200	150	150	150	150

Case A) Escalated $, Rate of Escalation = Annual Inflation = 3.0%

Escalated Dollar BTCF

Time 0 = -100
Year 1 = -200$(F/P_{3\%,1})$ = -206.0
Year 2 = 150$(F/P_{3\%,2})$ = 159.1
Year 3 = 150$(F/P_{3\%,3})$ = 163.9 or, 159.1(1.03) = 163.9
Year 4 = 150$(F/P_{3\%,4})$ = 168.8 or, 163.9(1.03) = 168.8
Year 5 = 150$(F/P_{3\%,5})$ = 173.9 or, 168.8(1.03) = 173.9

A) Escalated Dollar Cash Flows

Year	0	1	2	3	4	5
BTCF	-100	-206.0	159.1	163.9	168.8	173.9

PW Eq; $0 = -100 - 206.0(P/F_{i,1}) + 159.1(P/F_{i,2}) + 163.9(P/F_{i,3})$

$+ 168.8(P/F_{i,4}) + 173.9(P/F_{i,5})$

Escalated Dollar ROR = 33.1% > i* = 13.3%, acceptable *(see below)*

Escalated Minimum ROR, i* = (1+i*')(1+f) - 1
i* = (1.10)(1.03) - 1 = 0.133 or 13.3%

NPV = $-100 - 206.0(P/F_{13.3,1}) + 159.1(P/F_{13.3,2})$

$+ 163.9(P/F_{13.3,3}) + 168.8(P/F_{13.3,4}) + 173.9(P/F_{13.3,5})$

NPV = +$150.4

5-10 Case B) Constant $ Analysis of Case A Results,
     Annual Inflation = 3.0%

Escalated $ Discounted for Inflation = Constant Dollar BTCFs
_____

Time 0 = -100
Year 1 = -206.0(P/F$_{3\%,1}$) = -200.0
Year 2 = 159.1(P/F$_{3\%,2}$) = 150.0
Year 3 = 163.9(P/F$_{3\%,3}$) = 150.0
Year 4 = 168.8(P/F$_{3\%,4}$) = 150.0
Year 5 = 173.9(P/F$_{3\%,5}$) = 150.0

B) Constant Dollar Cash Flows

Year	0	1	2	3	4	5
BTCF	-100	-200.0	150.0	150.0	150.0	150.0

PW Eq; $0 = -100 - 200(P/F_{i',1}) + 150(P/F_{i',2}) + 150(P/F_{i',3})$

$\qquad + 150(P/F_{i',4}) + 150(P/F_{i',5})$

Constant Dollar ROR i'= 29.2% > i*' = 10%, acceptable

Or, Constant Dollar ROR, $i' = (1+i)/(1+f) - 1$
$\qquad\qquad\qquad i' = (1.331)/(1.03) - 1 = 0.292$ or 29.2%

NPV = $-100 - 200(P/F_{10,1}) + 150(P/F_{10,2}) + 150(P/F_{10,3})$

$\qquad + 150(P/F_{10,4}) + 150(P/F_{10,5})$

NPV = +$150.4 > 0, acceptable

5-10 Case C) Escalation = 0%, Annual Inflation = 3.0%

Escalated Dollar BTCF

Year	0	1	2	3	4	5
BTCF	-100	-200	150	150	150	150

$NPV = -100 - 200(P/F_{13.3\%,1}) + 150(P/A_{13.3\%,4})(P/F_{13.3\%,1})$

$= +\$114.9 > 0$, acceptable

Escalated $ ROR = 29.2% > 13.3%, acceptable

*In cases C and D, even though the analysis uses a forecast of
inflation at 3.0% per year, inflation is just one component of
escalation. This analysis assumes that the net effect from all
influences is that no change in costs and revenues will result,
so today's dollar values represent the actual dollars forecasted
to be realized over the next five years. The constant dollar
analysis of this scenario is Case D presented below.*

5-10 Case D) Constant Dollar Cash Flows,
     Annual Escalation = 0%, Annual Inflation = 3.0%

Time 0 = -100
Year 1 = -200.0 $(P/F_{3\%,1})$ = -194.2
Year 2 = 150.0 $(P/F_{3\%,2})$ = 141.4
Year 3 = 150.0 $(P/F_{3\%,3})$ = 137.3
Year 4 = 150.0 $(P/F_{3\%,4})$ = 133.3
Year 5 = 150.0 $(P/F_{3\%,5})$ = 129.4

D) Constant Dollar BTCF

Year	0	1	2	3	4	5
BTCF	-100	-194.2	141.4	137.3	133.3	129.4

PW Eq;

$0 = -100 - 194.2(P/F_{i',1}) + 141.4(P/F_{i',2}) + 137.3(P/F_{i',3})$

$+ 133.3(P/F_{i',4}) + 129.4(P/F_{i',5})$

Constant Dollar ROR i' = 25.4% > i*' = 10%, acceptable

Constant $ NPV @ 10% = 114.9 > 0, acceptable

CHAPTER 6 PROBLEM SOLUTIONS

6-1 Solution, Expected Value, (EV):

a) $EV = (1/38)(\$35) - (37/38)(\$1) = -\$0.0526$
b) $EV = (2/38)(\$17) - (36/38)(\$1) = -\$0.0526$
c) $EV = (4/38)(\$\ 8) - (34/38)(\$1) = -\$0.0526$
d) $EV = (18/38)(\$1) - (20/38)(\$1) = -\$0.0526$

6-2 Solution:

$Expected\ Cost = 0.10(5,000) + 0.30(8,000) + 0.40(10,000) + 0.20(14,000)$
$$= 500 + 2,400 + 4,000 + 2,800 = \$9,700$$

6-3 Solution:

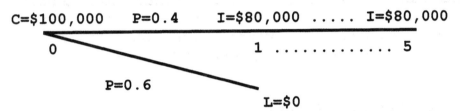

$$2.991$$
$Expected\ NPV = \$80,000(P/A_{20,5})(0.4) - \$100,000 = -\$4,288,\ Reject.$

Alternative Solution:

$Expected\ NPV = [\$80,000(P/A_{20,5}) - \$100,000](0.4) - \$100,000(0.6)$
$$= -\$4,288,\ Reject.$$

Expected ROR is the "i" value that makes ENPV = 0

Expected PW Equation: $\ 0 = \$80,000(P/A_{i,5})(0.4) - \$100,000$

By trial and error, i = Expected ROR = 18.3% < i* of 20%, Reject.

6-4 Solution:

There are 8 possible combinations of winning and losing teams for 3 games. The bettor wins on only 1 of these outcomes.

Expected Value = $(1/8)(\$25-\$5) - (7/8)(\$5) = -\$1.875$

Over the long run, for many repeated bets of this type the bettor would lose an average of $1.875 for each $5 bet placed.

6-5 Solution: *All Values in Thousands*

Expected Cash Flow Year 1 = 0.4(25) + 0.6(18) = $20.80
Expected Cash Flow Year 2 = 0.5(30) + 0.5(20) = $25.00
Expected Cash Flow Year 3 = 0.7(35) + 0.3(25) = $32.00

$$\begin{array}{ccc} 0.8696 & 0.7561 & 0.6575 \end{array}$$
ENPV = 20.80(P/F$_{15,1}$) + 25.00(P/F$_{15,2}$) + 32.00(P/F$_{15,3}$) - 50 = +$8.03

6-6 Solution:

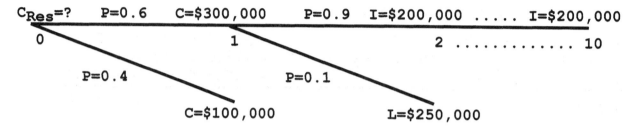

Expected Value (Chance Factor) Approach:

$$\begin{array}{ccc} 3.4631 & 0.8000 & 0.8000 \end{array}$$
{200,000(P/A$_{25,9}$)(P/F$_{25,1}$) - 300,000(P/F$_{25,1}$)}(0.54) = 169,612

{250,000(P/F$_{25,2}$) - 300,000(P/F$_{25,1}$)}(0.06)   = -4,800

{-100,000(P/F$_{25,1}$)}(0.40)   = -32,000
_____
Expected Value   = 132,812

Risk Adjusted Cash Flow Approach to ENPV:

	C=300,000(.6)	I=200,000(.6)(.9)		
	C=100,000(.4)	L=250,000(.6)(.1)	I=200,000(.6)(.9)	. . .
C$_{Res}$=?	Net C=220,000	Net I=123,000	Net I=108,000 ..	Net I=108,000
0	1	2	3	. . 10

ENPV = 108,000((P/A$_{25,8}$)(P/F$_{25,2}$))+123,000(P/F$_{25,2}$)-220,000(P/F$_{25,1}$)

    = +$132,812 = *Maximum acceptable time zero research cost.*

$$\begin{array}{ccc} 3.4631 & 0.8000 & 0.8000 \end{array}$$
ENPV = 200,000(P/A$_{25,9}$)(0.9)(P/F$_{25,1}$)(0.6) - 300,000(P/F$_{25,1}$)(0.6)

$$\begin{array}{cc} 0.6400 & 0.8000 \end{array}$$
    + 250,000(P/F$_{25,2}$)(0.1)(0.6) - 100,000(P/F$_{25,1}$)(0.4)

    = +$132,812 = *Maximum acceptable time zero research cost.*

Neglecting risk of failure gives the following risk free NPV:

$$\begin{array}{cc} 3.463 & 0.8000 \end{array}$$
NPV = [200,000(P/A$_{25,9}$) - 300,000](P/F$_{25,1}$) = $314,080

6-7 Solution:

C=$70,000   P=0.5   C=$120,000   P=0.7   I=$125,000 ... I=$125,000

Expected Value Approach (000's):

A) $[125(P/A_{20,6}) - 120](P/F_{20,1}) - 70 = \boxed{176.4}(0.35) = 61.74$
B) $[\ 50(P/F_{20,1}) - 120](P/F_{20,1}) - 70 = 135.3(0.15) = -20.29$
C) $-10(P/F_{20,1}) - 70 \qquad\qquad\qquad = -78.3(0.50) = -39.17$

Expected Value $=$ 2.28

Expected Value Using Risk Adjusted BTCF (000's):

	-120(.5)	125(.7)(.5)		
	-10(.5)	50(.3)(.5)	125(.7)(.5)	125(.7)(.5)
-70	-65	51.25	43.75 . . .	43.750

0	1	2	3 7

$ENPV = -70 - 65(P/F_{20,1}) + 51.25(P/F_{20,2}) + 43.75(P/A_{20,5})(P/F_{20,2})$

$= 2.28$

ENPV Using the Present Worth Equation Approach @ 20%, (000's)

$$= [125\underset{3.3255}{(P/A_{20,6})}(0.7) - 120]\underset{0.8333}{(P/F_{20,1})}(0.5) + 50\underset{0.6944}{(P/F_{20,2})}(0.3)(0.5)$$

$$- 10\underset{0.8333}{(P/F_{20,1})}(0.5) - 70 = 2.28 > 0, \text{ acceptable}$$

Risk Free Analysis:

The risk free analysis is based on assuming 100% certainty that the project will be successful and follow the top branch of the time diagram (decision tree) through year 7.

$$\text{Risk Free NPV @ 20\%} = [125,000\underset{3.3255}{(P/A_{20,6})} - 120,000]\underset{0.8333}{(P/F_{20,1})} - 70,000$$
$$= +\$176,397 \quad \textbf{\textit{Same as above in Expected Value Sol.}}$$

Risk Free Rate of Return = 50.7% Using a financial calculator.

Problem 6-7 *Solution Continued;*

Breakeven Additional Cost Calculations

In the second part of the problem, the objective is to determine the additional cost that could be incurred and give the investor an ENPV of $2,000 or 2.0 working in thousands.

To solve, let X represent the additional cost at time zero. The risk adjusted ENPV of the project with this new cost should result in an ENPV of $2.0 working in thousands as follows:

$$\boxed{\text{Desired ENPV After New Expenditure is 2.0!}}$$

$$
2.0 = [125\,\overset{3.3255}{(P/A_{20,6})}(0.7) - 120]\,\overset{0.8333}{(P/F_{20,1})}(0.8) + 50\,\overset{0.6944}{(P/F_{20,2})}(0.3)(0.8)
$$

$$
- 10\,\overset{0.8333}{(P/F_{20,1})}(0.2) - 70 - X
$$

$$
2.0 = 113.98 + 8.33 - 1.67 - 70 - X
$$

$$
X = 48.6
$$

Or, an equally valid approach would be to determine the ENPV of the project based on the new probabilities. The resulting difference in the old ENPV of 2.28 and the new ENPV* would represent the additional cost that could be incurred.

$$
\text{ENPV*} = [125\,\overset{3.3255}{(P/A_{20,6})}(0.7)-120]\,\overset{0.8333}{(P/F_{20,1})}(0.8) + 50\,\overset{0.6944}{(P/F_{20,2})}(0.3)(0.8)
$$

$$
- 10\,\overset{0.8333}{(P/F_{20,1})}(0.2) - 70
$$

$$
= 113.98 + 8.33 - 1.67 - 70
$$

$$
\text{ENPV*} = 50.6
$$

The difference in the two ENPV's is the breakeven additional cost:

50.6 - 2.28 = 48.32 slight round-off error difference with the above
                    solution at 48.6

6-8 Solution: *All Values in Thousands*

```
                                  I=$60        I=$60 ............... I=$60
                                _____
                        p=0.4  /     1           2 ................... 10
                              /
                             /        I=$50        I=$50 ............. I=$50
                    p=0.3   /    _____
          C=$170 _____/         1           2 ................... 10
                   \   p=0.2
                    \              I=$40        I=$40 ............. I=$40
                     \        _____
                      \  p=0.1      1           2 ................... 10
                       \
                        \
                       L=$20
```

$$ENPV = 60(P/A_{20,10})(0.4) + 50(P/A_{20,10})(0.3) + 40(P/A_{20,10})(0.20)$$

$$+ 20(P/F_{20,1})(0.1) - 170$$

$$= [60(0.4) + 50(0.3) + 40(0.2)](P/A_{20,10}) + 20(P/F_{20,1})(0.1) - 170$$

$$\underset{4.192}{} \qquad \underset{0.8333}{}$$

$$= [24+15+8](P/A_{20,10}) + 20(P/F_{20,1})(0.1) - 170$$

$$= \underline{+\$28.69} > 0, \; So \; satisfactory.$$

Expected ROR is the i value that makes the ENPV Equation = 0.
By trial and error, EROR = 24.9% > i* = 20%, so satisfactory.

6-9 Solution: *All Values in Millions*

*Sale value today of $1.0 = $ $CF_{Sell} = NPV_{Sell}$. *The develop analysis*
follows:

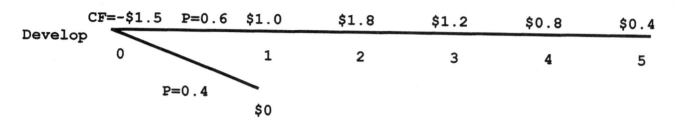

$$ENPV_{Develop} = -1.5 + [1.0(\overset{0.8333}{P/F_{20,1}}) + 1.8(\overset{0.6944}{P/F_{20,2}}) + 1.2(\overset{0.5787}{P/F_{20,3}})$$

$$+ (0.8)(\overset{0.4823}{P/F_{20,4}}) + (0.4)(\overset{0.4019}{P/F_{20,5}})](0.6)$$

$$= +\$0.49 < NPV_{Sell} = +\$1.0 \text{ } \textit{Therefore, select sell.}$$

6-10 Solution: *All Values in Millions of Dollars*

```
          C=20
   C=10    R=6      R=12      R=12      R=12                    R=12
A) ─────────────────────────────────────────────────────────────────
    0       1         2         3        4 . . . . . . . .  . . . .10
```

```
                            C=30
    -       -      C=15     R= 9      R=18     R=18      R=18      R=18
B) ─────────────────────────────────────────────────────────────────
    0       1        2        3        4 .... 10        11        12
```

Incremental Time Diagram A-B

```
   C=10    C=14     R=27     R=33     C=6      C=6      C=18      C=18
   ─────────────────────────────────────────────────────────────────
    0       1        2        3        4 ..... 10        11        12
```

Case A *100% Probability of Success Solutions*

$$\text{NPV}_A \text{ @ } 20\% = -10 - 14\overset{0.8333}{(P/F_{20,1})} + 12\overset{4.031}{(P/A_{20,9})}\overset{0.8333}{(P/F_{20,1})} = +\$18.64$$

$$\text{NPV}_B \text{ @ } 20\% = [(18\overset{4.031}{(P/A_{20,9})}-21)\overset{0.8333}{(P/F_{20,1})}-15]\overset{0.6944}{(P/F_{20,2})}= +\$19.42, Select\ B$$

For mutually exclusive alternatives, select largest NPV which is alternative B. This is verified using incremental analysis.

$$\text{NPV}_A - \text{NPV}_B = 18.64 - 19.42 = -0.78,\ Reject\ A\ and\ select\ B.$$

$$\text{PVR}_A = 18.64 / [10 + 14(P/F_{20,1})] = +0.86$$

$$\text{PVR}_B = 19.42 / [15(P/F_{20,2}) + 21(P/F_{20,3})] = +0.86$$

$$\text{PVR}_{A-B} = (18.64-19.42) / [10 + 14(P/F_{20,1})] = -0.04, Reject\ A, select\ B.$$

Case B *Expected Value Analysis Solutions*

$$\text{ENPV}_A \text{ @ } 20\% = -10 + [-14\overset{0.8333}{(P/F_{20,1})} + 12\overset{4.031}{(P/A_{20,9})}\overset{0.8333}{(P/F_{20,1})}](0.6)= +\$7.18$$

$$\text{ENPV}_B \text{ @ } 20\% = [(18\overset{4.031}{(P/A_{20,9})}-21)\overset{0.8333}{(P/F_{20,1})}(0.8)-15]\overset{0.6944}{(P/F_{20,2})} = +\$13.4$$

$$\text{EPVR}_A = 7.18 / [10 + 14(P/F_{20,1})(0.6)] = +\$0.42$$

$$\text{EPVR}_B = 13.45 / [15(P/F_{20,2}) + 21(P/F_{20,3})(0.8)] = +\$0.67$$

$$\text{EPVR}_{A-B} = (7.18-13.45) / [10 + 14(P/F_{20,1})(0.6)] = -\$0.37,\ Select\ B.$$

6-11 Solution: *Values in Thousands of Dollars*

$$C=100 \quad P=0.7 \quad \begin{array}{l} R=5X \\ OC=8 \end{array} \quad \begin{array}{l} R=5.5X=5X(F/P_{10,1}) \\ OC=9.2=8(F/P_{15,1}) \end{array} \quad \begin{array}{l} R=5.83X=5X(F/P_{10,1})(F/P_{6,1}) \\ OC=9.94=8(F/P_{15,1})(F/P_{8,1}) \end{array}$$

```
    0              1              2                         3
```

$P=0.3$

$CF=\$0$

Constant Dollar PW Equation

$0 = -100 + [(5X-8)(P/F_{7,1})(P/F_{12,1}) + (5.5X-9.2)(P/F_{7,2})(P/F_{12,2})$

$\quad + (5.83X-9.94)(P/F_{7,3})(P/F_{12,3})](0.70)$

To work in escalated dollars, calculate i* that is equivalent to i*' of 12.0% as follows:

$\quad (1+i) = (1+f)(1+i')$ so $i^* = 19.84\%$

19.84% is equivalent to $i^{*'} = 12\%$ for inflation of 7% per year.

Escalated Dollar PW Equation

$$\begin{array}{cc} 0.83445 & 0.69630 \end{array}$$
$0 = -100 + [(5X-8)(P/F_{19.84,1}) + (5.5X-9.2)(P/F_{19.84,2})$

$$0.58102$$
$\quad + (5.83X-9.94)(P/F_{19.84,3})](0.70)$

For either approach, the constant dollar or escalated dollar present worth equation simplifies to the following:

$0 = -100 + [11.389X - 18.8569](0.70)$

$113.19 = 7.9723X$

Escalated Dollar Selling Price X = \$14.20 per unit in year 1.

$X(1.1) = \$15.62$ per unit in year 2

$X(1.1)(1.06) = \$16.56$ per unit in year 3

6-12 Solution: All Values in Millions

```
                  Rev=$200        Rev=$200
   C=$400         OC=$100         OC=$100
```

```
   ────────────────────────────────────────
   0                1             5, 10 or 15 yr(s)
```

Present Worth Equation

$0 = -400 + (200-100)(P/A_{i,n})$ where n = 5, 10, or 15 years

Project Life Yrs		Cost=$400	Cost=$600	Cost=$800
5	ROR =	7.9%	-5.8%	-13.9%
10	ROR =	21.4%	10.5%	4.3%
15	ROR =	24.0%	14.5%	9.1%

CHAPTER 7 PROBLEM SOLUTIONS

7-1 Solution: *All Dollar Values in Thousands*

Modified ACRS & Straight Line Depreciation With Half-Year Convention

Period	200% DB Switching to St Line			Straight Line Depreciation		
Yr 1	(2,000)(2/7)(.5)	=	285.7	2,000(1/7)(.5)	=	142.9
Yr 2	(2,000-285.7)(2/7)	=	489.8	2,000(1/7)	=	285.7
Yr 3	(1,714.3-489.8)(2/7)	=	349.9	2,000(1/7)	=	285.7
Yr 4	(1,224.5-349.9)(2/7)	=	249.9	2,000(1/7)	=	285.7
Yr 5	(874.6-249.9)(1/3.5)	=	178.5*	2,000(1/7)	=	285.7
Yr 6	(624.7)(1/3.5)	=	178.5	2,000(1/7)	=	285.7
Yr 7	(624.7)(1/3.5)	=	178.5	2,000(1/7)	=	285.7
Yr 8	(624.7)(1/3.5)(.5)	=	89.2	2,000(1/7)(.5)	=	142.9

Total Cumulative Depreciation $2,000.0 $2,000.0

* *Switch in the year you get equal or more depreciation with straight line than you would get by continuing with 200% declining balance.*

Alternatively, you could also calculate the depreciation using modified ACRS rates from Table 7-3 of the text. Some round-off error does exist due to the number of decimals carried in the table.

Using Table 7-3

Period	Modified ACRS Depreciation		
Yr 1	2,000(0.1429)	=	285.8
Yr 2	2,000(0.2449)	=	489.8
Yr 3	2,000(0.1749)	=	349.8
Yr 4	2,000(0.1249)	=	249.8
Yr 5	2,000(0.0893)	=	178.6
Yr 6	2,000(0.0892)	=	178.4
Yr 7	2,000(0.0893)	=	178.6
Yr 8	2,000(0.0446)	=	89.2

Total Cumulative Depreciation $2,000.0

7-2 Solution: *Values in Thousands of Dollars*

Period	Modified ACRS Depreciation		
Yr 1	(100)(30/120)	=	25.0
Yr 2	(100)(30/120)	=	25.0
Yr 3	(100)(20/120)	=	16.7
Yr 4	(100)(10/120)	=	8.3
Yr 5	(100)(10/120)	=	8.3
Yr 6	(100)(10/120)	=	8.3
Yr 7	(100)(10/120)	=	8.3

Total Cumulative Depreciation $100.0 *Within Round-off*

7-3 Solution: *All Dollar Amounts in Thousands*

Modified ACRS & Straight Line Depreciation With Mid-Quarter Convention

Modified ACRS Depreciation

Yr	Light Trucks, Purchased, 1st Qtr		R&D Equipment Purchased, 4th Qtr	
1	(100.0)(2/5)(10.5/12)	= 35.0	(500.0)(2/5)(1.5/12)	= 25.0
2	(100.0-35.0)(2/5)	= 26.0	(500.0-25.0)(2/5)	= 190.0
3	(65.0-26.0)(2/5)	= 15.6	(475.0-190.0)(2/5)	= 114.0
4	(39.0-15.6)(1/2.125)	= 11.0*	(285.0-114.0)(2/5)	= 68.4
5	(39.0-15.6)(1/2.125)	= 11.0	(171.0-68.4)(1/1.875)	= 54.7
6	(23.5)(1/2.125)(1.5/12)	= 1.4	(102.6)(1/1.875)(10.5/12)	= 47.9
Cumulative Depreciation		$100.0		$500.0

* Switch in the year you get equal or more depreciation with straight line than you would by continuing with 200% double declining balance.

Straight Line Depreciation

Yr	Light Trucks, Purchased, 1st Qtr		R&D Equipment Purchased, 4th Qtr	
1	(100.0)(1/5)(10.5/12)	= 17.5	(500.0)(1/5)(1.5/12)	= 12.5
2	(100.0)(1/5)	= 20.0	(500.0)(1/5)	= 100.0
3	(100.0)(1/5)	= 20.0	(500.0)(1/5)	= 100.0
4	(100.0)(1/5)	= 20.0	(500.0)(1/5)	= 100.0
5	(100.0)(1/5)	= 20.0	(500.0)(1/5)	= 100.0
6	(100.0)(1/5)(1.5/12)	= 2.5	(500.0)(1/5)(10.5/12)	= 87.5
Cumulative Depreciation		$100.0		$500.0

7-4 Solution:

Depreciable Residential Rental Real Property

Straight Line Depreciation			
Year 1	$800,000(1/27.5)(9.5/12) =	23,030.3	
Year 2-27	$800,000(1/27.5) =	29,090.9	
Year 28*	$800,000(1/27.5)(8.5/12) =	20,606.1	
Cumulative Depreciation		$800,000.0 *Within Round-off*	

* The ratio of 8.5:12 in year 28 occurs because in the first year we generated 9.5 out of 12 months depreciation leaving 2.5 months to be depreciated, plus half-a-year at the 27.5 year rate remaining, therefore, 2.5 months + 6 months = 8.5 months.

7-5 Solution: Petroleum Property Evaluation - Project Cash Flows

Year	0	1
Min. Rts. Acq. Cost	500,000	
Intangible (IDC)	2,000,000	
Tangible Equipment	1,000,000	
Production (Bbls)		200,000
Selling Price ($/Bbl)		18.00
Operating Cost		200,000

Case A, Independent, i.e.
Non-Integrated Producer (< 1,000 Bbl's/day)

Case B
Integrated Producer

Year	Time 0	1		Time 0	1
Production		200,000			200,000
Gross Revenue		3,600,000			3,600,000
-Royalties (16%)		-576,000			-576,000
Net Revenue		3,024,000			3,024,000
-Operating Costs		-200,000			-200,000
-IDC	-2,000,000			-1,400,000	
-Depreciation		-142,900			-142,900
-Amortization				-60,000	-120,000
Taxable Before Depl.	-2,000,000	2,681,100		-1,460,000	2,561,100
-100% Limit		2,681,100			n/a
-Percentage Depletion		-453,600			n/a
-Cost Depletion		100,000			-100,000
-Loss Forward		⟋-2,000,000			⟋-1,460,000
Taxable Income	-2,000,000	227,500		-1,460,000	1,001,100
-Tax Due @ 40%	0	-91,000		0	-400,440
Net Income	-2,000,000	136,500		-1,460,000	600,660
+Depreciation		142,900			142,900
+Amortization				60,000	120,000
+Depletion Taken		453,600			100,000
+Loss Forward		2,000,000			1,460,000
-Tang. Equip.(Depr)	-1,000,000			-1,000,000	
-30% IDC (Amort)				-600,000	
-Min. Rts.(Cost Depl)	-500,000			-500,000	
Cash Flow	-3,500,000	2,733,000		-3,500,000	2,423,560

Depreciation ($1,000,000)(0.1429) = $142,900
Cost Depletion = ($500,000)(200,000 bbls / 1,000,000 bbls) = $100,000

Independent Only
Petroleum 100% Percent Depletion Limit = $2,681,100(1.0) = $2,681,100
Percentage Depletion = 0.15($3,024,000) = $453,600

7-6 Solution: Corporate Mining Cash Flows

Year	0	1
Min Rts Acq Cost	500,000	
Mine Development	2,000,000	
Mining Equipment	1,000,000	
Production (Tons Ore)		200,000
Selling Price ($/Ton)		18.00
Operating Cost		200,000

Year	Time 0	1
Production		200,000
Gross Revenue		3,600,000
-Royalties (16%)		-576,000
Net Revenue		3,024,000
-Operating Costs		-200,000
-Mine Development	-1,400,000	
-Depreciation		-142,900
-Amortization	-60,000	-120,000
Taxable Before Depl.	-1,460,000	2,561,100
-50% Limit		1,280,550
-Percentage Depletion		-453,600
-Cost Depletion		100,000
-Loss Forward		-1,460,000
Taxable Income	-1,460,000	647,500
-Tax Due @ 40%	0	-259,000
Net Income	-1,460,000	388,500
+Depreciation		142,900
+Amortization	60,000	120,000
+Depletion Taken		453,600
+Loss Forward		1,460,000
-Mining Equip (Deprec)	-1,000,000	
-30% Mine Dev (Amort)	-600,000	
-Min Rts (Cost Depl)	-500,000	
Cash Flow	-3,500,000	2,565,000

Depreciation ($1,000,000)(0.1429) = $142,900
Mining 50% Percentage Depletion Limit = 2,561,100(0.5) = $1,280,550
Percentage Depletion = (0.15)($3,024,000) = $453,600
Cost Depletion = ($500,000)(200,000 tons/1,000,000 tons) = $100,000

If no other income exists, losses (negative taxable income) must be carried forward and used against project income in later years. This loss forward deduction is a non-cash deduction similar to depreciation, depletion and amortization so it is added back to net income in determining project cash flow.

7-7 Solution: Gold Property, Corporate Investor, Values in (000's)

Development Cost	900	
Min. Rights Acq. Cost	800	
Mining Equipment Cost	1,000	*Assume year 5 working capital return*
Working Capital Cost	1,000	*from inventory liquidation is $1,000.*
		(Not given in the problem statement.)

Year	0	1	2	3	4	5	Salv
Gross Revenue		2,400	2,700	3,000	3,300	3,600	1,000
-Royalties @ 5.0%		-120	-135	-150	-165	-180	-
Net Revenue		2,280	2,565	2,850	2,135	3,420	1,000
-Operating Cost		-900	-1,000	-1,100	-1,200	-1,300	
-Depreciation		-143	-245	-175	-125	-89	
-Deprec. Write-off							-223
-Work.Cap.Write-off							-1,000
-Development	-630						
-Amortization	-27	-54	-54	-54	-54	-27	
Taxable Before Depl.	-657	1,183	1,266	1,521	1,756	2,004	-223
-50% Limit		591	633	760	878	1,002	0
-Percentage Depl.(15%)		-342	-385	-427	-469	-513	0
-Cost Depletion		160	114	23			
-Loss Forward		-657					
Taxable Income	-657	184	881	1,094	1,287	1,491	-223
-Tax @ 40%	0	-74	-352	-438	-515	-596	89*
Net Income	-657	110	529	656	772	895	-134
+Depreciation		143	245	175	125	89	
+Deprec. Write-off							223
+Work.Cap.Write-off							1,000
+Depletion Taken		342	385	427	469	513	
+Amortization	27	54	54	54	54	27	
+Loss Forward		657					
-Equip Cost (Deprec)	-1,000						
-Min.Rts (Cost Depl)	-800						
-30% Develop (Amort)	270						
-Work.Cap.Investment	-1,000						
Cash Flow	-3,700	1,306	1,213	1,312	1,420	1,524	1,089

2,613

MACRS Depreciation based on the $1,000 equipment cost
using Table 7-3 and rounding the decimal places:
Yr 1 = 1,000(0.1429) = 143,   Yr 2 = 1,000(0.2449) = 245 etc.

Amortization = 270(6/60) = 27, Years 1-4 = 270(12/60) = 54, etc.

Cost Depletion calculations follow:
Yr 1 = (800)(20/100) = 160   Yr 2 = (800-342)(20/80) = 114, etc.

DCFROR = 27.7%

7-8 Solution: *Values in Thousands of Dollars & Gallons*

Processing Facility Input Data Summary

Year	0	1	2	3
Patent Cost	2,000			
Equipment Cost	3,000			
R & D Cost	1,500			
Production (Gallons)		350	350	350
Selling Price ($/Gal)		$22.00	$23.00	$24.00
Operating Costs		3,000	3,300	3,600
Royalty Cost (%)		10%	10%	10%

Cash Flow Calculations

Year	0	1	2	3
Gross Revenue		7,700	8,050	8,400
-Royalties		-770	-805	-840
-Operating Cost		-3,000	-3,300	-3,600
-R & D Cost	-1,500			
-Depreciation*		-429	-735	-525
-Amortization**	-200	-400	-400	-400
-Loss Forward		-1,700	–	–
Taxable Income	-1,700	1,401	2,810	3,035
-Tax Due @ 40%	0	-560	-1,124	-1,214
Net Income	-1,700	841	1,686	1,821
+Depreciation		429	735	525
+Amortization	200	400	400	400
+Loss Forward		1,700	–	–
-Equipment (Deprec)	-3,000			
-Patent Costs (Amort)	-2,000			
Cash Flow	-6,500	3,370	2,821	2,746

* Depreciation calculations using Table 7-3:

    Yr 1: 3,000(0.1429) = $429
    Yr 2: 3,000(0.2449) = $735
    Yr 3: 3,000(0.1749) = $525

** Amortization calculations:

    Yr 0:   2,000(6/60) = 200
    Yrs 1-4: 2,000(12/60) = 400
    Yr 5:   2,000(6/60) = 200

All Write-offs are neglected in the year three cash flow.

7-9 Solution: Case A, Corporate Mining, Values in (000's)

Acquisition Cost	2,000			
Equipment Cost	3,000			
Development Cost	1,500			
Total Reserves(tons)	5,000			
Production (tons)		350	350	350

Cash Flow Calculations

Year	0	1	2	3
Gross Revenue		7,700	8,050	8,400
-Royalties (10%)		-770	-805	-840
Net Revenue		6,930	7,245	7,560
-Operating Cost		-3,000	-3,300	-3,600
-Development (70%)	-1,050			
-Depreciation*		-429	-735	-525
-Amortization**	-45	-90	-90	-90
Before Depletion	-1,095	3,411	3,120	3,345
-50% Limit		1,706	1,560	1,673
-Percent Depletion (15%)		-1,040	-1,087	-1,134
-Cost Depletion***		140	72	0
-Loss Forward		-1,095	0	0
Taxable Income	-1,095	1,276	2,033	2,211
-Tax Due @ 40%	0	-510	-813	-884
Net Income	-1,095	766	1,220	1,327
+Depreciation		429	735	525
+Depletion Taken		1,040	1,087	1,134
+Amortization	45	90	90	90
+Loss Forward		1,095	0	0
-Equipment (Deprec)	-3,000			
-30% Dev. (Amort)	-450			
-Min Rts (Cost Depl)	-2,000			
Cash Flow	-6,500	3,420	3,132	3,076

*Depreciation Calculated Using Table 7-3 in Text:
    Yr 1   3,000(0.1429) = 429
    Yr 2   3,000(0.2449) = 735   No write-off was asked for in stmt.
    Yr 3   3,000(0.1749) = 525   so it is neglected in year 3 cash flow

**Amortization Calculations on   ***Cost Depletion Calculations:
30% of Mine Develop=0.3(1,500):
    Yr 0   450(6/60) = 45   Yr 1 (2,000)(350/5,000)   = 200
    Yr 1   450(12/60) = 90   Yr 2 (2,000-1,040)(350/4,650) = 72
    Yr 2&3 450(12/60) = 90   Yr 3 (960-1,087) < 0, so stop

7-9 Solution: Case B, Individual Mining, Values (000's)

Acquisition Cost   2,000
Equipment Cost   3,000
Development Cost   1,500
Total Reserves(tons) 5,000
Production (tons)   350   350   350

Individual Cash Flow Calculations

Year	0	1	2	3
Gross Revenue		7,700	8,050	8,400
-Royalties (10%)		-770	-805	-840
Net Revenue		6,930	7,245	7,560
-Operating Cost		-3,000	-3,300	-3,600
-Development (100%)	-1,500			
-Depreciation*		-429	-735	-525
Before Depletion	-1,500	3,501	3,210	3,435
-50% Limit		1,751	1,605	1,718
-Percent Depletion (15%)		-1,040	-1,087	-1,134
-Cost Depletion**		140	72	0
-Loss Forward		-1,500	0	0
Taxable Income	-1,500	961	2,123	2,301
-Tax Due @ 40%	0	-384	-849	-920
Net Income	-1,500	577	1,274	1,381
+Depreciation		429	735	525
+Depletion Taken		1,040	1,087	1,134
+Loss Forward		1,500	0	0
-Equipment (Deprec)	-3,000			
-Min Acq (Cost Depl)	-2,000			
Cash Flow	-6,500	3,546	3,096	3,040

*Depreciation Calculated Using Table 7-3:

    Yr 1   3,000(0.1429) = 429
    Yr 2   3,000(0.2449) = 735   No writeoff was asked for so it is
    Yr 3   3,000(0.1749) = 525   neglected in year 3 cash flow.

**Cost Depletion Calculations Follow:

    Yr 1   (2,000)(350/5,000)   = 140
    Yr 2   (2,000-1,040)(350/4,650) = 72
    Yr 3   (960-1,087) < 0 stop cost depletion

7-10 Solution: Case A, Integrated Producer, All Values in (000's)

Acquisition Cost	2,000			
Equipment Cost	3,000			
IDC	1,500			
Total Reserves(Bbl)	5,000			
Production (Bbl)		350	350	350

Cash Flow Calculations:

Year	0	1	2	3
Gross Revenue		7,700	8,050	8,400
-Royalties (10%)		-770	-805	-840
Net Revenue		6,930	7,245	7,560
-Operating Cost		-3,000	-3,300	-3,600
-IDC (70%)	-1,050			
-Depreciation*		-429	-735	-525
-Amortization**	-45	-90	-90	-90
-Cost Depletion***		-140	-140	-140
-Loss Forward	0	-1,095	0	0
Taxable Income	-1,095	2,176	2,980	3,205
-Tax Due @ 40%	0	-870	-1,192	-1,282
Net Income	-1,095	1,306	1,788	1,923
+Depreciation		429	735	525
+Cost Depletion		140	140	140
+Amortization	45	90	90	90
+Loss Forward		1,095	0	0
-Tang Equip (Deprec)	-3,000			
-30% IDC (Amort)	-450			
-Min Acq (Cost Depl)	-2,000			
Cash Flow	-6,500	3,060	2,753	2,678

*Depreciation Calculated Using Table 7-3 in Text:

    Yr 1   3,000(0.1429) = 429
    Yr 2   3,000(0.2449) = 735   No write-off was asked for so it
    Yr 3   3,000(0.1749) = 525   is neglected in year 3 cash flows.

**Amortization Calculations on   ***Cost Depletion Calculations:
    30% of IDC = 0.3(1500):
    Yr 1   450(6/60) = 45   Yr 1   (2,000)(350/5,000)   = 140
    Yr 2   450(12/60) = 90   Yr 2   (2,000-140)(350/4,650) = 140
    Yr 3   450(12/60) = 90   Yr 3   (1,860-140)(350/4,300) = 140

7-10 Solution: Case B, Independent Producer < 1,000 Bbl/day
              All Values in (000's)

Acquisition Cost	2,000			
Equipment Cost	3,000			
IDC	1,500			
Total Reserves (Bbl)	5,000			
Production (Bbl)		350	350	350
Year	0	1	2	3
Gross Revenue		7,700	8,050	8,400
-Royalties (10%)		-770	-805	-840
Net Revenue		6,930	7,245	7,560
-Operating Cost		-3,000	-3,300	-3,600
-Development (100%)	-1,500			
-Depreciation*		-429	-735	-525
Before Depletion	-1,500	3,501	3,210	3,435
-100% Limit		3,501	3,210	3,435
-Percent Depletion (15%)		-1,040	-1,087	-1,134
-Cost Depletion**		140	72	0
-Loss Forward		-1,500	0	0
Taxable Income	-1,500	961	2,123	2,301
-Tax Due @ 40%	0	-384	-849	-920
Net Income	-1,500	577	1,274	1,381
+Depreciation		429	735	525
+Depletion Taken		1,040	1,087	1,134
+Loss Forward		1,500	0	0
-Equipment (Deprec)	-3,000			
-Min Acq (Cost Depl)	-2,000			
Cash Flow	-6,500	3,546	3,096	3,040

* Depreciation Calculated Using Table 7-3 in Text:

    Yr 1   3,000(0.1429) = 429
    Yr 2   3,000(0.2449) = 735   No write-off was asked for so it
    Yr 3   3,000(0.1749) = 525   neglected in year 3 cash flow.

**Cost Depletion Calculations Follow:

    Yr 1   (2,000)(350/5,000)   = 140
    Yr 2   (2,000-1,040)(350/4,650) = 72
    Yr 3   (960-1,087) < 0 stop cost depletion

7-10 Solution: Case C, Independent Producer > 1,000 Bbl/day
              All Values in (000's)

Acquisition Cost	2,000			
Equipment Cost	3,000			
IDC	1,500			
Total Reserves(Bbl)	5,000			
Production (Bbl)		350	350	350

Cash Flow Calculations:

Year	0	1	2	3
Gross Revenue		7,700	8,050	8,400
-Royalties (10%)		-770	-805	-840
Net Revenue		6,930	7,245	7,560
-Operating Cost		-3,000	-3,300	-3,600
-Development (100%)	-1,500			
-Depreciation*		-429	-735	-525
-Cost Depletion**		-140	-140	-140
-Loss Forward		-1,500	0	0
Taxable Income	-1,500	1,861	3,070	3,295
-Tax Due @ 40%	0	-744	-1,228	-1,318
Net Income	-1,500	1,117	1,842	1,977
+Depreciation		429	735	525
+Depletion Taken		140	140	140
+Loss Forward		1,500	0	0
-Equipment (Deprec)	-3,000			
-Min Acq (Cost Depl)	-2,000			
Cash Flow	-6,500	3,186	2,717	2,642

*Depreciation Calculated Using Table 7-3 in Text:

    Yr 1   3,000(0.1429) = 429
    Yr 2   3,000(0.2449) = 735   No write-off was asked for so it is
    Yr 3   3,000(0.1749) = 525   neglected in year 3 cash flow.

**Cost Depletion Calculations:

    Yr 1   (2,000)(350/5,000)   = 140
    Yr 2   (2,000-140)(350/4,650) = 140
    Yr 3   (1,860-140)(350/4,300) = 140

7-11 Solution: Case A, Integrated, Values in (000's)

	Acquisition Cost	200				

Acquisition Cost   200
Intangible Drilling   500
Tangible Completion   400
Initial Reserves(bbl) 200

Production/Year(bbl)		30	27	24	21	18	
Year	0	1	2	3	4	5	Sale
Gross Revenue		700	600	500	400	300	250
-Royalties		-105	-90	-75	-60	-45	-
Net Revenue		595	510	425	340	255	250
-Operating Costs		-50	-50	-50	-50	-50	
-Intangible	-350						
-Depreciation		-57	-98	-70	-50	-36	
-Deprec Write-off							-89
-Amortization	-15	-30	-30	-30	-30	-15	
-Cost Depletion		-30	-27	-24	-21	-18	
-Cost Depl Write-off							-80
-Loss Forward		-365					
Taxable Income	-365	63	305	251	189	136	81
-Tax @ 40%	0	-25	-122	-100	-76	-54	-32
Net Income	-365	38	183	151	113	82	49
+Depreciation		57	98	70	50	36	
+Cost Depletion		30	27	24	21	18	
+Write-offs							169
+Amortization	15	30	30	30	30	15	
+Loss Forward		365					
-Tang Equip (Deprec)	-400						
-30% IDC	-150						
-Min Rts (Cost Depl)	-200						
Cash Flow	-1,100	520	338	275	214	151	218

369

Depreciation Calculations:
Yr 1: 400(0.1429) = 57
Yr 2: 400(0.2449) = 98
Yr 3: 400(0.1749) = 70
Yr 4: 400(0.1249) = 50
Yr 5: 400(0.0893) = 36
Write-off: 400-311 = 89

Cost Depletion Calculations:
Yr 1:   (200)(30/200)   = 30
Yr 2:   (200-30)(27/170)   = 27
Yr 3:   (170-27)(24/143)   = 24
Yr 4:   (143-24)(21/119)   = 21
Yr 5:   (119-21)(18/98)   = 18
Write-off: 200-120   = 80

Amortization (30% of IDC):
Yr 0&5: 500(0.3)(6/60) = 15, Yr 1-4: 500(0.3)(12/60) = 30

i = DCFROR = 19.0%   (by calculator)

7-11 Solution: Case B, Independent < 1,000 Bbl/day, Values in (000's)

Acquisition Cost	200						
Intangible Drilling	500						
Tangible Completion	400						
Initial Reserves(bbl)	200						
Production/Year(bbl)		30	27	24	21	18	

Year	0	1	2	3	4	5	Sale
Gross Revenue		700	600	500	400	300	250
-Royalties		-105	-90	-75	-60	-45	-
Net Revenue		595	510	425	340	255	250
-Operating Costs		-50	-50	-50	-50	-50	
-Intangible	-500						
-Depreciation		-57	-98	-70	-50	-36	
-Deprec Write-off							-89
Taxable Before Depl	-500	488	362	305	240	169	161
-100% Limit		488	362	305	240	169	-
-Percentage Depl.		-89	-77	-64	-51	-38	-
-Cost Depletion		30	18	6			
-Loss Forward		↗-500	↗-101				
Taxable Income	-500	-101	184	241	189	131	161
-Tax @ 40%	0	0	-74	-96	-76	-52	-64
Net Income	-500	-101	110	145	113	79	97
+Depreciation		57	98	70	50	36	
+Depletion Taken		89	77	64	51	38	
+Deprec Write-off							89
+Loss Forward		500	101				
-Equipment (Deprec)	-400						
-Min Rts(Cost Depl)	-200						
Cash Flow	-1,100	545	386	278	214	153	186

$$\underbrace{}_{339}$$

Depreciation Calculations:

Yr 1:   400(0.1429) = 57
Yr 2:   400(0.2449) = 98
Yr 3:   400(0.1749) = 70
Yr 4:   400(0.1249) = 50
Yr 5:   400(0.0893) = 36
Writeoff: 400-311 = 89

Cost Depletion Calculations:

Yr 1:   (200)(30/200)   = 30
Yr 2:   (200-89)(27/170) = 18
Yr 3:   (111-77)(24/143) = 6
Yr 4:   (34-64)(21/119) < 0, stop

PW Eq: $0 = -1,100 + 545(P/F_{i,1}) + 386(P/F_{i,2}) + 278(P/F_{i,3})$

$$+ 214(P/F_{i,4}) + 339(P/F_{i,5})$$

i = DCFROR = 21.1%   (by calculator)

7-11 Solution: Case C, Independent > 1,000 Bbl/day, Values in (000's)

Acquisition Cost   200
Intangible Drilling   500
Tangible Completion   400
Initial Reserves (bbl) 200

Production/Year (bbl)		30	27	24	21	18	
Year	0	1	2	3	4	5	Sale
Gross Revenue		700	600	500	400	300	250
-Royalties		105	90	75	60	45	-
Net Revenue		595	510	425	340	255	250
-Operating Costs		-50	-50	-50	-50	-50	
-IDC (100%)	-500						
-Depreciation		-57	-98	-70	-50	-36	
-Deprec Write-off							-89
-Cost Depletion		-30	-27	-24	-21	-18	
-Cost Depl. Write-off							-80
-Loss Forward		-500	-42				
Taxable Income	-500	-42	293	281	219	151	81
-Tax Due @ 40%	0	0	-100	-96	-74	-60	-32
Net Income	-500	-42	193	185	145	91	49
+Depreciation		57	98	70	50	36	
+Cost Depletion		30	27	24	21	18	
+Write-offs							169
+Loss Forward		500	42				
-Tang.Equip (Deprc)	-400						
-Min Acq (Cost Depl)	-200						
Cash Flow	-1,100	545	360	279	216	145	218

363

Depreciation Calculations: Cost Depletion Calculations:
Yr 1:   400(0.1429) = 57   Yr 1:   (200)(30/200)   = 30
Yr 2:   400(0.2449) = 98   Yr 2:   (200-30)(27/170) = 27
Yr 3:   400(0.1749) = 70   Yr 3:   (170-27)(24/143) = 24
Yr 4:   400(0.1249) = 50   Yr 4:   (143-24)(21/119) = 21
Yr 5:   400(0.0893) = 36   Yr 5:   (119-21)(18/98)   = 18
Writeoff: 400-311 = 89   Writeoff: 200-120 = 80

PW Eq: $0 = -1,100 + 545(P/F_{i,1}) + 360(P/F_{i,2}) + 279(P/F_{i,3})$

$+ 216(P/F_{i,4}) + 363(P/F_{i,5})$

i = DCFROR = 20.7%   (by financial calculator)

7-12 Solution: General Process Evaluation, All Values (000's) $.

Patent Acquisition	600					
Research & Exper.	500					
Equipment	1,000					
Revenues		2,000 escalating 10% per yr ...				
Operating Costs		1,000 escalating 10% per yr ...				

Year	0	1	2	3	4	5
Revenue		2,000	2,200	2,420	2,662	2,928
-Operating Costs		-1,000	-1,100	-1,210	-1,331	-1,464
-Research & Exper.	-500					
-Depreciation		-200	-320	-192	-115	-115
-Deprec. Write-off						-58
-Amortization	-60	-120	-120	-120	-120	-60
-Loss Forward		-560				
Taxable Income	-560	120	660	898	1,096	1,231
-Tax Due @ 40%		-48	-264	-359	-438	-493
Net Income	-560	72	396	539	657	738
+Depreciation		200	320	192	115	115
+Deprec. Write-off						58
+Amortization	60	120	120	120	120	60
+Loss Forward		560				
-Equipment (Deprec)	-1,000					
-Patent (Amort)	-600					
Cash Flow	-2,100	952	836	851	893	972

Revenue Calculations: Operating Costs:
Yr 2 = 2,000(1.1) = 2,200   Yr 2 = 1,000(1.1) = 1,100
Yr 3 = 2,200(1.1) = 2,420 etc.   Yr 3 = 1,100(1.1) = 1,210 etc.

The patent is assumed to have a remaining life of 5 years upon which
amortization has been based. Assuming the patent cost was incurred in
the middle of tax year zero gives the following amortization:

Year   0 = (600)(6 months / 60 months) = 60
Year 1-4 = (600)(12 months / 60 months) = 120
Year   5 = (600)(6 months / 60 months) = 60

Depreciation of Equipment (Using MACRS Table 7-3):

Year 1 = 1,000(0.2000) = 200
Year 2 = 1,000(0.3200) = 320
Year 3 = 1,000(0.1920) = 192 etc...

DCFROR = 32.2% by financial calculator

7-13 Megawatt Hydroelectric Plant Economics

Before-tax Economic Analysis:

Annual Revenue = 5,000,000 watts * 6,000 hrs/yr * 1 kwh/1,000 watts

$$= 30,000,000 \text{ kwh per year}$$

30,000,000 kwh * \$0.035 profit / kwh = \$1,050,000 profit per year.

NPV Eq: $-6,000,000 + 1,050,000(P/A_{i,n})$

Sensitivity Analysis Summary:

Life (Years)	ROR	NPV @ i* = 10.0%	NPV @ i* = 15.0%
10	11.72%	451,795	-730,293
20	16.70%	2,939,242	572,298
30	17.35%	3,898,260	894,278
40	17.47%	4,268,003	973,867

After-tax Economic Analysis:

Assume straight line 10 year depreciation life, starting in year one with a full year deduction. Assume an effective income tax rate of 30%. All values in (000's).

Year	0	1-10	11-n
Revenue @ \$0.04/kwh	–	1,200	1,200
- O.C. @ \$0.005/kwh	–	-150	-150
- Depreciation*	–	-600	–
Taxable Income	–	450	1,050
- Tax @ 30%	–	-135	-315
Net Income	–	315	735
+ Depreciation	–	600	–
- Capital Cost	-6,000	–	–
Cash Flow	-6,000	915	735

NPV = $-6,000 + 915(P/A_{i},10) + 735(P/A_{i},n-10)(P/F_{i},10)$

Life (Years)	ROR	NPV @ i* = 10.0%
10	8.51%	-377,700
20	13.41%	1,363,491
30	14.23%	2,034,804
40	14.41%	2,293,624

7-14 Non-Resource Problem, Values in Thousands:

Land Acq	5,000						
Building	10,000						
Equipment	15,000						
Revenues		25,000 per yr ...				Yr 5 Salv = 30,000	
Operating Costs		10,000 per yr ...					

Year	0	1	2	3	4	5	Sale
Revenue	–	25,000	25,000	25,000	25,000	25,000	30,000
-Operating Costs	–	-10,000	-10,000	-10,000	-10,000	-10,000	
-Equip. Deprec.	–	-3,000	-4,800	-2,880	-1,728	-1,728	-864
-Building Deprec.	–	-203	-256	-256	-256	-256	-8,773
-Land Write-off	–						-5,000
-Loss Forward	–						
Taxable Income	–	11,797	9,944	11,864	13,016	13,016	15,363
-Tax Due @ 40%	–	-4,719	-3,977	-4,745	-5,206	-5,206	-6,145
Net Income	–	7,078	5,966	7,118	7,809	7,809	9,218
+Equip. Deprec.	–	3,000	4,800	2,880	1,728	1,728	864
+Building Deprec.	–	203	256	256	256	256	8,773
+Land Writeoff	–						5,000
-Land Cost	-5,000						
-Equipment	-15,000						
-Building	-10,000						
Cash Flow	-30,000	10,281	11,023	10,255	9,794	9,794	23,855
							33,649

Depreciation of Equipment (Using MACRS Table 7-3):

Year 1 = 15,000(0.2000) = 3,000
Year 2 = 15,000(0.3200) = 4,800
Year 3 = 15,000(0.1920) = 2,880 etc...

Depreciation SL (on Building)

Year   1 = 10,000(1/39)(9.5/12 mid month convention) = 202.99 or 203
Years 2-5 = 10,000(1/39) = 256.41 or 256

Write-offs = Cost Basis - Cumulative Depreciation

PW Eq: $0 = -30,000 + 10,281(P/F_{i,1}) + 11,023(P/F_{i,2}) + 10,255(P/F_{i,3})$

$+ 9,794(P/F_{i,4}) + 33,649(P/F_{i,5})$

DCFROR = 32.3% by calculator.

NPV @ 12% = $20,584

7-15 Case A) Corporate Mineral Version to Problem 7-14 With
              Additional Mine Development Cost in Time Zero and
              Treating The Land Cost as a Mineral Acquisition Cost,
              All Values in Thousands:

Mineral Acq.	5,000	
Mine Develop	5,000	
Building	10,000	
Equipment	15,000	
Revenues	25,000 per yr ...	Yr 5 Salv. = 30,000
Operating Costs	10,000 per yr ...	

Year	0	1	2	3	4	5	Sale
Revenue	–	25,000	25,000	25,000	25,000	25,000	30,000
-Operating Costs	–	-10,000	-10,000	-10,000	-10,000	-10,000	–
-Mine Develop	-3,500	–	–	–	–	–	–
-Amortization		-300	-300	-300	-300	-300	–
-Equip. Deprec.	–	-3,000	-4,800	-2,880	-1,728	-1,728	-864
-Building Deprec.	–	-203	-256	-256	-256	-256	-8,773
Taxable Inc. Bef.	-3,500	11,497	9,644	11,564	12,716	12,716	–
-50% Limit on %	–	5,749	4,822	5,782	6,358	6,358	–
-Percentage Depl.	–	-2,500	-2,500	-2,500	-2,500	-2,500	–
-Cost Depletion	–	500	278	–	–	–	–
-Loss Forward	–	-3,500	–	–	–	–	–
Taxable Income	-3,500	5,497	7,144	9,064	10,216	10,216	20,363
-Tax Due @ 40%	–	-2,199	-2,858	-3,626	-4,086	-4,086	-8,145
Net Income	-3,500	3,298	4,286	5,438	6,130	6,130	12,218
+Amortization	–	300	300	300	300	300	–
+Equip. Deprec.	–	3,000	4,800	2,880	1,728	1,728	864
+Building Deprec.	–	203	256	256	256	256	8,773
+Allowed Depl	–	2,500	2,500	2,500	2,500	2,500	–
+Loss Forward	–	3,500	–	–	–	–	–
-Mineral Acq	-5,000						
-30% Develop	-1,500						
-Equipment	-15,000						
-Building	-10,000						
Cash Flow	-35,000	12,801	12,142	11,374	10,914	10,914	21,855

                                                    32,769

DCFROR = 29.8%

NPV @ 12% = $19,735

7-15 Case B)   Integrated Oil and Gas Version to Problem 7-14 With
               Additional Intangible Drilling Cost (IDC) in Time Zero
               and Treating The Land Cost as a Lease Acquisition Cost,
               All Values in Thousands:

Lease Acq.	5,000					
IDC	5,000					
Building	10,000					
Tang. Equip.	15,000					
Revenues		25,000 per yr ...			Yr 5 Salv. = 30,000	
Operating Costs		10,000 per yr ...				

Year	0	1	2	3	4	5	Sale
Revenue	–	25,000	25,000	25,000	25,000	25,000	30,000
-Operating Costs	–	-10,000	-10,000	-10,000	-10,000	-10,000	–
-IDC	-3,500	–	–	–	–	–	–
-Amortization		-300	-300	-300	-300	-300	–
-Equip. Deprec.	–	-3,000	-4,800	-2,880	-1,728	-1,728	-864
-Building Deprec.	–	-203	-256	-256	-256	-256	-8,773
-Cost Depletion	–	-500	-500	-500	-500	-500	-2,500
-Loss Forward	–	-3,500	–	–	–	–	–
Taxable Income	-3,500	7,497	9,144	11,064	12,216	12,216	17,863
-Tax Due @ 40%	–	-2,999	-3,657	-4,426	-4,886	-4,886	-7,145
Net Income	-3,500	4,498	5,486	6,638	7,330	7,330	10,718
+Amortization	–	300	300	300	300	300	–
+Equip. Deprec.	–	3,000	4,800	2,880	1,728	1,728	864
+Building Deprec.	–	203	256	256	256	256	8,773
+Allowed Depl.	–	500	500	500	500	500	2,500
+Loss Forward	–	3,500	–	–	–	–	–
-Mineral Acq.	-5,000						
-30% Intangible	-1,500						
-Equipment	-15,000						
-Building	-10,000						
Cash Flow	-35,000	12,001	11,342	10,574	10,114	10,114	22,855

                                                                32,969

DCFROR = 27.6%

NPV @ 12% = $17,419

7-15 Case C) Non-Integrated Oil and Gas Producer With More Than 1,000 BOE per Day. This is a Version of Problem 7-14 and Includes an Additional Intangible Drilling Cost (IDC) in Time Zero and Treating The Land Cost as a Lease Acquisition Cost, All Values in Thousands:

Lease Acq.	5,000			
IDC	5,000			
Building	10,000			
Tang. Equip.	15,000			
Revenues		25,000 per yr ...		Yr 5 Salv. = 30,000
Operating Costs		10,000 per yr ...		

Year	0	1	2	3	4	5	Sale
Revenue	–	25,000	25,000	25,000	25,000	25,000	30,000
-Operating Costs	–	-10,000	-10,000	-10,000	-10,000	-10,000	–
-IDC	-5,000	–	–	–	–	–	–
-Equip. Deprec.	–	-3,000	-4,800	-2,880	-1,728	-1,728	-864
-Building Deprec.	–	-203	-256	-256	-256	-256	-8,773
-Cost Depletion	–	-500	-500	-500	-500	-500	-2,500
-Loss Forward	–	-5,000	–	–	–	–	–
Taxable Income	-5,000	6,297	9,444	11,364	12,516	12,516	17,863
-Tax Due @ 40%	–	-2,519	-3,778	-4,546	-5,006	-5,006	-7,145
Net Income	-5,000	3,778	5,666	6,818	7,510	7,510	10,718
+Equip. Deprec.	–	3,000	4,800	2,880	1,728	1,728	864
+Building Deprec.	–	203	256	256	256	256	8,773
+Allowed Depl	–	500	500	500	500	500	2,500
+Loss Forward	–	5,000	–	–	–	–	–
-Mineral Acq	-5,000						
-Equipment	-15,000						
-Building	-10,000						
Cash Flow	-35,000	12,481	11,222	10,454	9,994	9,994	22,855

$$32,849$$

DCFROR = 27.8%

NPV @ 12% = $17,522

7-16A Repair Business, SL Depreciation - Values in Actual Dollars:

Spare Parts   20,000
Equipment   200,000
Revenues   100,000 per yr ...   Yr 3 Salv = 140,000
Operating Costs   40,000 per yr ...

Year	0	1	2	3	Yr 3 Sale
Revenue	-	100,000	100,000	100,000	140,000
-Operating Costs	-	-40,000	-40,000	-40,000	-
-Equip. Deprec.	-	-20,000	-40,000	-40,000	-100,000
-Spare Parts W/O					-20,000
Taxable Income	-	40,000	20,000	20,000	20,000
Tax Due @ 40%	-	-16,000	-8,000	-8,000	-8,000
Net Income	-	24,000	12,000	12,000	12,000
+Equip. Deprec.	-	20,000	40,000	40,000	100,000
+Spare Parts W/O	-	-	-	-	20,000
-Spare Parts Cost	-20,000				
-Equipment	-200,000				
Cash Flow	-220,000	44,000	52,000	52,000	132,000

184,000

Depreciation SL (on Equipment)

Year   1 = 200,000(1/5)(1/2) = 20,000
Years 2-3 = 200,000(1/5) = 40,000

Depreciation Write-off = Cost Basis - Cumulative Depreciation Taken

        200,000 - 100,000 = 100,000

DCFROR = 10.25% < 12.0% so unsatisfactory.

NPV @ 12% = -$8,293 < 0, so unsatisfactory as well.

7-16B Repair Business, MACRS Depreciation - Values in Actual Dollars:

Spare Parts   20,000
Equipment   200,000
Revenues   100,000 per yr ... Yr 3 Salv = 140,000
Operating Costs   40,000 per yr ...

Year	0	1	2	3	Yr 3 Sale
Revenue	-	100,000	100,000	100,000	140,000
-Operating Costs	-	-40,000	-40,000	-40,000	-
-Equip. Deprec.	-	-40,000	-64,000	-38,400	-57,600
-Spare Parts W/O					-20,000
Taxable Income	-	20,000	-4,000	21,600	62,400
Tax Due @ 40%	-	-8,000	1,600	-8,640	-24,960
Net Income	-	12,000	-2,400	12,960	37,440
+Equip. Deprec.	-	40,000	64,000	38,400	57,600
+Spare Parts W/O	-	-	-	-	20,000
-Spare Parts Cost	-20,000				
-Equipment	-200,000				
Cash Flow	-220,000	52,000	61,600	51,360	115,040

166,400

Depreciation MACRS (on Equipment)

Year 1 = 200,000(0.2000) = 40,000
Year 2 = 200,000(0.3200) = 64,000
Year 3 = 200,000(0.1920) = 38,400

Depreciation Write-off = Cost Basis - Cumulative Depreciation Taken

$$200,000 - 142,400 = 57,600$$

DCFROR = 10.68% < 12.0% so unsatisfactory.

NPV @ 12% = -$6,024 < 0, so unsatisfactory as well.

A relatively short 3 year life with a write-off in year 3 eliminates most of the time value of money differential in the economics compared to part A of this problem where straight line depreciation was utilized.

CHAPTER 8 PROBLEM SOLUTIONS

8-1A Stand Alone Solution: *All Values in Thousand of Dollars*

Year	0	1	2	3	3 Salvage
Revenue	-	3,000	3,240	3,499	4,000
- Research	-1,000	-	-	-	-
- Operating Costs	-	-1,000	-1,080	-1,166	-
- Bldg Deprec.	-	-36*	-36	-36	-1,292
- Equip Deprec.	-	-400	-640	-384	-576
- WC (Inventory)	-	-	-	-	-300
- Land	-	-	-	-	-400
- Loss Forward	-	-1,000	-	-	-
Taxable Income	-1,000	564	1,484	1,913	1,432
- Income Tax @ 40%	0	-226	-594	-765	-573
Net Income	-1,000	338	890	1,148	859
+ Bldg Deprec	-	36	36	36	1,292
+ Bldg Equip	-	400	640	384	576
+ Loss Forward	-	1,000	-	-	-
+ WC (Invent&Land)	-	-	-	-	700
- Building Cost	-1,400				
- Equipment Cost	-2,000				
- Land Cost	-400				
- Inventory, WC	-300				
ATCF	-5,100	1,774	1,566	1,568	3,427

4,995

* *The year one real property depreciation neglects the mid-month convention.*

PW EQ: $0 = -5,100 + 1,774(P/F_{i,1}) + 1,566(P/F_{i,2}) + 4,995(P/F_{i,3})$

DCFROR = 23.7% by calculator > 15%, acceptable

NPV @ 15% = $911 by calculator > 0, acceptable

PVR @ 15% = 911 / 5,100 = 0.179 > 0, acceptable

8-1B Expense Solution: *All Values in Thousand of Dollars*

Year	0	1	2	3	3 Salvage
Revenue		3,000	3,240	3,499	4,000
- Research	-1,000	-	-	-	-
- Operating Costs		-1,000	-1,080	-1,166	-
- Bldg Deprec.		-36*	-36	-36	-1,292
- Equip Deprec.		-400	-640	-384	-576
- WC (Inventory)		-	-	-	-300
- Land		-	-	-	-400
Taxable Income	-1,000	1,564	1,484	1,913	1,432
- Income Tax @ 40%	400	-626	-594	-765	-573
Net Income	-600	938	890	1,148	859
+ Bldg Deprec		36	36	36	1,292
+ Bldg Equip		400	640	384	576
+ WC (Invent&Land)		-	-	-	700
- Building Cost	-1,400				
- Equipment Cost	-2,000				
- Land Cost	-400				
- Inventory, WC	-300				
ATCF	-4,700	1,374	1,566	1,568	3,427
					4,995

* *The year one real property depreciation neglects the mid-month convention.*

PW EQ: $0 = -4,700 + 1,374(P/F_{i,1}) + 1,566(P/F_{i,2}) + 4,995(P/F_{i,3})$

DCFROR = 24.5% by calculator > 15%, acceptable

NPV @ 15% = $964 by calculator > 0, acceptable

PVR @ 15% = 964 / 4,700 = 0.205 > 0, acceptable

8-2 Solution: *All Values in Dollars*

Case A) *Expense R&D as an Operating Cost Against Other Income*

	0	1-4	5
Working Capital	50,000		
Research & Experimentation	100,000 (Expense at year 0)		
Working Capital Return Revenue			70,000
Sales Revenue		500,000	500,000
Operating Costs		400,000	400,000
Year	**0**	**1-4**	**5**

Cash Flow Calculations:

Year	0	1-4	5
Revenue		500,000	570,000*
-Operating Costs		-400,000	-400,000
-R&D as O.C.	-100,000		
-Working Capital Write-off			-50,000
Taxable Income	-100,000	100,000	120,000
Tax @ 40%	40,000	-40,000	-48,000
Net Income	-60,000	60,000	72,000
+Working Capital Write-off			50,000
-Capital Costs (Work Cap.)	-50,000		
ATCF	-110,000	60,000	122,000

* *Year 5 revenue includes working capital return.*

PW Eq: $0 = -110,000 + 60,000(P/A_{i,4}) + 122,000(P/F_{i,5})$

$i = DCFROR = 51.3\%$

8-2 Solution: *Continued - All Values in Dollars*

Case B) *Expense R&D as an Operating Cost and Carry Forward to Use Against Project Income (Stand Alone Economics)*

	0	1-4	5
Working Capital	50,000		
Research & Experimentation	100,000		
Working Capital Return Revenue			70,000
Sales Revenue		500,000	500,000
Operating Costs		400,000	400,000
Year	0	1-4	5

Cash Flow Calculations:

Year	0	1	2-4	5
Revenue		500,000	500,000	570,000*
-Operating Costs		-400,000	-400,000	-400,000
-R&D as O.C.	-100,000			
-Working Capital Write-off				-50,000
-Loss Forward		-100,000		
Taxable Income	-100,000	0	100,000	120,000
Tax @ 40%	0	0	-40,000	-48,000
Net Income	-100,000	0	60,000	72,000
+Working Capital Write-off				50,000
+Loss Forward		100,000		
-Capital Costs	-50,000			
ATCF	-150,000	100,000	60,000	122,000

* Year 5 revenue includes working capital return.

PW Eq: $0 = -150,000 + 100,000(P/F_{i,1}) + 60,000(P/A_{i,3})(P/F_{i,1})$

$\qquad\qquad + 122,000(P/F_{i,5})$

i = DCFROR = 44.9%

8-2 Solution: *Continued*

Case C) Capitalize R&D and Deduct by Amortization

Working Capital	50,000		
Research & Experimentation	100,000		
Working Capital Return Revenue		–	70,000
Sales Revenue		500,000	500,000
Operating Costs		400,000	400,000

Year	0	1-4	5
Revenue		500,000	570,000*
-Operating Costs		-400,000	-400,000
-Amortization		-20,000	-20,000
-Working Capital Write-off		–	-50,000
Taxable Income		80,000	100,000
Income Tax @ 40%		-32,000	-40,000
Net Income		48,000	60,000
+Amortization		20,000	20,000
+Working Capital Write-off		–	50,000
-Capital Costs	-150,000		
ATCF	-150,000	68,000	130,000

* Year 5 revenue includes working capital return.

PW Eq: $0 = -150,000 + 68,000(P/A_{i,4}) + 130,000(P/F_{i,5})$

    $i = DCFROR = 40\%$

Case D) Expense R&D, Deutschemark (DM) Analysis

Case D1): ($0.70 US/DM)(833,330 DM) = $583,333 US revenue per year
Case D2): ($0.50 US/DM)(833,330 DM) = $416,667 US revenue per year

Case D1) Cash Flows:

Year	0	1-4	5
Revenue		583,333	653,333
-Oper. Costs		-400,000	-400,000
-R&D	-100,000		
-WC Write-off			-50,000
Taxable Income	-100,000	183,333	203,333
-Tax @ 40%	+40,000	-73,333	-81,333
Net Income	-60,000	110,000	122,000
+WC Write-off			50,000
-Capital Costs	-50,000		
ATCF	-110,000	110,000	172,000

Case D1 DCFROR = 98.6%

Case D2) Cash Flows:

Year	0	1-4	5
Revenue		416,667	486,667
-Oper. Costs		-400,000	-400,000
-R&D	-100,000		
-WC Write-off			-50,000
Taxable Income	-100,000	16,667	36,667
-Tax @ 40%	+40,000	-6,667	-14,667
Net Income	-60,000	10,000	22,000
+WC Write-off			50,000
-Capital Costs	-50,000		
ATCF	-110,000	10,000	72,000

Case D2 DCFROR = 0.4%

Foreign sales projects are very sensitive to exchange rate variations!

8-3 Solution: *All Values in Thousands of Dollars*

Case A) *Stand Alone Economics*

```
Acquisition Cost= 10,000
Working Capital =  2,000
Equipment Cost  = 15,000   I=30,000   I=33,000   I=36,300   I=39,930   I=43,923
Mine Develop    = 10,000   OC=12,000  OC=13,200  OC=14,520  OC=15,972  OC=17,569
```

	0	1	2	3	4	5

Cash Flow Calculations:

Year	Time 0	1	2	3	4	5	Salv
Production		1,000	1,000	1,000	1,000	1,000	
Gross Revenue		30,000	33,000	36,300	39,930	43,923	5,000
-Royalties		-2,400	-2,640	-2,904	-3,194	-3,514	
Net Revenue		27,600	30,360	33,396	36,736	40,409	
-Operating Costs		-12,000	-13,200	-14,520	-15,972	-17,569	
-Development	-7,000						
-Depreciation	-2,143	-3,673	-2,624	-1,874	-1,339	-1,339	-2,008
-Amortization	-600	-600	-600	-600	-600		
-WC Write-off							-2,000
Before Depletion	-9,743	11,327	13,936	16,402	18,825	21,501	992
50% Limit		5,663	6,968	8,201	9,412	10,751	
Percent Depletion		-2,760	-3,036	-3,340	-3,112*	-3,233	
Cost Depletion		2,000	1,810	1,401	432		
-Loss Forward		-9,743	-1,176				
Taxable Income	-9,743	-1,176	9,724	13,062	15,713	18,268	992
-Tax Due @ 40%	0	0	-3,890	-5,225	-6,285	-7,307	-397
Net Income	-9,743	-1,176	5,834	7,837	9,428	10,961	595
+Depreciation	2,143	3,673	2,624	1,874	1,339	1,339	2,008
+Depletion Taken		2,760	3,036	3,340	3,112	3,233	
+Amortization	600	600	600	600	600		
+Loss Forward		9,743	1,176				
+WC Write-off							2,000
-Capital; Equip	-15,000						
-Capital; Dev (30%)	-3,000						
-Working Cap.	-2,000						
-Mineral Acq.	-10,000						
ATCF	-37,000	15,600	13,270	13,651	14,478	15,533	4,603

* *Cumulative percentage depletion in years 1, 2 and 3 is $9,136, so $864 more depletion equals $10,000 mineral rights acquisition cost. $864/.10 = $8,640 net revenue after royalty is needed for 10% depletion, balance is 8% depletion. 8% depletion revenue = ($36,736-$8,640)(0.08) = $28,096(0.08) = $2,248. Cumulative year 4 percentage depletion = $2,248 + $864 = $3,112.*

8-3 Solution: *Case A Continued*

Depreciation Calculations:

Yr 0 $15,000(.1429) = 2,143$
Yr 1 $15,000(.2449) = 3,673$
Yr 2 $15,000(.1749) = 2,624$
Yr 3 $15,000(.1249) = 1,874$
Yr 4 $15,000(.0893) = 1,339$
Yr 5 $15,000(.0892) = 1,339$

Yr 5 Remaining Book Write-off
       $15,000(.1339) = 2,008$

Cost Depletion Calculations:

Yr 1 $10,000(1,000/5,000)$ $= 2,000$
Yr 2 $(10,000-2,760)(1,000/4,000) = 1,810$
Yr 3 $(7,240-3,036)(1,000/3,000) = 1,401$
Yr 4 $(4,204-3,340)(1,000/2,000) =   432$
Yr 5 $(864-3,112) < 0$, stop cost depl.

Amortization of 30% of Development:

Yrs 0-4 $10,000(.30) = 3,000(12/60) = 600$

PW Eq: $0 = -37,000 + 15,600(P/F_{i,1}) + 13,270(P/F_{i,2}) + 13,651(P/F_{i,3})$
           $+ 14,478(P/F_{i,4}) + 20,047(P/F_{i,5})$

DCFROR = 29.4% > 20%, acceptable

NPV $= -37,000 + 15,600(P/F_{20,1}) + 13,270(P/F_{20,2}) + 13,651(P/F_{20,3})$
       $+ 14,478(P/F_{20,4}) + 20,047(P/F_{20,5})$

NPV = $8,154 > 0, acceptable

8-3 Solution Continued: Case B) Expense Economics

Year	0	1	2	3	4	5	Salv
Production		1,000	1,000	1,000	1,000	1,000	
Gross Revenue		30,000	33,000	36,300	39,930	43,923	5,000
-Royalties		-2,400	-2,640	-2,904	-3,194	-3,514	
Net Revenue		27,600	30,360	33,396	36,736	40,409	
-Operating Costs		-12,000	-13,200	-14,520	-15,972	-17,569	
-Development	-7,000						
-Depreciation	-2,143	-3,673	-2,624	-1,874	-1,339	-1,339	-2,008
-Amortization	-600	-600	-600	-600	-600		
-Write-off							-2,000
Before Depletion	-9,743	11,327	13,936	16,402	18,825	21,501	992
Percent Depletion		-2,760	-3,036	-3,340	-3,112*	-3,233	
50% Limit		5,663	6,968	8,201	9,412	10,751	
Cost Depletion		2,000	1,810	1,401	432		
Taxable Income	-9,743	8,567	10,900	13,062	15,713	18,268	992
-Tax Due @ 40%	3,897	-3,427	-4,360	-5,225	-6,285	-7,307	-397
Net Income	-5,846	5,140	6,540	7,837	9,428	10,961	595
+Depreciation	2,143	3,673	2,624	1,874	1,339	1,339	2,008
+Depletion		2,760	3,036	3,340	3,112	3,233	
+Amortization	600	600	600	600	600		
+Write-off							2,000
-Capital, Equip	-15,000						
-Capital, Dev (30%)	-3,000						
-Working Capital	-2,000						
-Mineral Acq.	-10,000						
ATCF	-33,103	12,173	12,800	13,651	14,478	15,533	4,603

$$20,136$$

* Cumulative percentage depletion in years 1, 2 and 3 = $9,136 so
$864 more depletion equals $10,000 mineral rights acquisition cost.
$864/0.10 = $8,640 which is the net revenue after royalty needed for
10% depletion, the balance of revenue is 8% depletion.
8% depletion revenue = ($36,736-$8,640)(0.08) = $28,096(0.08) =
$2,248. Cumulative year 4 percentage depletion = $2,248 + $864 =
$3,112.

$$NPV = -33,103 + 12,173(P/F_{20,1}) + 12,800(P/F_{20,2}) + 13,651(P/F_{20,3})$$

$$+ 14,478(P/F_{20,4}) + 20,136(P/F_{20,5}) = +\$8,904$$

DCFROR = 30.8%

8-4 Solution: *Values in Dollars*

Growth Rate of Return

Cash Flows	-150,000	60,000	70,000	80,000	90,000
Year	0	1	2	3	4

Project DCFROR PW Eq: $150,000 = [60,000 + 10,000(A/G_{i,4})](P/A_{i,4})$

$$i = DCFROR = 32\%$$

To calculate the project Growth DCFROR, you must account for 40% tax to be paid on 12% Treasury bond interest each year; therefore, money grows at 7.2% per year after taxes.

$$\overset{1.2319}{F = 60,000(F/P_{7.2,3})} + \overset{1.1492}{70,000(F/P_{7.2,2})} + \overset{1.072}{80,000(F/P_{7.2,1})} + 90,000$$

$$= 330,118$$

Solving for Growth ROR:

PW EQ: $0 = -150,000 + 330,118(P/F_{i,4})$

Growth DCFROR = 21.8%

8-5 Solution: *All Values in Thousands of Dollars*

Manufacturing Plant Evaluation

```
Working Capital         =  20    I =100 ........  I =100
Depreciable Equipment = 180      OC=40 .........  OC=40   WC Ret =  20
                                 ─────────────────────    Salvage = 150

                         0       1 .............. 15
```

Project Cash Flow Calculations:

Salvage Year	0	1	2-7	8	9-15	15 Salv
Revenue		100.00	100.00	100.00	100.00	170.00
-Operating Costs		-40.00	-40.00	-40.00	-40.00	
-Depreciation		-12.86	-25.71	-12.86		
-WC Write-off						-20.00
Taxable Income		47.14	34.29	47.14	60.00	150.00
-Tax @ 40%		-18.86	-13.71	-18.86	-24.00	-60.00
Net Income		28.29	20.57	28.29	36.00	90.00
+Depreciation		12.86	25.71	12.86		
+WC Return						20.00
Capital Costs	-200.00					
ATCF	-200.00	41.14	46.29	41.14	36.00	110.00

$$\text{NPV @ 15\%} = -200.00 + 41.14(P/F_{15,1}) + 46.29(P/A_{15,6})(P/F_{15,1})$$

$$+ 41.14(P/F_{15,8}) + 36.00(P/A_{15,7})(P/F_{15,8})$$

$$+ 110.00(P/F_{15,15})$$

$$= +\$64.0$$

DCFROR = 21.1%

8-6 Solution: *Values in Thousands*

Corporate Mining, Stand Alone Economics

Acquisition Cost $1,000
Development Cost $500 *(Amort 12/60 of 30% beginning in year 1)*
Equipment Cost   − $1,000 *(Depreciate, MACRS, 7 Years)*
Units Produced   −   −   100   100   150   150

Year	Time 0	1	2	3	4	5	Salvage
Production			100	100	150	150	
Net Revenue			2,000	2,000	3,000	3,000	
−Operating Costs			−800	−800	−1,200	−1,200	
−Development		−350					
−Depreciation			−143	−245	−175	−125	−312
Amortization		−30	−30	−30	−30	−30	
Before Depletion		−380	1,027	925	1,595	1,645	−312
50% Limit on % Depletion			514	463	798	823	
Percent Depletion			−440	−440	−660	−660	
Cost Depletion			200	140	60	0	
−Loss Forward			−380				
Taxable Income		−380	207	485	935	985	−312
−Tax Due @ 40%		0	−83	−194	−374	−394	125
Net Income		−380	124	291	561	591	−187
+Depreciation			143	245	175	125	312
+Depletion Taken			440	440	660	660	
+Amortization		30	30	30	30	30	
+Loss Forward			380				
−Capital Costs	−1,000	−1,150					
ATCF	−1,000	−1,500	1,117	1,006	1,426	1,406	125

1,531

Depreciation Calculations:

Yr 2   1,000(0.1429) = 143
Yr 3   1,000(0.2449) = 245
Yr 4   1,000(0.1749) = 175
Yr 5   1,000(0.1249) = 125
Depreciable Write-off = 312

Cost Depletion Calculations:

Yr 2   1,000(100/500) = 200
Yr 3   560(100/400)   = 140
Yr 4   120(150/300)   = 60
Yr 5   *Basis < 0, no cost depletion*

PW Eq: $0 = -1,000 - 1,500(P/F_{i,1}) + 1,117(P/F_{i,2}) + 1,006(P/F_{i,3})$

$+ 1,426(P/F_{i,4}) + 1,531(P/F_{i,5})$

DCFROR = 27.3%,   NPV @ 15% = +$778,   PVR = $778/[1,000+1,500(P/F_{15,1})]$ = 0.34

Pay-back from start of project = 3 years + (377/1,426) = 3.26 years

8-7 Solution: *All Values in Thousands*

Petroleum Property Evaluation, Independent Producer

Acquisition Cost:	$100						
Intang. Drill :	$750	$250					
Tangible Compl. :	–	$1,000					
Production :	–	–	70	56	42	28	14
Year	0	1	2	3	4	5	6

Case A and B Cash Flows for Expensing Against Other Income:

				Success					Fail
Year	0	1	2	3	4	5	6	6	1
Gross Revenue			1,540	1,331	1,078	776	419		
-Royalties			-216	-186	-151	-109	-59		
Net Revenue			1,324	1,145	927	667	360		
-Oper. Costs			-175	-193	-212	-233	-256		-50
-Intangible	-750	-250							
-Depreciation			-143	-245	-175	-125	-89		
-Write-off								-223	
Before Depl.	-750	-250	1,006	707	540	309	15	-223	-50
-100% Limit			1,006	707	540	309	-15		
-% Depln(15%)			-199	-172	-139	-100	54		
-Cost Depl.			33	0	0	0	0		-100
Taxable Inc	-750	-250	807	535	401	209	0	-223	-150
-Tax @ 38%	285	95	-307	-203	-152	-80	0	85	57
Net Income	-465	-155	500	332	249	130	0	-138	-93
+Depreciation			143	245	175	125	89		
+Write-off								223	
+Depletion			199	172	139	100	15		100
-Acq. Cost	-100								
-Tangible Cost		-1,000							
ATCF	-565	-1,155	842	749	563	355	104	85	7
								189	

PW Eq: $0 = -565 - 1{,}155(P/F_{i,1}) + 842(P/F_{i,2}) + 749(P/F_{i,3}) + 563(P/F_{i,4})$

$$+ 355(P/F_{i,5}) + 189(P/F_{i,6})$$

DCFROR = 19.0%   NPV @ 15% = +$140

Problem 8-7 Solution Continued:

*Risk adjust Case A for a 40% probability of success after the year 0
expenditures. A $50,000 abandonment cost is incurred in year 1 if the project
fails along with a write-off of the $100,000 acquisition cost.*

Risk Adjusted PW Eq:

$$0 = -565 + [-1,155(P/F_{i,1}) + 842(P/F_{i,2}) + 749(P/F_{i,3}) + 563(P/F_{i,4})$$

$$+ 355(P/F_{i,5}) + 189(P/F_{i,6})](.4) + 7(P/F_{i,1})(.6)$$

Expected DCFROR = 1.8%,   Expected NPV @ 15% = -$279

*Case C)   Integrated Producer 6-month deduction for amortization of IDC in the
year incurred.*

| Year | 0 | 1 | Success P(0.4) | | | | | Failure P(0.6) |
			2	3	4	5	6*	1
Gross Revenue			1,540	1,331	1,078	776	419	
-Royalties			-216	-186	-151	-109	-59	
Net Revenue			1,324	1,145	927	667	360	
-Oper Costs			-175	-193	-212	-233	-256	-50
-IDC's	-525	-175						
-Depreciation			-143	-245	-175	-125	-89	
-Write-off							-223	
-Amortization	-23	-53	-60	-60	-60	-38	-8	-202
-Cost Depln			-33	-27	-20	-13	-7	-100
Taxable Inc	-548	-227	913	620	460	258	-223	-352
-Tax @ 38%	208	86	-347	-236	-175	-98	89	134
Net Income	-339	-141	566	384	285	160	-134	-218
+Depreciation			143	245	175	125	89	
+Write-off							223	
+Amortization	23	53	60	60	60	38	8	202
+Depletion			33	27	20	13	7	100
-Cap. Costs	-325	-1,075						
ATCF	-642	-1,164	802	716	540	336	193	84

* Year Includes Write-offs

PW Eq: $0 = -642 - 1,164(P/F_{i,1}) + 802(P/F_{i,2}) + 716(P/F_{i,3}) + 540(P/F_{i,4})$

$$+ 336(P/F_{i,5}) + 193(P/F_{i,6})$$

DCFROR = 14.5%   NPV @ 15% = -$18

Problem 8-7 Solution Continued:

*Risk adjust Case C for a 40% probability of success after the year 0
expenditures. A $50,000 abandonment cost is incurred in year 1 if the project
fails along with a write-off of the $100,000 acquisition cost.*

Risk Adjusted PW Eq:

$$0 = -642 + [-1,164(P/F_{i,1}) + 802(P/F_{i,2}) + 716(P/F_{i,3}) + 540(P/F_{i,4})$$
$$+ 336(P/F_{i,5}) + 193(P/F_{i,6})](0.4) + 84(P/F_{i,1})(0.6)$$

Applying the probabilities to the cash flow streams and combining gives:

$$0 = -642 + -415.2(P/F_{i,1}) + 320.8(P/F_{i,2}) + 286.4(P/F_{i,3}) + 216.0(P/F_{i,4})$$
$$+ 134.4(P/F_{i,5}) + 77.2(P/F_{i,6})$$

Expected DCFROR = -0.7%, Expected NPV @ 15% = -$348

Case D) *Independent Producer, Stand Alone Economic Analyses*

				Success					Fail
Year	0	1	2	3	4	5	6	6	1
Gross Revenue			1,540	1,331	1,078	776	419		
-Royalties			-216	-186	-151	-109	-59		
Net Revenue			1,324	1,145	927	667	360		
-Oper Costs			-175	-193	-212	-233	-256		-50
-Intangible	-750	-250							
-Depreciation			-143	-245	-175	-125	-89		
-Write-off								-223	
Before Depln	-750	-250	1,006	707	540	309	15	-223	-50
-100% Limit			1,006	707	540	309	-15		
-% Depl (15%)			-199	-172	-139	-100	54		
-Cost Depln			33	0	0	0	0		-100
-Loss Forward		-750	-1,000	-193					
Taxable Inc	-750	-1,000	-193	342	401	209	0	-223	-150
-Tax @ 38%	0	0	0	-130	-152	-79	0	85	57
Net Income	-750	-1,000	-193	212	249	130	0	-138	-93
+Depreciation			143	245	175	125	89		
+Write-off								223	
+Depletion			199	172	139	100	15		100
+Loss Forward		750	1,000	193					
-Cap. Costs	-100	-1,000							
ATCF	-850	-1,250	1,149	822	563	355	104	85	7

Problem 8-7 Solution Continued:

Year	Success								Fail
	0	1	2	3	4	5	6	6	1
ATCF	-850	-1,250	1,149	822	563	355	104	85	7

PW Eq: $0 = -850 - 1,250(P/F_{i,1}) + 1,149(P/F_{i,2}) + 822(P/F_{i,3}) + 563(P/F_{i,4})$

$+ 355(P/F_{i,5}) + 189(P/F_{i,6})$

DCFROR = 16.3%

NPV @ 15% = +$52.4

Risk adjust Case D for a 40% probability of success after the time 0 expenditures. A $50,000 abandonment cost is incurred in year 1 if the project fails along with a write-off of the $100,000 acquisition cost.

Risk Adjusted PW Eq:

$0 = -850 + [-1,250(P/F_{i,1}) + 1,149(P/F_{i,2}) + 822(P/F_{i,3}) + 563(P/F_{i,4})$

$+ 355(P/F_{i,5}) + 189(P/F_{i,6})](.4) + 7(P/F_{i,1})(.6)$

Applying the probabilities to the cash flow streams and combining gives:

$0 = -850 - 495.8(P/F_{i,1}) + 459.6(P/F_{i,2}) + 328.8(P/F_{i,3}) + 225.2(P/F_{i,4})$

$+ 142.0(P/F_{i,5}) + 75.6(P/F_{i,6})$

Expected DCFROR = -3.0%, Expected NPV @ 15% = -$485

8-8 Solution: *Values in Thousands of Dollars*

Case A) 9 Year Evaluation Life

Year	0	1	2-7	8	9
Revenue		400	400	400	500*
-Operating Costs		-200	-200	-200	-200
-Depreciation		-30	-60	-30	
-Write-offs					-100
Taxable Income		170	140	170	200
-Tax @ 35%		-59	-49	-59	-70
Net Income		111	91	111	130
+Depreciation		30	60	30	
+Write-offs					100
-Capital Costs	-520				
ATCF	-520	141	151	141	230

* Revenue includes Working Capital Return.

PW Eq: $0 = -520 + 141(P/F_{i,1}) + 151(P/A_{i,6})(P/F_{i,1})$
$+ 141(P/F_{i,8}) + 230(P/F_{i,9})$

DCFROR = 25.2%   NPV @ 15% = +$210

Case B) 18 Year Evaluation Life

Year	0	1	2-7	8	9-17	18
Revenue		400	400	400	400	500*
-Operating Costs		-200	-200	-200	-200	-200
-Depreciation		-30	-60	-30		
-Write-offs						-100
Taxable Income		170	140	170	200	200
-Tax @ 35%		-59	-49	-59	-70	-70
Net Income		111	91	111	130	130
+Depreciation		30	60	30		
+Write-offs						100
-Capital Costs	-520					
ATCF	-520	141	151	141	130	230

PW Eq: $0 = -520 + 141(P/F_{i,1}) + 151(P/A_{i,6})(P/F_{i,1}) + 141(P/F_{i,8})$

$+ 130(P/A_{i,9})(P/F_{i,8}) + 230(P/F_{i,18})$

DCFROR = 27.7%   NPV @ 15% = +$366

8-9 Solution: *Costs ($) and Production (Gal) in Thousands*

Processing Facility

Year	Time 0	1	2	3	4	5
Production, (Gal)		62	53	35	24	17
Research & Exper.	750	250				
Equipment		670				
Patent Rights	100					
Operating Costs		175	193	212	233	256
Price, ($/Gal)		26.0	26.0	26.0	27.3	28.7
Royalty (% of Gross)		14%	14%	14%	14%	14%

Case 1A, Expense Cash Flows

Year	Time 0	1	2	3	4	5	Salv
Production		62	53	35	24	17	
Gross Revenue		1,612	1,378	910	655	488	
-Royalties		-226	-193	-127	-92	-68	
Net Revenue		1,386	1,185	783	563	420	
-Operating Costs		-175	-193	-212	-233	-256	
-Research	-750	-250					
-Depreciation		-96	-164	-117	-84	-60	-149
-Amortization	-20	-20	-20	-20	-20		
Taxable Income	-770	846	808	433	227	104	-149
-Tax Due @ 40%	308	-338	-323	-173	-91	-42	60
Net Income	-462	507	485	260	136	62	-89
+Depreciation		96	164	117	84	60	149
+Amortization	20	20	20	20	20		
-Depreciable Equip.		-670					
-Patent Cost	-100						
ATCF	-542	-47	669	397	240	122	60

$$\underbrace{\qquad\qquad}_{182}$$

PW Eq: $0 = -542 - 47(P/F_{i,1}) + 669(P/F_{i,2}) + 397(P/F_{i,3})$

$\qquad\qquad + 240(P/F_{i,4}) + 182(P/F_{i,5})$

DCFROR = 40.6% > i^* of 15%, *accept*

NPV @ 15% = +$412 > 0, *accept*

PVR = 412 / [542 + 47($P/F_{15,1}$)] = +0.71 > 0, *accept*

8-9 Solution: *Continued*

Case 1B, Stand Alone Cash Flows

Year	Time 0	1	2	3	4	5	Salv
Production		62	53	35	24	17	
Gross Revenue		1,612	1,378	910	655	488	
-Royalties		-226	-193	-127	-92	-68	
Net Revenue		1,386	1,185	783	563	420	
-Operating Costs		-175	-193	-212	-233	-256	
-Research	-750	-250					
-Depreciation		-96	-164	-117	-84	-60	-149
-Amortization	-20	-20	-20	-20	-20		
-Loss Forward		-770					
Taxable Income	-770	76	808	433	227	104	-149
-Tax Due @ 40%	0	-30	-323	-173	-91	-42	60
Net Income	-770	45	485	260	136	62	-89
+Depreciation		96	164	117	84	60	149
+Amortization	20	20	20	20	20		
+Loss Forward		770					
-Depreciable Equip.		-670					
-Patent Cost	-100						
ATCF	-850	261	669	397	240	122	60

182

PW Eq: $0 = -850 + 261(P/F_{i,1}) + 669(P/F_{i,2}) + 397(P/F_{i,3})$

$+ 240(P/F_{i,4}) + 182(P/F_{i,5})$

DCFROR = 33.9% > i^* of 15%, *accept*

NPV @ 15% = $371 > 0, *accept*

PVR = 371 / 850 = +0.44 > 0, *accept*

8-9 Solution: *Continued*

Case 2, Risk Analysis for Part 1A
Non-Risk Adjusted Cash Flows

ATCF	-542 p=0.40	-47	669	397	240	182
Year	0	1	2	3	4	5

p=0.60

-Abandonment Cost	-70
-Patent Bk Value Write-off	-80
Taxable Income	-150
-Tax @ 40%	60
Net Income	-90
+ Write-off	80
Failure ATCF	-10

Risk Adjusted Cash Flows

Expected
Value

ATCF	-542	-25*	268	159	96	73
Year	0	1	2	3	4	5

* Yr 1 cash flow is determined by combining the two expected cash flows
  as follows: (-10)(.6) + (-47)(.4) = -25.

Expected Discounted Cash Flow Rate of Return:

PW Eq: $0 = -542 - 25(P/F_{i,1}) + 268(P/F_{i,2}) + 159(P/F_{i,3}) + 96(P/F_{i,4})$
$+ 73(P/F_{i,5})$

Expected DCFROR = 1.7% < i^* of 15%, *reject*

ENPV @ 15% = -$166 < 0, reject

$$\text{EPVR} = -166 / [542 + 25(\overset{0.8696}{P/F_{15,1}})] = -0.29 < 0, \textit{reject}$$

8-9 Solution: Continued

Case 3, Break-even Analysis of Case 1A Cash Flows

Year	Time 0	1	2	3	4	5	Salv
Total Production		62	53	35	24	17	
Net Production (86%)		53	46	30	21	15	
Selling Price ($/Gal)		X	X	X	X	X	
Net Revenue		53X	46X	30X	21X	15X	
-Operating Costs		-175	-193	-212	-233	-256	
-Research	-750	-250					
-Depreciation		-96	-164	-117	-84	-60	-149
-Amortization	-20	-20	-20	-20	-20		
Taxable Income	-770	53X-541	46X-377	30X-349	21X-337	15X-316	-149
-Tax Due @ 40%	308	-21X+216	-18X+151	-12X+140	-8X+135	-6X+126	60
Net Income	-462	32X-325	28X-226	18X-209	13X-202	9X-190	-89
+Depreciation		96	164	117	84	60	149
+Amortization	20	20	20	20	20		
-Capital Costs	-100	-670					
ATCF	-542	32X-879	28X-42	18X-72	13X-98	9X-130	60

$$9X-70$$

Present Worth Equation:

$$0 = -542 + (32X-879)(P/F_{15,1}) + (28X-42)(P/F_{15,2}) + (18X-72)(P/F_{15,3})$$

with factors 0.8696, 0.7561, 0.6575

$$+ (13X-98)(P/F_{15,4}) + (9X-70)(P/F_{15,5})$$

with factors 0.5718, 0.4972

$$0 = 72.74X - 1{,}476.32, \text{ therefore, } X = \$20.30$$

Break-even Selling Price X = $20.30 per gallon

The "Goal Seek" routine in Excel can make breakeven calculations of this type very simple. Be sure to link all cash flows so that a change in one parameter will influence each subsequent year appropriately. The same is true for the next application (Case 4). In each case, the objective is to find the before-tax value that will make the after-tax NPV equal zero at the desired after-tax minimum rate of return (or hurdle rate).

8-9 Solution: *Continued*

Case 4, Before-tax Acquisition Cost Analysis
A break-even cost analysis assuming the acquisition cost will be treated like a patent cost for tax purposes and amortized over 5 years.

Cash Flows From Part 1A

ATCF	-542	-47	669	397	240	182
Year	0	1	2	3	4	5

NPV from Part 1A = $412

This NPV represents additional after-tax acquisition cost that can be incurred and still give the investor a 15% DCFROR. Let the before-tax acquisition cost equal "X" and be subject to 5 year amortization. The tax savings generated from the additional amortization deductions above those associated with the $100,000 patent rights fee are calculated as follows:

	Before-Tax Deduction	Tax Savings
Yr 0:	X(1/5) = .20X	.20X(.4) = .08X
Yr 1:	X(1/5) = .20X	.20X(.4) = .08X
Yr 2:	X(1/5) = .20X	.20X(.4) = .08X
Yr 3:	X(1/5) = .20X	.20X(.4) = .08X
Yr 4:	X(1/5) = .20X	.20X(.4) = .08X

Applying Equation 9-1:

X = After-Tax NPV + PW of Tax Savings from Deductions Related to X

$$X = 412 + 0.08X + 0.08X \overset{2.855}{(P/A_{15,4})}$$

Break-even Acquisition Cost = $596

Therefore, X = $596 is the before-tax break-even acquisition cost that could be incurred and still have the project earn the desired 15% after-tax minimum rate of return.

8-10 Solution: *Costs ($) and Production (Bbl) in Thousands*

Petroleum Project

Year	0	1	2	3	4	5
Production (Bbls)		62	53	35	24	17
Intangibles (IDC's)	750	250				
Tangible (Completion)		670				
Mineral Rights Acq.	100					
Operating Costs		175	193	212	233	256
Price, ($/Bbl)		26.0	26.0	26.0	27.3	28.7

Case 1A) Integrated Producer, Expense Cash Flows

Year	0	1	2	3	4	5
Gross Revenue		1,612	1,378	910	655	488
-Royalties		-226	-193	-127	-92	-68
Net Revenue		1,386	1,185	783	563	420
-Oper. Costs		-175	-193	-212	-233	-256
-Intangible (70%)	-525	-175				
-Depreciation		-96	-164	-117	-84	-60
-Deprec Write-off						-149
-Amortization	-45	-60	-60	-60	-60	-15
-Cost Depletion		-32	-28	-18	-13	-9
Taxable Income	-570	848	740	376	173	-69
-Tax @ 40%	228	-339	-296	-150	-70	27
Net Income	-342	509	444	226	103	-42
+Deprec/Write-off		96	164	117	84	209
+Depletion		32	28	18	13	9
+Amortization	45	60	60	60	60	15
-Tangible Completion		-670				
-30% Intangible	-225	-75				
-Mineral Acquisition	-100					
ATCF	-622	-48	696	421	260	191

PW Eq: $0 = -622 - 48(P/F_{i,1}) + 696(P/F_{i,2}) + 421(P/F_{i,3}) + 260(P/F_{i,4})$

$\qquad + 191(P/F_{i,5})$, i = DCFROR = 36.3% > i^* of 15%, *accept*

$\qquad\qquad\qquad 0.8696 \qquad\qquad 0.7561 \qquad\qquad 0.6575 \qquad\qquad 0.5718$

NPV@15% = $-622 - 48(P/F_{15,1}) + 696(P/F_{15,2}) + 421(P/F_{15,3}) + 260(P/F_{15,4})$

$\qquad\qquad 0.4972$

$\qquad + 191(P/F_{15,5}) = +383 > 0$, *accept*

PVR = $383 / \{622 + 48(P/F_{15,1})\} = 0.58 > 0$, *accept*

8-10 Solution: *Continued*

Case 1B) Integrated Producer, Stand Alone Cash Flows

Year	0	1	2	3	4	5
Gross Revenue		1,612	1,378	910	655	488
-Royalties		-226	-193	-127	-92	-68
Net Revenue		1,386	1,185	783	563	420
-Oper Costs		-175	-193	-212	-233	-256
-Intangible	-525	-175				
-Depreciation		-96	-164	117	-84	-60
-Deprec Write-off						-149
-Amortization	-45	-60	-60	-60	-60	-15
-Cost Depletion		-32	-28	-18	-13	-9
-Loss Forward		-570				
Taxable Income	-570	278	740	376	173	-69
-Tax @ 40%	0	-111	-296	-150	-70	27
Net Income	-570	167	444	226	103	-42
+Deprec/Write-off		96	164	117	84	209
+Cost Depletion		32	28	18	13	9
+Amortization	45	60	60	60	60	15
+Loss Forward		570				
-Acquisition Cost	-100					
-30% Intangibles	-225	-75				
-Tangible Compl.		-670				
ATCF	-850	180	696	421	260	191

PW Eq: $0 = -850 + 180(P/F_{i,1}) + 696(P/_{i,2}) + 421(P/F_{i,3}) + 260(P/F_{i,4})$

$+ 191(P/F_{i,5})$

DCFROR = 32.1% > i* of 15%, *accept*

NPV @ 15% = +353 > 0, *accept*

PVR = 353 / 850 = 0.42 > 0, *accept*

8-10 Solution: *Continued*

Case 2) Integrated Producer, Risk Adjusted Case 1A Cash Flows
Non-Risk Adjusted Cash Flows

ATCF	-622 p=0.40	-48	696	421	260	191
Year	0	1	2	3	4	5

p=0.60

-Abandonment Cost	-70
-30% Unamortized IDC	-180
-Cost Depl Write-off	-100
Taxable Income	-350
-Tax @ 40%	140
Net Income	-210
+ Write-offs	280
Failure ATCF	+70

Risk Adjusted Cash Flows (40% Probability of Success)

Expected Value ATCF	-622	23*	278	168	104	76
Year	0	1	2	3	4	5

* *Cash Flow = -48(0.4) + 70(0.6) = +23*

Expected Discounted Cash Flow Rate of Return (EDCFROR):

PW Eq: $0 = -622 + 23(P/F_{i,1}) + 278(P/F_{i,2}) + 168(P/F_{i,3}) + 104(P/F_{i,4})$

$\qquad + 76(P/F_{i,5})$

EDCFROR = 1.5% < i* of 15%, *reject*

ENPV @ 15% = -184.1 < 0, *reject*

EPVR = -184.1 / 622 = -0.296 < 0, *reject*

8-10 Solution: *Continued*

Case 3) *Independent Producer > 1,000 Bbls/Day, Expense Cash Flows*

Year	0	1	2	3	4	5	Salv
Production		62	53	35	24	17	
Gross Revenue		1,612	1,378	910	655	488	
-Royalties		-226	-193	-127	-92	-68	
Net Revenue		1,386	1,185	783	563	420	
-Operating Costs		-175	-193	-212	-233	-256	
-Intangible Drilling	-750	-250					
-Depreciation		-96	-164	-117	-84	-60	-149
-Cost Depletion		-32	-28	-18	-13	-9	
Taxable Income	-750	833	800	435	234	95	-149
-Tax Due @ 40%	300	-333	-320	-174	-94	-38	60
Net Income	-450	500	480	261	141	57	-89
+Depreciation		96	164	117	84	60	149
+Cost Depletion		32	28	18	13	9	
-Tangible Equipment		-670					
-Mineral Acquisition	-100						
ATCF	-550	-42	672	397	237	126	60

$$186$$

PW Eq: $0 = -550 - 42(P/F_{i,1}) + 672(P/F_{i,2}) + 397(P/F_{i,3}) + 237(P/F_{i,4})$
$$+ 186(P/F_{i,5})$$

DCFROR = 40.3% > i^* of 15%, *accept*

NPV @ 15% = +$410 > 0, *accept*

$$0.8696$$
PVR = 410 / {550 + 42(P/F_{15,1})} = +0.70 > 0, *accept*

8-10 Solution: *Continued*

Case 3) Independent Producer > 1,000 Bbls/Day, Stand Alone Cash Flows

Year	Time 0	1	2	3	4	5	Salv.
Production		62	53	35	24	17	
Gross Revenue		1,612	1,378	910	655	488	
-Royalties		-226	-193	-127	-92	-68	
Net Revenue		1,386	1,185	783	563	420	
-Operating Costs		-175	-193	-212	-233	-256	
-Intangible Drilling	-750	-250					
-Depreciation		-96	-164	-117	-84	-60	-149
-Cost Depletion		-32	-28	-18	-13	-9	
-Loss Forward		-750					
Taxable Income	-750	83	800	435	234	95	-149
-Tax Due @ 40%	0	-33	-320	-174	-94	-38	60
Net Income	-750	50	480	261	141	57	-89
+Depreciation		96	164	117	84	60	149
+Cost Depletion		32	28	18	13	9	
+Loss Forward		750					
-Mineral Acq Cost	-100						
-Tangible Completion		-670					
ATCF	-850	258	672	397	237	126	60

186

PW Eq: $0 = -850 + 258(P/F_{i,1}) + 672(P/F_{i,2}) + 397(P/F_{i,3}) + 237(P/F_{i,4})$

$+ 186(P/F_{i,5})$

DCFROR = 33.9% > i* of 15%, *accept*

NPV @ 15% = +$371 > 0, *accept*

PVR = 371 / 850 = +0.44 > 0, *accept*

8-10 Solution: *Continued*

Case 3)   Independent Producer > 1,000 Bbls/Day, Risk Analysis
Non-Risk Adjusted ATCF

ATCF	-550 p=0.40	-42	672	397	237	186
Year	0	1	2	3	4	5

p=0.60

-Abandonment Cost	-70
-Cost Depl Write-off	-100
Taxable Income	-170
-Tax @ 40%	68
Net Income	-102
+ Write-offs	100
Failure ATCF	-2

Risk Adjusted Cash Flows for 40% Probability of Success

ATCF	-550	-18*	269	159	95	74
Year	0	1	2	3	4	5

* Cash Flow = -42(.4) - 2(.6) = -18

Expected Present Worth Equation:

PW Eq: $0 = -550 - 18(P/F_{i,1}) + 269(P/F_{i,2}) + 159(P/F_{i,3}) + 95(P/F_{i,4})$
$+ 74(P/F_{i,5})$

Expected DCFROR = 1.7% < i^* of 15%, *reject*

ENPV @ 15% = -167 < 0, *reject*

$$EPVR = -167 / [550 + \overset{0.8696}{18(P/F_{15,1})}] = -0.30 < 0, \text{ } reject$$

8-10 Solution: *Continued*

Case 4)   Independent Producer < 1,000 Bbls/Day, Expense ATCF

Year	0	1	2	3	4	5	5 Salv
Gross Revenue		1,612	1,378	910	655	488	
-Royalties		-226	-193	-127	-92	-68	
Net Revenue		1,386	1,185	783	563	420	
-Operating Costs		-175	-193	-212	-233	-256	
-Intangible	-750	-250					
-Depreciation		-96	-164	-117	-84	-60	
-Deprec Write-off							-149
Before Depletion	-750	866	828	453	247	104	-149
-100% Limit		866	828	453	247	104	
-Percent Depletion		-208	-178	-117	-85	-63	
-Cost Depletion		32	0	0	0	0	
Taxable Income	-750	658	650	336	162	41	-149
-Income Tax @ 40%	300	-263	-260	-134	-65	-16	60
Net Income	-450	395	390	202	97	25	-89
+Depreciation		96	164	117	84	60	149
+Depletion Taken		208	178	117	85	63	
-Tangible Equipment		-670					
-Mineral Acq.	-100						
ATCF	-550	28	732	436	266	148	60

$$\underbrace{}_{208}$$

PW Eq: $0 = -550 + 28(P/F_{i,1}) + 732(P/F_{i,2}) + 436(P/F_{i,3}) + 266(P/F_{i,4})$
$$+ 208(P/F_{i,5})$$

DCFROR = 50.3% > i^* of 15%, *accept*

NPV @ 15% = 570.0 > 0, *accept*

PVR = 570 / 550 = 1.04 > 0, *accept*

8-10 Solution: *Continued*

Case 4)   *Independent Producer < 1,000 Bbls/Day, Stand Alone ATCF*

Year	0	1	2	3	4	5	5 Salv
Gross Revenue		1,612	1,378	910	655	488	
-Royalties		-226	-193	-127	-92	-68	
Net Revenue		1,386	1,185	783	563	420	
-Oper Costs		-175	-193	-212	-233	-256	
-Intangible	-750	-250					
-Depreciation		-96	-164	-117	-84	-60	
-Deprec Write-off							-149
Before Depl.	-750	866	828	453	247	104	-149
-100% Limit		866	828	453	247	104	
-Percent Depl		-208	-178	-117	-85	-63	
-Cost Depl.		32	0	0	0	0	
-Loss Forward		-750	-92				
Taxable Income	-750	-92	558	336	162	41	-149
-Tax @ 40%			-223	-134	-65	-16	60
Net Income	-750	-92	335	202	97	25	-89
+Depreciation		96	164	117	84	60	149
+Depletion		208	178	117	85	63	
+Loss Forward		750	92				
-Mineral Acq Cost	-100						
-Tangible Compl		-670					
ATCF	-850	291	769	436	266	148	60

208

PW Eq: $0 = -850 + 291(P/F_{i,1}) + 769(P/F_{i,2}) + 436(P/F_{i,3}) + 266(P/F_{i,4})$
$+ 208(P/F_{i,5})$

DCFROR = 41.25% > i* of 15%, *accept*

NPV @ 15% = +526.7 > 0, *accept*

PVR = 526.7 / 850 = 0.62 > 0 accept

8-10 Solution: *Continued*

Case 4)   Independent Producer < 1,000 Bbls/Day, Risk Analysis

Non-Risk Adjusted ATCF

ATCF	-550	p=0.40	28	732	436	266	208

Year	0	1	2	3	4	5

p=0.60

-Abandonment Cost	-70
-Cost Depl Write-off	-100
Taxable Income	-170
-Tax @ 40%	68
Net Income	-102
+ Write-offs	100
Failure ATCF	-2

Risk Adjusted ATCF

Expected
Value

ATCF	-550	10*	293	174	106	83

Year	0	1	2	3	4	5

*   Cash Flow is 28(0.4) - 2(0.6) = +10

Expected Present Worth Equation:

PW Eq: $0 = -550 + 10(P/F_{i,1}) + 293(P/F_{i,2}) + 174(P/F_{i,3}) + 106(P/F_{i,4})$
$+ 83(P/F_{i,5})$

Expected DCFROR = 6.8% < i^* of 15%, *reject*

ENPV @ 15% = -103 < 0, *reject*

EPVR = -103 / 550 = -0.19 < 0, *reject*

8-10 Solution: *Continued*

Case 5)   Integrated Producer, Break-even Price/Unit Analysis
*   Case 1A, Expense Economics*

Year	0	1	2	3	4	5
Net Revenue		.86X(62)	.86X(53)	.86X(35)	.86X(24)	.86X(17)
-Oper Costs		-175	-193	-212	-233	-256
-Intangible	-525	-175				
-Depreciation		-96	-164	-117	-84	-60
-Deprec Write-off						-149
-Amortization	-45	-60	-60	-60	-60	-15
-Cost Depletion		-32	-28	-18	-13	-9
Taxable Income	-570	53X-538	46X-445	30X-408	21X-389	15X-489
-Tax @ 40%	228	-21X+215	-18X+178	-12X+163	-8X+156	-6X+196
Net Income	-342	32X-323	28X-267	18X-245	13X-234	9X-294
+Depreciation		96	164	117	84	209
+Cost Depletion		32	28	18	13	9
+Amortization	45	60	60	60	60	15
-Acq Cost	-100					
-30% Intangible	-225	-75				
-Tangible Compl.		-670				
ATCF	-622	32X-880	28X-15	18X-49	13X-77	9X-60

$$0 = -622 + \underset{0.8696}{(32X-880)(P/F_{15,1})} + \underset{0.7561}{(28X-15)(P/F_{15,2})} + \underset{0.6575}{(18X-49)(P/F_{15,3})}$$

$$+ \underset{0.5718}{(13X-77)(P/F_{15,4})} + \underset{0.4972}{(9X-60)(P/F_{15,5})}$$

$$0 = 72.74X - 1,504.63, \textit{ therefore, } X = \$20.69$$

Break-even Selling Price Per Unit = $20.69 per barrel

8-10 Solution: *Continued*

Case 6) *Integrated Producer, Acquisition Break-even Cost*

ATCF from Part 1A:

Year	0	1	2	3	4	5
ATCF	-622	-48	696	421	261	191

Part 1A Net Present Value = $383.54

This NPV represents additional after-tax acquisition cost that can be incurred and still give the investor a 15% DCFROR. Let the before-tax acquisition cost equal "X" and be subject to cost depletion. The tax savings generated from the additional cost depletion deductions above those associated with the $100,000 acquisition fee are calculated as follows:

	Before-Tax Value		Tax Savings
Yr 1:	X(62/191)	= .32X	.32X(.4) = .13X
Yr 2:	.68X(53/129)	= .28X	.28X(.4) = .11X
Yr 3:	.40X(35/76)	= .18X	.18X(.4) = .07X
Yr 4:	.22X(24/41)	= .13X	.13X(.4) = .05X
Yr 5:	.09X(17/17)	= .09X	.09X(.4) = .04X

Present Worth (PW) Tax Savings from Deductions Equal:

$$0 = .13X(P/F_{15,1}) + .11X(P/F_{15,2}) + .07X(P/F_{15,3})$$

with factors 0.8696, 0.7561, 0.6575

$$+ .05X(P/F_{15,4}) + .04X(P/F_{15,5}) = .2907X$$

with factors 0.5718, 0.4972

Using Equation 9-1:

X = After-Tax NPV + PW Tax Savings from Deductions Related to X

Re-arranging:

X - PW Tax Savings from Deductions Related to X = After-Tax NPV

So, X - .2907X = $383.54 NPV, therefore, X = 540.73

An integrated producer who can expense deductions against other income could invest $540,730 to acquire the mineral rights to this project and still have the project earn a 15% DCFROR.

8-11 Solution: *Costs and Production in Thousands*

Mining Project

Year	0	1	2	3	4	5
Production in Tons		62	53	35	24	17
Mineral Develop	750	250				
Mining Equipment		670				
Mineral Rights Acq.	100					
Operating Costs		175	193	212	233	256
Price, $ Per Ton		26	26	26	27.3	28.7

Case 1A) Corporate Mining, Expense Cash Flows

Year	0	1	2	3	4	5	Salv
Gross Revenue		1,612	1,378	910	655	488	
-Royalties		-226	-193	-127	-92	-68	
Net Revenue		1,386	1,185	783	563	420	
-Oper Costs		-175	-193	-212	-233	-256	
-Development	-525	-175					
-Depreciation		-96	-164	-117	-84	-60	
-Deprec Write-off							-149
-Amortization	-45	-60	-60	-60	-60	-15	
Before Depletion	-570	881	768	393	187	89	-149
-50% Limit		440	384	197	93	-45	
-Percent Depletion		-208	-178	-117	-85	63	
-Cost Depletion		32					
Taxable Income	-570	673	590	276	102	44	-149
-Income Tax @ 40%	228	-269	-236	-110	-41	-18	60
Net Income	-342	404	354	166	61	26	-89
+Deprec/Write-off		96	164	117	84	60	149
+Depletion Taken		208	178	117	85	45	
+Amortization	45	60	60	60	60	15	
-Mine Equipment		-670					
-30% Mine Develop	-225	-75					
-Mineral Acq.	-100						
ATCF	-622	22	756	460	290	146	60

206

PW Eq: $0 = -622 + 22(P/F_{i,1}) + 756(P/F_{i,2}) + 460(P/F_{i,3})$

$+ 290(P/F_{i,4}) + 206(P/F_{i,5})$

DCFROR = 45.1%   NPV @ 15% = +$539   PVR = 539 / 622 = 0.87

8-11 *Solution Continued:*

Case 1B) *Corporate Mining, Stand Alone Cash Flows*

Year	0	1	2	3	4	5	Salv
Gross Revenue		1,612	1,378	910	655	488	
-Royalties		-226	-193	-127	-92	-68	
Net Revenue		1,386	1,185	783	563	420	0
-Oper Costs		-175	-193	-212	-233	-256	
-Development	-525	-175					
-Depreciation		-96	-164	-117	-84	-60	
-Deprec Write-offs							-149
-Amortization	-45	-60	-60	-60	-60	-15	
Before Depletion	-570	881	768	393	187	89	-149
-50% Limit		440	384	197	93	-45	
-Percent Depl.		-208	-178	-117	-85	63	
-Cost Depletion		32					
-Loss Forward		-570					
Taxable Income	-570	103	590	276	102	44	-149
-Tax @ 40%	0	-41	-236	-110	-41	-18	60
Net Income	-570	62	354	166	61	26	-89
+Deprec/Write-offs		96	164	117	84	60	149
+Depletion Taken		208	178	117	85	45	
+Amortization	45	60	60	60	60	15	
+Loss Forward		570					
-Mineral Acq	-100						
-30% Development	-225	-75					
-Equipment Cost		-670					
ATCF	-850	250	756	460	290	146	60

206

PW Eq: $0 = -850 + 250(P/F_{i,1}) + 756(P/F_{i,2}) + 460(P/F_{i,3})$

$+ 290(P/F_{i,4}) + 206(P/F_{i,5})$

DCFROR = 39.7%

NPV @ 15% = +$510

PVR = 510 / 850 = .60

8-11 *Solution Continued:*

Case 2)   *Corporate Mining, Risk Adjustment Based on Case 1A*
Non-Risk Adjusted ATCF

ATCF	-622 p=0.40	22	756	460	290	206
Year	0	1	2	3	4	5

p=0.60

-Abandonment Cost	-70
-30% Unamortized Develop.	-180
-Cost Depl Write-off	-100
Taxable Income	-350
-Tax @ 40%	140
Net Income	-210
+ Write-offs	280
Failure ATCF	+70

Risk Adjusted ATCF

ATCF	-622	51*	302	184	116	82
Year	0	1	2	3	4	5

* ATCF is 22(.4) + 70(.6) = +51

Expected Discounted Cash Flow Rate of Return:

PW Eq: $0 = -622 + 51(P/F_{i,1}) + 302(P/F_{i,2}) + 184(P/F_{i,3})$

$+ 116(P/F_{i,4}) + 82(P/F_{i,5})$

Expected DCFROR = 6.1% < i^* of 15%, *reject*

ENPV @ 15% = -121 < 0, *reject*

EPVR = -121 / 622 = -0.195 < 0, *reject*

8-11 *Solution Continued:*

Case 3) Individual Mineral Producer, Expense Cash Flows

Year	0	1	2	3	4	5	Salv
Gross Revenue		1,612	1,378	910	655	488	
-Royalties		-226	-193	-127	-92	-68	
Net Revenue		1,386	1,185	783	563	420	
-Oper Costs		-175	-193	-212	-233	-256	
-Development	-750	-250					
-Depreciation		-96	-164	-117	-84	-60	
-Deprec Write-off							-149
Before Depln	-750	866	828	453	247	104	-149
-50% Limit		433	414	227	123	-52	
-Percent Depln		-208	-178	-117	-85	63	
-Cost Depletion		32					
Taxable Income	-750	658	650	336	162	52	-149
-Tax @ 40%	300	-263	-260	-134	-65	-21	60
Net Income	-450	395	390	202	97	31	-89
+Depreciation		96	164	117	84	60	
+Write-off							149
+Depletion Taken		208	178	117	85	52	
-Mineral Acq.	-100						
-Mine Equipment		-670					
ATCF	-550	28	732	436	266	143	60
						203	

PW Eq: $0 = -550 + 28(P/F_{i,1}) + 732(P/F_{i,2}) + 436(P/F_{i,3}) + 266(P/F_{i,4})$

$+ 203(P/F_{i,5})$

DCFROR = 50.3% > 15%, accept

NPV @ 15% = 567.5 > 0, accept

PVR = 567.5 / 550 = 1.03 > 0, accept

8-11 *Solution Continued:*

Case 3) *Individual Mineral Producer, Stand Alone Cash Flows*

Year	0	1	2	3	4	5	Salv
Gross Revenue		1,612	1,378	910	655	488	
-Royalties		-226	-193	-127	-92	-68	
Net Revenue		1,386	1,185	783	563	420	
-Oper Costs		-175	-193	-212	-233	-256	
-Development	-750	-250					
-Depreciation		-96	-164	-117	-84	-60	
-Deprec Write-off							-149
Before Depletion	-750	866	828	453	247	104	
-50% Limit		433	414	227	123	-52	
-Percent Depl.		-208	-178	-117	-85	63	
-Cost Depletion		32					
-Loss Forward		-750	-92				
Taxable Income	-750	-92	558	336	162	52	-149
-Tax @ 40%	0	0	-223	-134	-65	-21	60
Net Income	-750	-92	335	202	97	31	-89
+Depreciation		96	164	117	84	60	149
+Depletion Taken		208	178	117	85	52	
+Loss Forward		750	92				
-Acquisition Cost	-100						
-Mine Equipment		-670					
ATCF	-850	291	769	436	266	143	60

$$203$$

PW Eq: $0 = -850 + 291(P/F_{i,1}) + 769(P/F_{i,2}) + 436(P/F_{i,3}) + 266(P/F_{i,4})$
$$+ 203(P/F_{i,5})$$

DCFROR = 41.2% > 15%, *accept*

NPV @ 15% = +524.2 > 0, *accept*

PVR = 524.2 / 850 = 0.62 > 0, *accept*

8-11 *Solution Continued:*

*Case 3)   Individual Mineral Producer,
          Risk Adjustment Based on "Expense" ATCF*

Non-Risk Adjusted ATCF

ATCF	−550 p=0.40	28	732	436	266	203
Year	0	1	2	3	4	5

p=0.60

−Abandonment Cost	−70
−Cost Depl Write-off	−100
Taxable Income	−170
−Tax @ 40%	68
Net Income	−102
+ Write-offs	100
Failure ATCF	−2

Risk Adjusted ATCF:

Expected Value ATCF	−550	10*	293	174	106	80
Year	0	1	2	3	4	5

* ATCF is 28(.4) − 2(.6) = +10

Expected DCFROR:

PW Eq: $0 = -550 + 10(P/F_{i,1}) + 293(P/F_{i,2}) + 174(P/F_{i,3}) + 106(P/F_{i,4}) + 80(P/F_{i,5})$

Expected DCFROR = 6.67% < i* of 15%, *reject*

ENPV @ 15% = −105 < 0, *reject*

PVR = −105 / 550 = −0.19 < 0, *reject*

8-11 *Solution Continued:*

Case 4) Corporate Mineral Producer, Break-even Selling Price Analysis

Year	Time 0	1	2	3	4	5	Salv
Total Production		62	53	35	24	17	
Net Production (86%)		53	46	30	21	15	
Selling Price ($/Ton)		X	X	X	X	X	
Net Revenue		53X	46X	30X	21X	15X	
-Operating Costs		-175	-193	-212	-233	-256	
-Development	-525	-175					
-Depreciation		-96	-164	-117	-84	-60	
-Deprec Write-off							-149
-Amortization	-45	-60	-60	-60	-60	-15	
Before Depletion	-570	53X-506	46X-417	30X-389	21X-377	15X-331	-149
-50% Limit		27X-253	23X-208	15X-195	0*	0	
-Percent Depl. (15%)		-8X	-7X	-5X			
-Cost Depletion		32					
Taxable Income	-570	45X-506	39X-417	25X-389	21X-377	15X-331	-149
-Tax @ 40%		228-18X	+202-16X	+167-10X	+156 -8X	+151 -6X	+132	60
Net Income	-342	27X-304	23X-250	15X-233	13X-226	9X-199	-89
+Depreciation		96	164	117	84	60	149
+Depletion Taken		8X	7X	5X			
+Amortization	45	60	60	60	60	15	
-Capital Costs	-325	-745					
ATCF	-622	35X-893	30X-26	20X-56	13X-82	9X-124	60
							9X-64

* By iterative calculations, percentage depletion is the largest
depletion deduction in years 1, 2 & 3 and the 50% limit is zero or near
zero in years 4 and 5. Since the cost depletion basis is recovered by
the year 1 percentage depletion, no depletion exists in years 4 and 5.

$$0 = -622 + (35X-893)(P/F_{15,1}) + (30X-26)(P/F_{15,2}) + (20X-56)(P/F_{15,3})$$

$$\overset{0.8696}{\qquad} \overset{0.7561}{\qquad} \overset{0.6575}{\qquad}$$

$$+ (13X-82)(P/F_{15,4}) + (9X-64)(P/F_{15,5})$$

$$\overset{0.5718}{\qquad} \overset{0.4972}{\qquad}$$

$$0 = 78.18X - 1,533.71, \text{ therefore, } X = \$19.62$$

Break-even Selling Price Per Unit = $19.62 per ton

8-11 *Solution Continued:*

Case 5) *Corporate Mineral Producer, Acquisition Break-even Cost Analysis*

Year	0	1	2	3	4	5	Salv
Revenue		1,612	1,378	910	655	488	
-Royalties		-226	-193	-127	-92	-68	
Net Revenue		1,386	1,185	783	563	420	
-Oper Costs		-175	-193	-212	-233	-256	
-Development	-525	-175					
-Depreciation		-96	-164	-117	-84	-60	
-Deprec Write-off							-149
-Amortization	-45	-60	-60	-60	-60	-15	
Before Depletion	-570	881	768	393	187	89	-149
-50% Limit		440	384	197	93	-45	
-Percent Depl. (15%)		-208	-178	-117	-85	63	
-Cost Depletion		32					
Taxable Income	-570	673	590	276	102	44	-149
-Tax @ 40%	228	-269	-236	-110	-41	-18	60
Net Income	-342	404	354	166	61	26	-89
+Deprec/Write-off		96	164	117	84	60	149
+Depletion		208	178	117	85	45	
+Amortization	45	60	60	60	60	15	
-Capital Costs	-325	-745					
ATCF	-622	22	756	460	290	146	60

206

Net Present Value = $539

Since percentage depletion is allowed for all mineral producers, if we assume percentage depletion deductions will continue to be larger than the new cost depletion deductions, the before-tax value we could afford to pay for the property is the same as the after-tax net present value of $539,000. Checking this assumption, additional mineral rights cost of $539,000 added to the $100,000 in the analysis statement gives $639,000 total acquisition cost. The first year cost depletion would be $639,000(62/191) = $207,420 which is less than year 1 percentage depletion of $208,000 so percent depletion would still be taken. The additional mineral rights acquisition cost would not affect the depletion deduction so $539,000 is the incremental break-even acquisition cost.

CHAPTER 9 PROBLEM SOLUTIONS

9-1 Solution: *Production and Cash Flow Values in Dollars*

	525,000(.259)	470,000(.259)	460,000(.259)
BTCF OLD:	-135,980	-121,730	-119,140

0	1	2	3

	-8,000		
	525,000(.143)	470,000(.143)	460,000(.143)
	525,000(.040)	470,000(.040)	460,000(.040)
BTCF -39,000	-96,080	-86,010	-84,180
New:			

0	1	2	3

	-8,000		
	525,000(.076)	470,000(.076)	460,000(.076)
NEW C=39,000	Savings=39,900	=35,720	=34,960
-OLD:			

0	1	2	3

Year	0	1	2	3
Savings		39,900	35,720	34,960
-Development		-8,000	–	–
-Depreciation		-3,900	-7,800	-7,800
-Deprec Write-off		–	–	-19,500
Taxable Income		28,000	27,920	7,660
-Tax @ 40%		-11,200	-11,168	-3,064
Net Income		16,800	16,752	4,596
+Depreciation		3,900	7,800	27,300
-Capital Costs	-39,000	–	–	–
ATCF	-39,000	20,700	24,552	31,896

A) PW Eq: $0 = -39,000+20,700(P/F_{i,1})+24,552(P/F_{i,2})+31,896(P/F_{i,3})$

   i = DCFROR = 39.9% > i* = 12%, NPV @ 12% = $21,758 > 0

B) *Non-Discounted Pay-back* = 1 + (39,000-20,700)/24,552 = 1.75

C) *From Equation 5-1:* 1 + i = (1 + f)(1 + i')

   Constant Dollar DCFROR = i' = {(1.399)/(1.1)} - 1 = .2716 or 27.2%

Alternatively, Constant Dollar Cash Flows:

-39,000	20,700(P/F_{10,1}) =18,818	24,552(P/F_{10,2}) =20,290	31,896(P/F_{10,3}) =23,963

0	1	2	3

PW Eq: $0 = -39,000 + 18,818(P/F_{i',1}) + 20,290(P/F_{i',2}) + 23,963(P/F_{i',3})$
i' = Constant Dollar DCFROR = 27.2%, *the same as from Eq 5-1.*

9-2 Solution: *All Values in Thousands of Dollars*

Abandon Now at Yr 0:

$$\overbrace{\text{Acq Cost}=400 \qquad\qquad \text{IDC}=600}^{\text{Sunk Costs}}$$

Write-off All Capital Costs Against Other Income at Yr0

| -2 | 0 | 0 *Now* | 1 |

Develop in Month 7 of Year 0 (now):
(Assume $600 IDC was in Month 5 of Yr 0)

Yr 1 Abandon
Salvage=100

$$\overbrace{\text{Acq Cost}=400 \qquad\qquad \text{IDC}=600}^{\text{Sunk Costs}}$$

$C_{IDC}=100$ P=0.4
$C_{tang}=200$

Rev=420
P=0.6   OC= 35

| -2 | 0 | 0 *Now* | 1 |

The $400 year -2 acquisition cost and the $600 year 0 IDC are sunk along with the tax deduction for 70% of the $600 year 0 IDC. These cost are not relevant to our analysis; the remaining tax effects are as illustrated below.

Year	Abandon 0 *Now*	Develop & Succeed 0 *Now*	1	Yr 1 Sale	Fail and Abandon Yr 1
Gross Revenue			420	350	100
-Royalties			-76		
Net Revenue			344	350	100
-Oper Costs			-60		
-Intangible		-70			
-Depreciation			-29	-171	-200
-Amortization	-180 *write-off*	-27	-36	-147	-183
-Cost Depletion	-400 *write-off*		-100	-300	-400
Taxable Income	-580	-97	119	-268	-683
-Tax @ 40%	232	39	-48	107	273
Net Income	-348	-58	71	-161	-410
+Depreciation			29	171	200
+Cost Depletion	400		100	300	400
+Amortization	180	27	36	147	183
-Capital Costs		-230			
ATCF	232	-261	236	457	373

P(Success=0.6)   P(Fail=0.4)

$NPV_{Abandon} = +\$232$

$ENPV_{Develop} = -261+[236(P/F_{20},1) + 457(P/F_{20},1)](.6) + 373(P/F_{20},1)(.4)$

$= +\$210 < NPV_{Abandon},$ *therefore, abandon now.*

9-3 Solution: *All Values in Thousands of Dollars*

Land Acquisition Break-even Sale Price: Let X = Sale Value

SELL Cash Flow Calculation:		*ABANDON Cash Flow Calculation:*	
Sale Value	X	Equipment Salvage Value	30
-Book Value Write-off	-5	-Abandon Cost	-20
Taxable Income	X-5	-Book Value Write-off	-5
-Tax @ 40%	-.4X+2	Taxable Income	5
Net Income	.6X-3	-Tax @ 40%	-2
+Book Value Write-off	5	Net Income	3
ATCF	.6X+2	+Book Value Write-off	5
		ATCF	8

Set "Sale Cash Flow" equal to "Abandon Cash Flow" and solve for the unknown break-even sale value "X":

.6X + 2 = 8, therefore, X = $10

9-4 Solution:

C = $60,000   Esc $ Sale Value = $X

0   2

Sale Value in Escalated Dollars	X
-Book Value Write-off	-60,000
Taxable Income	X-60,000
-Tax @ 30%	-.3X+18,000
Net Income	.7X-42,000
+Book Value Write-off	60,000
ATCF in Escalated Dollars	.7X+18,000

Constant Dollar Present Worth Equation:

$60,000 = (.7X+18,000)(P/F_{f=10\%,2})(P/F_{i*'=20\%,2})$

60,000 = .4017X + 10,330

Break-even Selling Price: X = $123,649

Alternate Solution:

$1 + i = (1 + f)(1 + i'); so\ i^* = (1 + .10)(1 + .20) - 1 = .32\ or\ 32\%$

$i^* = 32\%$ is equivalent to $i^{*'} = 20\%$ for 10%/yr inflation, f.

Escalated Dollar Present Worth Equation:

$60,000 = (.7X+18,000)(P/F_{32,2})$ therefore, X = $123,649

9-5 Solution: *Values in Thousands of Dollars*

Land Acquisition Break-even Sales Price Analysis:

DEVELOP:

C=500 *(Sunk)* ATCF=-1,500 P=0.6 1,000 1,800 1,200 800 400

-2 .... 0 .... 1 .. 2 .. 3 .. 4 .. 5

P=0.4

CF=0

SELL:

C=500 *(Sunk)* ATCF=800 *(Opportunity Cost if Developed)*

-2 .... 0 .... 1 .. 2 .. 3 .. 4 .. 5

Yr 0 Sell Cash Flow:

Sale Revenue	1,000
-Book Value Write-off	500
Taxable Income	500
-Tax @ 40%	-200
Net Income	300
+Book Value Write-off	500
ATCF	800

Sell NPV:

Sell CF = Sell NPV = +$800

Develop Expected NPV for $i^* = 20\%$:

$$ENPV = -1,500 + [1,000(P/F_{20,1}) + 1,800(P/F_{20,2}) + 1,200(P/F_{20,3})$$
$$+ 800(P/F_{20,4}) + 400(P/F_{20,5})](0.6) = +\$495$$

Therefore, select the maximum NPV and Sell.

Incremental ENPV generates the same economic conclusion:
$ENPV_{Develop-Sell} = 495 - 800 = -\$305$, *reject the develop alternative*

Break-even Probability of Occurrence :

Let "X" equal the break-even probability of success, which is the value of "X" that makes the $ENPV_{DEV} = NPV_{Sell} = +\$800$

$$\overset{0.8333}{} \quad \overset{0.6944}{} \quad \overset{0.5787}{}$$
$$800 = -1,500 + [1,000(P/F_{20,1}) + 1,800(P/F_{20,2}) + 1,200(P/F_{20,3})$$

$$\overset{0.4823}{} \quad \overset{0.4019}{}$$
$$+ 800(P/F_{20,4}) + 400(P/F_{20,5})](X)$$

$$800 = -1,500 + X(3,324.3), \text{ therefore, } X = 0.69 \text{ or } 69\%$$

9-6 Solution: *All Values in Dollars*

Depreciable Costs	100,000	50,000			
Working Capital	25,000	-			
Sale Value	-	-	-	-	250,000
Revenue	-	200,000	280,000	280,000	
Operating Costs	-	140,000	190,000	190,000	

Cash Flow Calculations

Year	0	1	2	3	3 Salv.
Revenue		200,000	280,000	280,000	250,000
-Operating Costs		-140,000	-190,000	-190,000	
-Depreciation		-21,435	-36,735	-26,235	
-Deprec Write-off					-65,595
-WC Write-off					-25,000
Taxable Income		38,565	53,265	63,765	159,405
-Tax @ 40%		-15,426	-21,306	-25,506	-63,762
Net Income		23,139	31,959	38,259	95,643
+Depreciation		21,435	36,735	26,235	65,595
+WC Write-off					25,000
-Working Capital	-25,000				
-Equipment Cost	-100,000	-50,000			
ATCF	-125,000	-5,426	68,694	64,494	186,238

250,732

PW Eq: $0 = -125,000 - 5,426(P/F_{i,1}) + 68,694(P/F_{i,2}) + 250,732(P/F_{i,3})$

DCFROR = 39%, NPV @ $i^* = 15\% = +\$87,085$

NPV represents additional after-tax cost (negative cash flow) that may be incurred at time zero in addition to $125,000 for the project to yield a DCFROR of 15%. Using Equation 9-1, developed in the text Example 9-8; if the equivalent before-tax cost is deductible as a development cost at time zero, convert after-tax NPV as follows:

Eq 9-1: X = After-Tax NPV + PW Tax Savings From Deductions Related to X

X = 87,085 + 0.4X

0.6X = 87,084   Therefore, 87,084 / (0.6) = $145,140

This is the before-tax research or development cost that could be incurred in year 0 and still have the project earn a 15% discounted cash flow rate of return.

9-7 Solution: *All Values in Dollars*

Land Acquisition:

			Rev=250,000
C_{Land}=100,000	OC=2,500	OC=2,500	OC=2,500
0	1	2	3

Cash Flow Calculations:

Year	0	1-3	Yr 3 Sale
Revenue			250,000
-Property Taxes		-2,500	
-Write-off Bk Value			-100,000
Taxable Income		-2,500	150,000
-Tax @ 30%		750	-45,000
Net Income		-1,750	105,000
+Write-off Bk Value			100,000
-Capital Cost	-100,000		
ATCF	-100,000	-1,750	205,000

PW Eq: $0 = -100,000 - 1,750(P/A_{i,3}) + 205,000(P/F_{i,3})$

Escalated Dollar DCFROR, i, = 25.6%

*Use Equation 5-1 to convert the escalated dollar DCFROR to the
equivalent constant dollar DCFROR as follows:*

$$1+i = (1+f)(1+i')$$

Constant Dollar DCFROR for 8% inflation:

$i' = (1.256 / 1.08) - 1 = 0.163$ or 16.3%.

9-8 Solution: *All Values in Thousands of Dollars*

Common Stock versus Bonds:

Investment Alternative #1, Purchase Common Stock

C=100

```
├─────────────────────────────────────────────┤    F = 100(F/P_{10,10}) = 259.4
0                                            10
```

Taxable Gain = 259.4 - 100 = $159.4
Tax on Gain = 159.4(0.30) = -$47.8

Yr 10 After-Tax Cash Flow (Future Value) = 259.4 - 47.8 = $211.6

Investment Alternative #2, Purchase Bond

C=100   I=10   I=10 . . . .   I=10

```
├────────────────────────────────────────────┤    L=100
0          1         2 . . . . . . . . . . .  10
```

Interest Income of $10,000 per year is before-tax and needs to be converted to an after-tax value that represents the actual dollars available to be reinvested at the after-tax money market interest rate of 7.0% (10% - 3%) as follows:

Net Cash Flow From Bond Dividends Each Year: 10 - 10(0.3) = $7.0

Year 10 after-tax cash flow (future value):

$$\qquad\qquad 13.816$$
Year 10 FW = 7.0(F/A_{7,10}) + 100 maturity value = $196.7

Purchase common stock to maximize future value of $211.6 versus $196.7

The required before-tax growth rate for common stock that would make the alternatives economically equivalent is shown below:

Let X = before-tax common stock sale value at year 10 to give after-tax cash flow of $196.7 which equals the bank investment projected future value.

196.7 = Required after-tax year 10 value
196.7 = X - (X-100)(0.3)
196.7 = X - 0.3X + 30
196.7 = 0.7X + 30

Therefore, 0.7X = 196.7 - 30, so X = $238.1

PW Eq: 100 = 238.1(P/F_{i,10}), Growth Rate, i = 9.06%

9-9 Solution: *Values in Thousands of Dollars*

Break-even Sales Analysis

Let X = the break-even sales revenue required to give a 25% DCFROR.

Year	0	1	2	3	4	5
Revenue		X	X+10	X+20	X+30	X+40
-Operating Costs		-50.0	-60.0	-70.0	-80.0	-90.0
-Depreciation	-71.5	-122.5	-87.5	-62.5	-45.0	-45.0
-Depr Write-off						-67.0
Taxable Income	-71.5	X-172.5	X-137.5	X-112.5	X-95.0	X-162.0
-Tax @ 40%	28.6	-.4X+69.0	-.4X+55.0	-.4X+45.0	-.4X+38.0	-.4X+64.8
Net Income	-42.9	.6X-103.5	.6X-82.5	.6X-67.5	.6X-57.0	.6X-97.2
+Depreciation	71.5	122.5	87.5	62.5	45.0	45.0
-Depr Write-off						67.0
-Capital Cost	-500.0					
Cash Flow	-471.4	.6X+19.0	.6X+5.0	.6X-5.0	.6X-12.0	.6X+14.8

$$\text{PW Eq: } 0 = -471.4 + (.6X + 19)\underset{0.8000}{(P/F_{25,1})} + (.6X + 5)\underset{0.6400}{(P/F_{25,2})}$$

$$+ (.6X - 5.0)\underset{0.512}{(P/F_{25,3})} + (.6X - 12.0)\underset{0.4096}{(P/F_{25,4})}$$

$$+ (.6X + 14.8)\underset{0.3277}{(P/F_{25,5})}$$

$$0 = 1.6136X - 455.63, \text{ therefore, } X = \$282.37$$

Year 1 Break-even Revenue: $282.37.

This amount will increase by $10 in each succeeding year.

9-10 Solution: *All Values in Thousands of Dollars*

Cash Flows

Year	0	1	2	3	4	5	6
Revenue			900	900	900	900	1,300*
-Operating Costs			-200	-200	-200	-200	-200
-Research/Develop	-100	-300					
-Depreciation		-50	-100	-100	-100	-100	-50
-Work Cap Book Value							-200
Taxable Income	-100	-350	600	600	600	600	850
-Tax @ 40%	40	140	-240	-240	-240	-240	-340
Net Income	-60	-210	360	360	360	360	510
+Depreciation		50	100	100	100	100	50
+Work Cap Book Value							200
-Equipment (Deprec)		-500					
-Working Capital		-200					
Cash Flow	-60	-860	460	460	460	460	760

* *Revenue includes working capital return and salvage.*

Case A) Net Present Value Analysis

NPV = -60 - 860(P/F$_{15,1}$) + 460(P/A$_{15,4}$)(P/F$_{15,1}$) + 760(P/F$_{15,6}$) = +$663

Case B) Additional Before-Tax Research and Development Cost at Year 0

An additional development cost of $X at year 0 that is expensed against other taxable income saves 0.4X in income tax, increasing the negative year 0 cash flow by -0.6X. Setting 0.6X equal to NPV of +663 and solving for X gives the year 0 break-even research or development cost that will exactly make NPV = 0 for i* = 15%.

NPV / (1-tax rate) = 663 / (1-0.4) = $1,105

Case C) Consider $900,000 Sale Offer at Year 1.

Sale CF = 900-(900-0)(0.4 tax rate)=540 after taxes at year 1 = NPV$_{Sell}$
Yr 1 NPV$_{Dev}$ = -860 + 460(P/A$_{15,4}$) + 760(P/F$_{15,5}$) = 831
NPV$_{Dev}$ > NPV$_{Sell}$ so select Develop.

Case D) What sale value at year 1 makes selling a break-even with developing?

Let X = break-even before-tax sale price at year 1.
X - (X-0)(0.4 tax rate) = 0.6X = CF$_{Sell}$ = NPV$_{Sell}$ = NPV$_{Dev}$ = 831
X = $1,385 = Break-even Project Sale Price

9-10 Solution Continued:

Case E) Additional Cost to Allow a 15% Minimum ROR

Let X = the unknown additional year zero depreciable cost

Year	0	1	2	3	4	5	6	6Salv
Total Rev			900	900	900	900	900	400
-Oper Costs			-200	-200	-200	-200	-200	
-Res/Dev	-100	-300						
-Yr 1 Deprec		-50	-100	-100	-100	-100	-50	
-Acq Deprec		-.1X	-.2X	-.2X	-.2X	-.2X	-.1X	
-Work Cap								-200

| Taxable Inc | -100 | -350-.10X | 600-.20X | 600-.20X | 600-.20X | 600-.20X | 650-.10X | 200 |
| -Tax Due@40% | 40 | 140+.04X | -240+.08X | -240+.08X | -240+.08X | -240+.08X | -260+.04X | -80 |

Net Income	-60	-210-.06X	360-.12X	360-.12X	360-.12X	360-.12X	390-.06X	120
+Deprec.		50+.10X	100+.20X	100+.20X	100+.20X	100+.20X	50+.10X	
+Work Cap Ret								200
-Equip Cost	-X	-500						
-Work Cap	-	-200						

| Cash Flow | -X-60 | -860+.04X | 460+.08X | 460+.08X | 460+.08X | 460+.08X | 440+.04X | 320 |

PW Equation:

$$
\begin{array}{c}
\quad\quad\quad\quad\quad 0.8696 \quad\quad\quad\quad\quad\quad\quad\quad 2.855 \quad 0.8696 \\
0 = -X - 60 + (-860+.04X)(P/F15,1) + (460+.08X)(P/A15,4)(P/F15,1)
\end{array}
$$

$$
\begin{array}{c}
\quad\quad\quad 0.4323 \\
+ (760+.04X)(P/F15,6)
\end{array}
$$

$$0 = -X - 60 - 747.85 + .0348X + 1,117.22 + 0.1986X + 328.55 + 0.0173X$$

Calculating the value of X to make NPV = 0.

$$0 = -X + 663 + 0.2507X$$

Re-arranging the above equation gives text Equation 9-1:

X = 663 + .2507X   or, X = NPV + Present Worth of Tax Savings on X (Eq 9-1)

Solving for X gives the following:

0.7493X = 663, therefore, X = $885

Verification of Problem 9-10, Case B

*Additional before-tax research/development cost = NPV/(1-tax rate)
= $663/(1-0.4) = $1,105.   This research/development cost, in addition to
the $100 research cost already built into the analysis at year 0, makes
NPV equal to 0 as the following cash flow and NPV calculations show.*

Problem 9-10 *Case B, Verification of Results*

Year	0	1	2	3	4	5	6
Revenue			900	900	900	900	1,300*
-Operating Costs			-200	-200	-200	-200	-200
-Development	-1,205	-300					
-Depreciation		-50	-100	-100	-100	-100	-50
-Work Cap Book Val							-200
Taxable Income	-1,205	-350	600	600	600	600	850
-Tax @ 40%	482	140	-240	-240	-240	-240	-340
Net Income	-723	-210	360	360	360	360	510
+Depreciation		50	100	100	100	100	50
+Work Cap Book Val							200
-Equipment Costs		-500					
-Working Capital		-200					
Cash Flow	-723	-860	460	460	460	460	760

* Revenue includes working capital return and salvage.

$$NPV = -723 - 860(P/F_{15,1}) + 460(P/A_{15,4})(P/F_{15,1}) + 760(P/F_{15,6}) = 0$$

9-11 Solution:

Problem 9-10 Net Income as Previous Calculated in 9-10, Part A.

Year	0	1	2	3	4	5	6
Revenue			900	900	900	900	1,300*
-Operating Costs			-200	-200	-200	-200	-200
-Research/Develop	-100	-300					
-Depreciation		-50	-100	-100	-100	-100	-50
-Work Cap Book Value							-200
Taxable Income	-100	-350	600	600	600	600	850
-Tax @ 40%	40	140	-240	-240	-240	-240	-340
Net Income	-60	-210	360	360	360	360	510

The beginning of year book value is based on the capital expenditures only, adjusted for the previous years depreciation. In this example, R&D was expensed and therefore, reflected on the net income side of the Value Added calculation. Further, the book value at the beginning of year 1 is zero. Since depreciation was also taken at the end of year 1 the book value at the beginning of year 2 (end of year 1) is 650.

Year	0	1	2	3	4	5	6
Beg. Asset Book Value	0	0	650.0	550.0	450.0	350.0	250.0
Opportunity Cost @ 15%	0	0	-97.5	-82.5	-67.5	-52.5	-37.5

Value Added is Net Income – Opportunity Cost of Keeping Capital:

No deferred tax adjustment is necessary since the straight line depreciation is assumed to represent both the financial and tax depreciation.

Year	0	1	2	3	4	5	6
Net Income	-60	-210	360.0	360.0	360.0	360.0	510.0
Opportunity Cost	–	–	-97.5	-82.5	-67.5	-52.5	-37.5
Value Added (VA)	-60	-210	262.5	277.5	292.5	307.5	472.5

PV of VA @ 15% = 663

Project After-Tax NPV @ 15% = 663, identical results

9-12 Solution: *All Values in Thousands of Dollars*

Accounting for Risk in Problem 9-10

Success Cash Flows: -60   P=0.4   -860   P=0.7   460   460   460   460   760

$$\begin{array}{ccccccc} 0 & & 1 & & 2 & 3 & 4 & 5 & 6 \\ P=0.6 & & P=0.3 & & & & & & \end{array}$$

Failure Cash Flows: 0   200+500(.4) = 400

Case A)

$$\text{ENPV @ 15\%} = -60 + [-860 \overset{0.8696}{(P/F_{15,1})} + \{460 \overset{2.855}{(P/A_{15,4})} \overset{0.8696}{(P/F_{15,1})}$$

$$+ 760 \overset{0.4323}{(P/F_{15,6})}\}(0.7)](0.4) + 400 \overset{0.7561}{(P/F_{15,2})}(.3)(.4) = +\$88.92$$

Case B)   *Additional Before-Tax Research and Development Cost That Could be Incurred on a Risk-Adjusted Analysis Basis:*

NPV / (1-tax rate) = 88.92 / (1 - .4) = $148.19

9-13 Solution: *All Values in Thousands of Dollars*

Break-even Before-Tax Revenue Analysis for Problem 9-10A

Year	0	1	2	3	4	5	6
Revenue			X	X	X	X	X+400*
-Operating Costs			-200	-200	-200	-200	-200
-Development	-100	-300					
-Depreciation		-50	-100	-100	-100	-100	-50
-Work Cap Bk Val							-200
Taxable Income	-100	-350	X-300	X-300	X-300	X-300	X-50
-Tax @ 40%	40	140	-.4X+120	-.4X+120	-.4X+120	-.4X+120	-.4X+20
Net Income	-60	-210	.6X-180	.6X-180	.6X-180	.6X-180	.6X-30
+Depreciation		50	100	100	100	100	50
+Work Cap Bk Val							200
-Equipment Cost		-500					
-Working Capital		-200					
Cash Flow	-60	-860	.6X-80	.6X-80	.6X-80	.6X-80	.6X+220

* Revenue includes working capital return and salvage.

9-13 *Solution Continued:*

Break-even Before-Tax Revenues an Selling Price ($/Unit Produced)

$$\text{PW Eq: } 0 = -60 - 860(P/F_{15,1})^{0.8696} + (.6X-80)(P/A_{15,4})^{2.855}(P/F_{15,1})^{0.8696}$$

$$+ (.6X+220)(P/F_{15,6})^{0.4323}$$

$$0 = 1.749X - 911.37, \quad therefore, \; X = \$521.07$$

$$\textbf{Break-even Selling Price: } = \frac{521{,}070 \text{ break - even revenue per year}}{10{,}000 \text{ units produced per year}}$$

$$= \$52.11/\text{unit break-even selling price}$$

9-14 Solution: *All Values in Dollars*

```
                                                    50,000
C_Equip=200,000                313,600  344,960   372,560
C_R&D  =100,000    P=0.6       -44,000  -48,400   -53,240
  |_____
  0                               1        2         3
           P=0.4
                          R=100,000 + Write-offs
```

Escalated Dollar Cash Flow Calculations

Year	0	60% Probability of Success			3 Salv	Fail40%
		1	2	3		1
Revenue		313,600	344,960	372,560	50,000	100,000
-Oper Costs		-44,000	-48,400	-53,240		
-Develop	-100,000					
-Deprec	-28,571	-48,980	-34,985	-24,990		
-Write-off					-62,474	-171,429
-Loss Forward		-128,571				-128,571
Taxable	-128,571	92,049	261,575	294,330	-12,474	-200,000
-Tax @ 40%	0	-36,819	-104,630	-117,732	4,990	80,000
Net Income	-128,571	55,228	156,945	176,598	-7,484	-120,000
+Deprec	28,571	48,980	34,985	24,990	62,474	171,429
+Loss Forward		128,571				128,571
-Equip Cost	-200,000					
ATCF	-300,000	232,779	191,930	201,588	54,990	180,000

$$256{,}578$$

9-14 *Solution Continued*:

Constant Dollar ENPV @ 10%:

$$= -300,000 + [232,779 \overset{0.9434}{(P/F_{6,1})} \overset{0.9091}{(P/F_{10,1})} + 191,930 \overset{0.9434}{(P/F_{6,1})} \overset{0.9259}{(P/F_{8,1})} \overset{0.8264}{(P/F_{10,2})}$$

$$+ 256,578 \overset{0.9434}{(P/F_{6,1})} \overset{0.9259}{(P/F_{8,1})} \overset{0.9091}{(P/F_{10,1})} \overset{0.7513}{(P/F_{10,3})}](.6)$$

$$+ 180,000 \overset{0.9434}{(P/F_{6,1})} \overset{0.9091}{(P/F_{10,1})}(.4) = +\$56,508$$

Using Equation 5-1, it is necessary to calculate the equivalent escalated dollar minimum rate of return accounting for the various inflation rates each year as follows:

$$i^* = (1+i^{*\prime})(1+f) - 1$$

> Yr 1: Escalated \$ Minimum DCFROR = (1.1)(1.06) - 1 = .1660 or 16.6%
> Yr 2: Escalated \$ Minimum DCFROR = (1.1)(1.08) - 1 = .1880 or 18.8%
> Yr 3: Escalated \$ Minimum DCFROR = (1.1)(1.10) - 1 = .2110 or 21.1%

Escalated Dollar ENPV:

$$\text{ENPV} = -300,000 + [232,779 \overset{0.8576}{(P/F_{16.6,1})} + 191,930 \overset{0.8576}{(P/F_{16.6,1})} \overset{0.8418}{(P/F_{18.8,1})}$$

$$+ 256,578 \overset{0.8576}{(P/F_{16.6,1})} \overset{0.8418}{(P/F_{18.8,1})} \overset{0.8258}{(P/F_{21.1,1})}](.6) + 180,000 \overset{0.8576}{(P/F_{16.6,1})}(.4)$$

$$= +\$56,440$$

Factor round-off error causes a slight difference between this result and the constant dollar NPV.

9-15 Solution: *All Values in Thousands of Dollars*

Natural Gas Pipeline Break-even Analysis With Mid-Period Compounding
Let X = Break-even Transportation Price

Year	0	0.5	1.5	2.5	3.5	4.5	5.5
Revenue		1900X	1440X	1030X	730X	440X	150X
-Oper Costs		-5	-5	-5	-5	-5	-5
-Depreciation		-31	-54	-38	-27	-20	-20
-Depr Write-off							-30
Taxable Income		1900X-36	1440X-59	1030X-43	730X-32	440X-25	150X-55
-Tax @ 40%		-760X+14	-576X+23	-412X+17	-292X+12	-176X+10	-60X+22
Net Income		1140X-22	864X-36	618X-26	438X-20	264X-15	90X-33
+Deprec/Write-off		31	54	38	27	20	50
-Cap Costs	-220						
Cash Flow	-220	1140X+9	864X+18	618X+12	438X+7	264X+5	90X+17

PW Eq: $0 = -220 + (1{,}140X + 9)\underset{0.9449}{(P/F_{12,0.5})} + (864X + 18)\underset{0.8437}{(P/F_{12,1.5})}$

$\qquad + (618X + 12)\underset{0.7533}{(P/F_{12,2.5})} + (438X + 7)\underset{0.6726}{(P/F_{12,3.5})}$

$\qquad + (264X + 5)\underset{0.6005}{(P/F_{12,4.5})} + (90X + 17)\underset{0.5362}{(P/F_{12,5.5})}$

$0 = 2{,}773X - 170.4$, *rearranging gives:* $170.4 = 2{,}773X$

Break-even Price Per MCF: X = $0.06145 per Mcf < $0.10 / Mcf offer, so reject the offer and build the gathering line.

The break-even transport charge for a 12% escalated dollar DCFROR on the $220,000 pipeline investment is $0.0614 per Mcf based on mid-year values and compounding which treats year 1 values at period n = 0.5, year 2 values as occurring at period n = 1.5, and so forth.

$P/F_{12,0.5} = (1/1.12)^{0.5} = \$0.9449$

$P/F_{12,1.5} = (1/1.12)^{1.5} = \$0.8437$

and so forth for n = 2.5, 3.5, etc. . .

9-16 Solution: *All Values in Thousands of Dollars*

```
Development         = 10,000   Rev = 30,000  33,000  36,300  39,930  43,923
Deprec Equipment = 15,000      OC  = 12,000  13,200  14,520  15,972  17,569
Working Capital  =  2,000
Salvage (Including Working Capital Return)                                5,000
```
                    0   1   2   3   4   5

The $10,000 mineral rights acquisition cost incurred at year -2 is sunk, but remaining tax effects and sale value are not.

Development Cash Flow Calculations

Year	0	1	2	3	4	5	Salv
Gross Revenue		30,000	33,000	36,300	39,930	43,923	5,000
-Royalties		-2,400	-2,640	-2,904	-3,194	-3,514	
Net Revenue		27,600	30,360	33,396	36,736	40,409	5,000
-Oper Costs		-12,000	-13,200	-14,520	-15,972	-17,569	
-Development	-7,000						
-Depreciation	-2,143	-3,673	-2,624	-1,874	-1,340	-1,338	-2,008
-Amortization	-600	-600	-600	-600	-600		
-WC Write-off							-2,000
Before Depltn	-9,743	11,327	13,936	16,402	18,824	21,502	992
-50% Limit		5,663	6,968	8,201	9,412	10,751	
-Percent Depl		-2,760	-3,036	-3,340	-3,112*	-3,233	
-Cost Depltn		2,000	1,810	1,401	432		
Taxable Income	-9,743	8,567	10,900	13,062	15,712	18,269	992
-Tax @ 40%	3,897	-3,427	-4,360	-5,225	-6,285	-7,308	-397
Net Income	-5,846	5,140	6,540	7,837	9,427	10,961	595
+Depreciation	2,143	3,673	2,624	1,874	1,340	1,338	2,008
+Depletion		2,760	3,036	3,340	3,112	3,233	
+Amortization	600	600	600	600	600		
+WC Write-off							2,000
-Working Cap	-2,000						
-30% Develop.	-3,000						
-Equipment	-15,000						
Cash Flow	-23,103	12,173	12,800	13,651	14,479	15,532	4,603

                                                                20,135

* Cumulative percentage depletion in years 1, 2 and 3 = $9,136 so $864 more depletion equals $10,000 mineral rights acquisition cost. $864/0.10 = $8,640 net revenue after royalty is needed for 10% depletion, balance is 8% depletion. 8% depletion revenue = ($36,736-$8,640)(0.08) = $28,096(0.08) = $2,248. Cumulative year 4 percentage depletion = $2,248 + $864 = $3,112.

9-16 *Solution Continued:*

Case 1)   *Calculating DCFROR and NPV ($10,000 acquisition cost is sunk)*

PW Eq: $0 = -23,103 + 12,173(P/F_{i,1}) + 12,800(P/F_{i,2}) + 13,651(P/F_{i,3})$

$$+ 14,479(P/F_{i,4}) + 20,135(P/F_{i,5}) \quad i = DCFROR = 50.7\%$$

$NPV = -23,103 + 12,173(P/F_{20,1}) + 12,800(P/F_{20,2}) + 13,651(P/F_{20,3})$

$$+ 14,479(P/F_{20,4}) + 20,135(P/F_{20,5}) = +\$18,904$$

After-tax Cash Flow of Yr 0 Sale Offer:

Before-tax sale value minus the tax due from the sale equals the sale cash flow and net present value. At the point of the sale, (time zero) the only cost incurred was 2 years ago. That cost is sunk and not relevant except for remaining tax effects. If we sell the property the remaining book value is deducted from the sale revenue to determine the taxable gain as follows:

$20,000 - (20,000 - 10,000)(0.4) = \$16,000 < \$18,904$ Develop NPV, *so develop*

Case 2)   *Break-even Selling Price with Developing*

In this analysis you are determining the break-even sale price the makes the sale NPV equal to the develop NPV. This calculation is very similar to the analysis just made, except the selling price becomes an unknown variable. Let "X" equal the break-even selling price.

$X - (X-10,000)(0.4) = \$18,904$

$0.6X + 4,000 = \$18,904$, therefore, $X = \$14,904/0.6 = \$24,840$

Case 3)   *Additional Development Cost that Could be Incurred*

Neglecting sale value opportunity cost considerations, this question asks you to determine the additional development cost (above the current $10,000) that can be incurred and still have the project earn a 20% DCFROR on invested dollars. As in the previous solutions to this problem, if we let "X" be the unknown break-even development cost, then "X" less the tax savings from deductions on "X" will be equal to the after-tax NPV of development ($18,904). 70% of "X" can be expensed at time zero by a corporate mineral producer with the remaining 30% amortized over 5 years (year 0 to 4) as follows:

$X - (0.7)X(0.4 \text{ tax rate}) - (0.06)X(0.4) - (0.06)X(0.4)(P/A_{20,4}) = \$18,904$

$X - 0.28X - 0.024X - 0.024X(2.589) = \$18,904$

$0.634X = 18,904$ therefore, $X = \$29,823$

9-17 Solution:

Alternative A)   100% Working Interest, 87.5% Net Revenue Interest

Production, Bbls/yr		17,500	9,000	6,500	3,000
Selling Price, $/Bbl		$20.00	$20.00	$21.00	$22.05
Royalty, $/Bbl		$2.50	$2.50	$2.62	$2.75
Operating Cost, $/Bbl		$4.00	$4.00	$4.00	$4.00
Intangible Drilling	$250,000				
Tangible Completion	$100,000				
Lease Cost	$0				

Cash Flows:

Year	0	1	2	3	4
Gross Revenue		350,000	180,000	136,500	66,150
-Royalties		-43,750	-22,500	-17,063	-8,269
Net Interest		306,250	157,500	119,438	57,881
-Operating Expenses		-70,000	-36,000	-26,000	-12,000
-Intangibles (70%)	-175,000	-	-	-	-
-Depreciation/Writeoff		-14,290	-24,490	-17,490	-43,730
-Amortization	-7,500	-15,000	-15,000	-15,000	-22,500
Taxable Income	-182,500	206,960	82,010	60,948	-20,349
-Tax @ 38%	69,350	-78,645	-31,164	-23,160	7,733
Net Income	-113,150	128,315	50,846	37,787	-12,616
+Depreciation/Write-off		14,290	24,490	17,490	43,730
+Amortization	7,500	15,000	15,000	15,000	22,500
-Tangible Equipment	-100,000				
-30% of IDC	-75,000				
ATCF	-280,650	157,605	90,336	70,277	53,614

$$\text{NPV @ 12\%} = -280,650 + 157,605 \overset{0.8929}{(P/F_{12,1})} + 90,336 \overset{0.7972}{(P/F_{12,2})}$$

$$+ 70,277 \overset{0.7118}{(P/F_{12,3})} + 53,614 \overset{0.6355}{(P/F_{12,4})} = \$16,179$$

$$\text{PVR} = 16,179/280,650 = 0.058$$

$$\text{PW Eq: } 0 = -280,650 + 157,605(P/F_{i,1}) + 90,336(P/F_{i,2})$$

$$+ 70,277(P/F_{i,3}) + 53,614(P/F_{i,4})$$

DCFROR = 15.3% *by financial calculator*

9-17 Solution Continued:

Case B) 5% Carried Interest, Back-in for 25% Working Interest and 21.875% Net Revenue Interest

Pay-out Calculation Using Production:

When the cumulative value of net revenue (defined here as production times the selling price less royalties and cash operating costs) gives revenue equal to the total dollars invested, the project is at pay-out. In this case, we know we've spent $350,000, and the price in years 1 and 2 is constant at $20.00 per barrel. Due to the two royalties, the producer only gets 82.5% of each barrel to pay off the investment. Hence, pay-out in production is calculated as follows:

```
Yr 1 Pay-out Basis $350,000 - [17,500x($20.00(0.825)-$4.00)] = $131,250
Yr 2 Pay-out Basis $131,250 - [ 9,000x($20.00(0.825)-$4.00)] = $ 18,750
Yr 3 Pay-out: $18,750 = (X bbl)($21.00(0.825)-$4.00)   X = 1,407 bbl
```

Therefore, in year 3, 1,407 barrels would be subject to the over-riding royalty interest of 5.0%, after which (the reversion point), 5,093 barrels are applicable to the 25.0% working interest, and a 21.875% net revenue interest (25.0% adjusted for 12.5% royalties).

Crude Price Rose to $21.00/bbl

Cash Flow Calculations:

Year	0	1	2	3	4
Carried Interest Rev. (5%)		17,500	9,000	1,477	0
Net Revenue Interest (21.875%)		0	0	23,396	14,470
Total Net Revenues		17,500	9,000	24,873	14,470
-Operating Expense (25%)		0	0	-5,093	-3,000
Taxable Income		17,500	9,000	19,780	11,470
-Tax @ 38%		-6,650	-3,420	-7,517	-4,359
Net Income		10,850	5,580	12,263	7,111
-Capital Costs					
ATCF		10,850	5,580	12,263	7,111

$$\text{NPV @ 12\%} = 10,850\underset{0.8929}{(P/F_{12,1})} + 5,580\underset{0.7972}{(P/F_{12,2})}$$

$$+ 12,263\underset{0.7118}{(P/F_{12,3})} + 7,111\underset{0.6355}{(P/F_{12,4})} = \$27,386 \text{ select carried interest}$$

From a purely economic viewpoint, selecting the largest NPV leads to the conclusion to farm out the property. However, from a practical viewpoint the NPV results are very close and effectively a break-even. This is verified by an appropriate incremental analysis (see next page).

9-17 *Solution Continued:*

The decision of whether to drill a property on a "heads up" basis or to take a carried interest is a classic example of mutually exclusive alternatives. From Chapter 4 it was learned that a proper incremental analysis of the alternatives would always lead to selecting the project with the largest NPV. Again, an incremental analysis attempts to justify spending more money so the comparison that follows looks at the difference in "Develop – Carried Interest" or, A-B, as follows:

Incremental Cash Flow Alternative A - Alternative B:

-280,650	146,755	84,756	58,014	46,503
0	1	2	3	4

ROR_{A-B} = 9.62% < 12%, *reject the incremental investment in A, accept B*

NPV_{A-B} = -$11,205 < 0, *reject the incremental investment in A, accept B*

PVR_{A-B} = -11,205/280,650 = -0.04 < 0,   *reject A, accept B*

The "carried interest farm out" (Case B) has a slight economic advantage with all methods. Since Cases A and B are mutually exclusive alternatives, Case B with maximum total investment NPV of $27,386 is the economic choice. Incremental PVR and ROR lead to the same conclusion.

Value Added for "Heads-Up" Development Scenario *(Not Asked For)*

Data for Calculations:

Year	0	1	2	3	4
-Depreciation/Writeoff		-14,290	-24,490	-17,490	-43,730
-Amortization	-7,500	-15,000	-15,000	-15,000	-22,500
-Tangible Equipment	100,000				
-30% of IDC	75,000				
Beg Period Asset Bk Value	0	167,500	138,210	98,720	66,230
Opportunity Cost @ 12%	0	-20,100	-16,585	-11,846	-7,948

Calculating Value Added:

Net Income	-113,150	128,315	50,846	37,787	-12,616
Opportunity Cost @ 12%		-20,100	-16,585	-11,846	-7,948
Value Added	-113,150	108,215	34,261	25,941	-20,564

PV Value Added @ 12% = 16,179 which equals the NPV.

9-18 Solution:

The following incremental cash flow calculations are based on the before-tax data provided in the problem statement. The in-fill drilling alternative reflects combined adjusted production from both the new and existing wells, versus the current production forecast for the current or existing well. Notice that beginning in year 3 and beyond, the incremental production is negative which translates into reduced revenues, implying the company would pay less in royalties and operating costs (the later in year 6 only).

Incremental Cash Flow Calculations:

Year	0	1	2	3	4	5	6
Production	90,000	140,000	45,000	-10,000	-25,000	-30,000	-25,000
Price ($/MCF)	1.25	1.25	1.50	1.75	2.00	2.25	2.50
Revenue	112,500	175,000	67,500	-17,500	-50,000	-67,500	-62,500
-Royalties	-14,063	-21,875	-8,438	2,188	6,250	8,438	7,813
Net Revenue	98,438	153,125	59,063	-15,313	-43,750	-59,063	-54,688
-Oper Costs	-1,000	-2,000	-2,000	-2,000	-2,000	-2,000	4,000
-IDC	-88,200	-	-	-	-	-	-
-Deprec	-6,000	-10,286	-7,347	-5,248	-3,748	-3,748	-5,622
-Amort	-3,780	-7,560	-7,560	-7,560	-7,560	-3,780	
Taxable Inc	-542	133,279	42,156	-30,120	-57,058	-68,591	-56,310
-Tax @ 38%	206	-50,646	-16,019	11,446	21,682	26,065	21,398
Net Income	-336	82,633	26,136	-18,675	-35,376	-42,526	-34,912
+Deprec	6,000	10,286	7,347	5,248	3,748	3,748	5,662
+Amort	3,780	7,560	7,560	7,560	7,560	3,780	
-Cap. Cost	-79,800						
Cash Flow	-70,356	100,479	41,043	-5,867	-24,068	-34,998	-29,290

Depreciation, Tangible Cost = $168,000(0.25) = $42,000

Year 0:	42,000(0.1429)	= $ 6,000
Year 1:	42,000(0.2449)	= $10,286
Year 2:	42,000(0.1749)	= $ 7,347
Etc..		

Amortization Deductions $168,000(0.75)(0.30) = $37,800

Year 0:	37,800(6/60)	= $3,780
Years 1-4:	37,800(12/60)	= $7,560
Year 5:	37,800(6/60)	= $3,780

9-18 *Solution Continued:*

Present Worth Equation: (Note Cost-Income-Cost in CF's)

$$0 = -70{,}356 + 100{,}479(P/F_{i,1}) + 41{,}043(P/F_{i,2})$$

$$- 5{,}867(P/F_{i,3}) - 24{,}068(P/F_{i,4}) - 34{,}998(P/F_{i,5}) - 29{,}290(P/F_{i,6})$$

NPV @ 12% = -$2,093,   *reject in-fill drilling*

Note the incremental project investment pay-out period is 0.7 per year, but the incremental investment is rejected indicating pay-out is a poor economic indicator.

DCFROR analysis of this cash flow stream leads to the dual rate of return problem and requires modifying cash flow streams.

Modified Present Worth Cost ROR Analysis:

$$\overset{0.7118}{70{,}356 + 5{,}867(P/F_{12\%,3})} + \overset{0.6355}{24{,}068(P/F_{12\%,4})}$$

$$+ \overset{0.5674}{34{,}998(P/F_{12\%,5})} + \overset{0.5066}{29{,}290(P/F_{12\%,6})} = \$124{,}524 = Modified\ Cost$$

$$124{,}524 = 100{,}479(P/F_{i\%,1}) + 41{,}043(P/F_{i\%,2})$$

Modified DCFROR = 10.51% < 12.0%, *reject in-fill drilling*

PVR = -2,093/70,356 = -0.0297 < 0, *reject in-fill drilling*

9-19 Solution: *All Dollar Values in Millions*

Escalated Dollar Cash Flow Calculations:

| | | | | | | | ⌐20%fail⌐ |
Year	Time 0	1	2	3	4	Salv.	Yr 1
Revenue		25.00	25.00	25.00	25.00	–	10.00
-Oper. Costs		-10.00	-10.00	-10.00	-10.00	–	–
-Development	-12.00						
-Depreciation		-2.14	-3.67	-2.62	-1.87	-4.69	-15.00
-Amortization		-0.50	-0.50	-0.50	-0.50	-0.50	-2.50
Taxable Income	-12.00	12.36	10.83	11.88	12.63	-5.19	-7.50
-Tax @ 38%	4.56	-4.70	-4.11	-4.51	-4.80	1.97	2.85
Net Income	-7.44	7.66	6.71	7.36	7.83	-3.22	-4.65
+Depreciation		2.14	3.67	2.62	1.87	4.69	15.00
+Amortization		0.50	0.50	0.50	0.50	0.50	2.50
-Equipment Cost	-15.00						
ATCF	-22.44	10.30	10.89	10.49	10.20	1.97	12.85

Depreciation Based on $15 Million Equip. Cost	Amortization Deductions on $2.5 million Patent	Year 0 Sell Cash Flow		
Yr 1 15(0.1429) = 2.14 Yr 2 15(0.2449) = 3.67 Yr 3 15(0.1749) = 2.62 Yr 4 15(0.1249) = 1.87 Yr 4 Book Value = 4.69	Years 1-4 2.5(1/5) = 0.50 Write-off 2.5(1/5) = 0.50	Revenue		4.50
		-Bk Value		-2.50
		Taxable		2.00
		-Tax @ 38%		-0.76
		Net Income		1.24
		+Bk Value		2.50
		Cash Flow$_0$		3.74

A) *Escalated Dollar Expected Net Present Value @ 15%:*

$$\qquad\qquad\quad 0.8696 \qquad\qquad\qquad 0.7561$$
$$ENPV = -22.44 + (0.8)[10.30(P/F_{15\%,1}) + 10.89(P/F_{15\%,2})$$

$$\qquad\quad 0.6575 \qquad\qquad 0.5718 \qquad\qquad\qquad 0.8696$$
$$+ 10.49(P/F_{15\%,3}) + 12.17(P/F_{15\%,4})] + (0.2)[12.85(P/F_{15\%,1})]$$

= +\$4.63 > \$3.74 *choose development*

B) *Constant Dollar Expected NPV @ i*=15% With 8.7% Inflation:*

Using Equation 5-1: i* = (1.15)(1.087) - 1 = 0.25 or 25.0%, *therefore*

$$\qquad\qquad\quad 0.8000 \qquad\qquad\qquad 0.6400$$
$$ENPV = -22.44 + (0.8)[10.30(P/F_{25\%,1}) + 10.89(P/F_{25\%,2})$$

$$\qquad\quad 0.5120 \qquad\qquad 0.4096 \qquad\qquad\qquad 0.8000$$
$$+ 10.49(P/F_{25\%,3}) + 12.17(P/F_{25\%,4})] + (0.2)[12.85(P/F_{25\%,1})]$$

= +\$0.07 < \$3.74 *choose selling*

9-20 Solution:

Purchase Compressor:

```
  -75,000
-1,000,000        -          -      -225,000      -        300,000
         ┌─────────────────────────────────────────────────────────
         0         1          2         3          4           5
```

Lease Compressor:

```
  -75,000
 -144,000   -288,000  -288,000  -288,000  -288,000  -144,000
         ┌─────────────────────────────────────────────────────────
         0         1          2         3          4           5
```

Before-Tax Incremental Time Diagram Purchase - Lease:

```
-1,000,000                     -225,000              300,000
   144,000   288,000  288,000   288,000   288,000   144,000
         ┌─────────────────────────────────────────────────────────
         0         1          2         3          4           5
```

After-Tax Incremental Cash Flows:

Year	0	1	2	3	4	5
Savings	144,000	288,000	288,000	288,000	288,000	444,000
-Repair	-	-	-	-225,000	-	-
-Depreciation	-142,900	-244,900	-174,900	-124,900	-89,300	-223,100
Taxable Income	1,100	43,100	113,100	-61,900	198,700	220,900
-Tax @ 40%	-440	-17,240	-45,240	24,760	-79,480	-88,360
Net Income	660	25,860	67,860	-37,140	119,220	132,540
+Depreciation	142,900	244,900	174,900	124,900	89,300	223,100
-Equip. Costs	-1,000,000	-	-	-	-	-
ATCF	-856,440	270,760	242,760	87,760	208,520	355,640

PW Eq: $0 = -856,440 + 270,760(P/F_{i,1}) + 242,760(P/F_{i,2})$

$\quad\quad\quad + 87,760(P/F_{i,3}) + 208,520(P/F_{i,4}) + 355,640(P/F_{i,5})$

Annual Effective Discount Rate = $(1+0.01)^{12} - 1 = 0.1268$ *or 12.68%*

ROR = i = 10.87% *by financial calculator* < i*=12.68%, *reject purchase*

NPV @ 12.68% = -$38,481 < 0, *reject purchase*

PVR = -38,461 / 856,457 = -0.045 < 0, *reject purchase*

9-21 Solution: *All Values in Dollars*

Case A) 10 Year Bond Analysis

C=10,000   I=800 .... I=800

Maturity Value = 10,000

0   1 .... 10 yr

Since Initial Cost and Salvage are equal:

Before-Tax Yield = 8%
After-Tax Yield = 8%(1-0.38) = 4.96%

Bond market values are based on before-tax yields (interest rates) and therefore are not affected by the investor's tax situation. Bond market value (price) is not identical to the investor's NPV from buying a bond. NPV is dependent upon an investor's tax situation.

$$\text{At 6\% interest:} \quad P = 800 \underset{7.360}{(P/A_{6,10})} + 10,000 \underset{0.5584}{(P/F_{6,10})} = \$11,472$$

$$\text{At 10\% interest:} \quad P = 800 \underset{6.144}{(P/A_{10,10})} + 10,000 \underset{0.3855}{(P/F_{10,10})} = \$8,770$$

Case B) 30 Year Bond Analysis

Value=?   I=$800 .... I=$800

Maturity Value = $10,000

0   1 .... 30 yr+

At 8% interest: P = Value = $10,000

$$\text{At 6\% interest:} \quad P = 800 \underset{13.765}{(P/A_{6,30})} + 10,000 \underset{0.1741}{(P/F_{6,30})} = \$12,753$$

$$\text{At 10\% interest:} \quad P = 800 \underset{9.427}{(P/A_{10,30})} + 10,000 \underset{0.0573}{(P/F_{10,30*})} = \$8,115$$

Case C) 30 Year Zero Coupon Bond

Value=?   –   –

Maturity Value = $10,000

0   1 .... 30 yr

$$\text{At 8\% interest:} \quad P = \text{Value} = 10,000 \underset{0.099377}{(P/F_{8,30})} = \$994$$

$$\text{At 6\% interest:} \quad P = \text{Value} = 10,000 \underset{0.174110}{(P/F_{6,30})} = \$1,741$$

$$\text{At 10\% interest:} \quad P = \text{Value} = 10,000 \underset{0.057309}{(P/F_{10,30})} = \$573$$

CHAPTER 10 PROBLEM SOLUTIONS

10-1 Solution: *Replacement Analysis in Actual Dollars*

	-15,000	-6,000	-7,000	-8,000
A, New Machine				── 2,000
	0	1	2	3

	-21,000	-5,000	-5,000	-5,000
B, Existing Machine				── 3,000
	0	1	2	3

"A" New Machine Cash Flows

Year	0	1	2	3	Salvage
Revenue					2,000
-Operating Costs		-6,000	-7,000	-8,000	
-Depreciation	-3,000	-4,800	-2,880	-1,728	-2,592
Taxable Income	-3,000	-10,800	-9,880	-9,728	-592
-Tax @ 40%	1,200	4,320	3,952	3,891	237
Net Income	-1,800	-6,480	-5,928	-5,837	-355
+Depreciation	3,000	4,800	2,880	1,728	2,592
-Capital Costs	-15,000				
Cash Flow	-13,800	-1,680	-3,048	-4,109	2,237

PW Cost$_A$ @ 20% = 13,800+1,680(P/F$_{20,1}$)+3,048(P/F$_{20,2}$)+1,872(P/F$_{20,3}$)

= $18,400   *Select A with Minimum PW Cost*

Break-even Cost/Unit = 18,400/[(1,000)(250)(P/A$_{20,3}$)(1-.4)]= $0.058/unit

10-1 *Solution Continued...*

"B" Existing Machine Cash Flows

Year	0	1	2	3	Salvage
Revenue					3,000
-Operating Costs		-5,000	-5,000	-5,000	
-Depreciation	-4,200	-6,720	-4,032	-2,419	-3,629
Taxable Income	-4,200	-11,720	-9,032	-7,419	-629
-Tax @ 40%	1,680	4,688	3,613	2,968	252
Net Income	-2,520	-7,032	-5,419	-4,452	-377
+Depreciation	4,200	6,720	4,032	2,419	3,629
-Capital Costs	-21,000				
Cash Flow	-19,320	-312	-1,387	-2,032	3,252

PW Cost$_B$ @ 20% = 19,320 + 312(P/F$_{20,1}$) + 1,387(P/F$_{20,2}$) - 1,220(P/F$_{20,3}$)

$\qquad$ = +$19,838 $\quad$ *Reject B, since A has Minimum PW Cost*

Break-even Cost/Unit = 19,838/[(1,000)(250)(P/A$_{20,3}$)(1-.4)]= $0.063/unit

If the additional 500 units of Machine B productivity can be utilized, PW Cost$_B$ of 1,000 units =19,838(2/3)=13,225 < 18,400 PW Cost$_A$. Select B.

10-2 Solution: *All Values in Actual Dollars*

```
                               -23,000
     -2,000(.6)=1,200   -3,000 -4,000  -2,000  -2,500  -3,000
"A"  ─────────────────────────────────────────────────────── 8,000
          0               1      2       3       4       5
```

```
      -20,000                  -1,500  -2,000  -2,500  -3,000  -3,500
"B"  ─────────────────────────────────────────────────────── 3,000
          0                      1       2       3       4       5
```

Machine A Cash Flows

Year	Time 0	1	2	3	4	5	Salvage
Revenue							8,000
-Operating Costs		-3,000	-4,000	-2,000	-2,500	-3,000	
-Depreciation			-3,286	-5,633	-4,023	-2,874	-7,185
Taxable Income		-3,000	-7,286	-7,633	-6,523	-5,874	815
-Tax Due @ 40%		1,200	2,914	3,053	2,609	2,350	-326
Net Income		-1,800	-4,371	-4,580	-3,914	-3,524	489
+Depreciation			3,286	5,633	4,023	2,874	7,185
-Capital Costs	-1,200		-23,000				
Cash Flow	-1,200	-1,800	-24,086	1,053	109	-650	7,674

$$\text{PW Cost}_A = 1,200 + 1,800(P/F_{15,1}) + 24,086(P/F_{15,2}) - 1,053(P/F_{15,3})$$

$$- 109(P/F_{15,4}) + 650(P/F_{15,5}) - 7,674(P/F_{15,5}) = \$16,731$$

10-2 Solution Continued..

Replacement Machine B Cash Flows

Year	Time 0	1	2	3	4	5	Salvage
Revenue							3,000
-Operating Costs		-1,500	-2,000	-2,500	-3,000	-3,500	
-Depreciation	-2,857	-4,898	-3,499	-2,499	-1,785	-1,785	-2,677
Taxable Income	-2,857	-6,398	-5,499	-4,999	-4,785	-5,285	323
-Tax Due @ 40%	1,143	2,559	2,199	2,000	1,914	2,114	-129
Net Income	-1,714	-3,839	-3,299	-2,999	-2,871	-3,171	194
+Depreciation	2,857	4,898	3,499	2,499	1,785	1,785	2,677
-Capital Costs	-20,000						
Cash Flow	-18,857	1,059	199	-500	-1,086	-1,386	2,871

$$PW\ Cost_B = 18,857 - 1,059(P/F_{15,1}) -199(P/F_{15,2}) + 500(P/F_{15,3})$$
$$+ 967(P/F_{15,4}) + 1,267(P/F_{15,5}) - 2,633(P/F_{15,5}) = \$17,997$$

Case A) Select Machine A with the lowest present worth cost of $16,731.

Case B) If extra service can be utilized, select Machine B, since
17,997/1.4 = $12,855 is less than the Machine A present worth
cost of $16,731.

10-3 Solution: *All Values in Thousands of Dollars*

Calculate the Year 0 Opportunity Cost

Sale Revenue	30,000
−Book Value	−21,000
Taxable Income	9,000
− Income Tax 40%	−3,600
Net Income	5,400
+ Book Value	21,000
ATCF Selling	26,400 *(Opportunity Cost)*

After-Tax Cash Flow If Machine is Kept

Year	0	1	2	3
−Repair Cost	−25,000	−	−	−
−Operating Costs	−	−15,000	−18,000	−21,000
−Depreciation	−21,000	−	−	−
Taxable Income	−46,000	−15,000	−18,000	−21,000
−Income Tax @ 40%	18,400	6,000	7,200	8,400
Net Income	−27,600	−9,000	−10,800	−12,600
+Depreciation	21,000	−	−	−
−Opportunity Cost	−26,400	−	−	−
Cash Flow	−33,000	−9,000	−10,800	−12,600

Case A) Present Worth Cost

$$-33,000 - 9,000\underset{0.8333}{(P/F_{20,1})} - 10,800\underset{0.6944}{(P/F_{20,2})} - 12,600\underset{0.5787}{(P/F_{20,3})} = -55,291$$

Case B) Annual Cost: $-55,291\underset{0.47473}{(A/P_{20,3})} = -26,248$

Case C) Break-even Lease Payments. Let the three uniform and equal beginning of year lease payments equal "X", 40% of "X" goes to tax, so yr 0, 1 & 2 cash flow increases by 0.6X.

PW Eq: $(.6X-33,000) + (.6X-9,000)\underset{0.8333}{(P/F_{20,1})} + (.6X-10,800)\underset{0.6944}{(P/F_{20,2})}$

$\qquad -12,600\underset{0.5787}{(P/F_{20,3})} = 0$

$\qquad 1.5168X = 55,291$ therefore, $X = 36,455$

10-4 Solution: *All Values in Thousands of Dollars*

Alternative A Time Diagram

-50	-12	-15	-18	-21	-24	
						3
0	1	2	3	4	5	

Alternative B Time Diagram

	-32	-50				
-15	-20	-16	-3	-4	-5	
						25
0	1	2	3	4	5	

Alternative A Cash Flows

Year	0	1	2	3	4	5	Salvage
Revenue							3.00
-Operating Costs		-12.00	-15.00	-18.00	-21.00	-24.00	
-Depreciation	-7.14	-12.24	-8.75	-6.25	-4.46	-4.46	-6.69
Taxable Income	-7.14	-24.24	-23.75	-24.25	-25.46	-28.46	-3.69
-Tax Due @ 40%	2.86	9.70	9.50	9.70	10.18	11.38	1.48
Net Income	-4.29	-14.55	-14.25	-14.55	-15.28	-17.08	-2.22
+Depreciation	7.14	12.24	8.75	6.25	4.46	4.46	6.69
-Capital Costs	-50.00						
ATCF	-47.14	-2.30	-5.50	-8.30	-10.82	-12.62	4.48

-8.14

Present Worth Cost @ 15% = -69.0, *Select A with slightly lower PW Cost.*

Alternative B Cash Flows

Year	0	1	2	3	4	5	Salvage
Revenue							25.00
-Operating Costs		-20.00	-16.00	-3.00	-4.00	-5.00	
-Depreciation	-2.14	-3.67	-14.34	-20.08	-14.34	-10.25	-25.61
-Write-off			-6.56				
Taxable Income	-2.14	-23.67	-36.90	-23.08	-18.34	-15.25	-0.61
-Tax Due @ 40%	0.86	9.47	14.76	9.23	7.34	6.10	0.25
Net Income	-1.29	-14.20	-22.14	-13.85	-11.01	-9.15	-0.37
+Depreciation	2.14	3.67	14.34	20.08	14.34	10.25	25.61
+Write-Off			6.56				
-Capital Costs	-15.00	-32.00	-50.00				
ATCF	-14.14	-42.53	-51.24	6.23	3.34	1.10	25.25

26.35

Present Worth Cost @ 15% = -70.8

10-4 Solution Continued:

Incremental Analysis, Alternative A - Alternative B

Year	0	1	2	3	4	5
A) ATCF	-47.14	-2.30	-5.50	-8.30	-10.82	-8.14
B) ATCF	-14.14	-42.53	-51.24	6.23	3.34	26.35
A-B) ATCF	-33.00	40.23	45.74	-14.53	-14.16	-34.49

Note the existence of cost-income-cost and dual i values as follows:

Calculate NPV for a range of discount rates "i" to determine the dual "i" values.

i	NPV
0	-10.2
5	- 4.4
10	- 0.6
15	1.8
20	3.2
30	4.2
40	3.7
50	2.5
60	1.0
70	-0.6

The 1.80 incremental NPV for i* = 15% equals the difference in the Present Worth Cost of "A" of -69.0 and the Present Worth Cost of "B" of -70.8

Dual DCFROR's are 11% and 66%, but they are not valid for decision making as ROR results. You must go to a modified ROR analysis, either Growth ROR or Present Worth Cost Modified ROR analysis discussed in Chapter Four.

Escrow Approach to DCFROR Analysis:

$$\text{PW Cost} = -33.00 - 14.53 \overset{0.6575}{(P/F_{15,3})} - 14.16 \overset{0.5717}{(P/F_{15,4})} - 34.49 \overset{0.4972}{(P/F_{15,5})}$$

$$= -67.79$$

Modified DCFROR PW Eq $0 = -67.79 + 40.23(P/F_{i,1}) + 45.74(P/F_{i,2})$

i = PW Cost Modified DCFROR = 17.0% > i^* = 15%, *accept Machine A*

If you prefer to obtain the incremental Machine A-B after-tax cash flow by taking the difference in the alternatives before-tax and converting the incremental costs and savings to after-tax cash flow, be very careful not to net incremental operating costs and capital costs against one another. Also note that the negative incremental "A-B" capital costs in years 1 and 2 are savings that result in negative depreciation in years 2, 3, 4 and 5 and a negative write-off at year 5.

10-4 Solution Continued:

Before-Tax Incremental Diagram, Machine A - Machine B

```
            -32        -50
 -35         -8         -1      -15      -17      -19
  |_____|_____|_____|_____|_____|
  0          1          2        3        4        5
```

Correct handling of the depreciation calculations is the key to correct
incremental cash flow analysis, but it is very easy to make mistakes.
From a practical viewpoint, this solution is presented to emphasize what
not to do!

Year	Incremental A-B Depreciation		Net Depreciation	
0	(35)(.1429)	= 5.0	Yr 0	5.00
1	(35)(.2449)	= 8.57	Yr 1	8.57
2	Write-off on (-15)	= -9.19		
2	(50)(.1749)	= 8.75		
2	(-82)(.1429)	= -11.72	Yr 2	-12.16
3	(50)(.1249)	= 6.25		
3	(-82)(.2449)	= -20.08	Yr 3	-13.83
4	(50)(.0893)	= 4.46		
4	(-82)(.1749)	= -14.34	Yr 4	-9.88
5	(50)(.0892)	= 4.46		
5	(-82)(.1249)	= -10.25	Yr 5	-5.79
5	write-off on 50	= 6.69		
5	write-off on (-82)	= -25.62	Yr 5	-18.92

Incremental Cash Flow Calculations

Year	0	1	2	3	4	5
Savings/Salvage		8.00	1.00			-22.00
-Oper Costs				-15.00	-17.00	-19.00
-Deprec/Write-off	-5.00	-8.57	12.16	13.83	9.88	24.71
Taxable Income	-5.00	-0.57	13.16	-1.17	-7.12	-16.29
-Tax @ 40%	2.00	0.23	-5.26	0.47	2.85	6.52
Net Income	-3.00	-0.34	7.90	-0.70	-4.27	-9.77
+Deprec/Write-off	5.00	8.57	-12.16	-13.83	-9.88	-24.71
-Capital Costs	-35.00	32.00	50.00			
Cash Flow	-33.00	40.23	45.74	-14.53	-14.15	-34.48

Within round-off error these incremental A-B after-tax cash flows are the
same as those from analyzing the difference in the total investment cash
flows.

10-5 Solution: *Values in Thousands of Dollars*

Old Machine

Case 1	Case 2	Case 3 (Accounting
C=90-36 tax if D9 sold	C=90	C=0　　　Viewpoint)
Yr 0 Book Value = 0	Yr 0 Book Value = 0	Yr 0 Book Value = 0

New Machine

Case 1	Case 2	Case 3
C=460	C=460+36 tax old sale	C=460+36 tax-90 sale
Yr 0 Bk Value = 460	Yr 0 Bk Value = 460	Yr 0 Bk Value = 460

Since the same relative differences exist between the New and Old Machines for all 3 cases (incremental cost of $406 for each), you must get the same economic conclusions using any of the 3 cases. However, do not mix the cases.

Present worth cost analysis results are presented. You can convert present worth cost results to equivalent annual cost by multiplying present worth cost times A/P$_{15,5}$, giving the same economic conclusions.

Case A) Assumes the New and Old assets give the same service

Old Machine Cash Flow Calculations

Year	0			1	2	3	4	5
Case #	1	2	3					
-Op Costs	-100.0	-100.0	-100.0	-150.0	-237.0	-184.0	-290.0	-156.0
Taxable	-100.0	-100.0	-100.0	-150.0	-237.0	-184.0	-290.0	-156.0
-Tax @ 40%	40.0	40.0	40.0	60.0	94.8	73.6	116.0	62.4
Net Income	-60.0	-60.0	-60.0	-90.0	-142.2	-110.4	-174.0	-93.6
-Cap Costs	-54.0	-90.0						
Cash Flow	-114.0	-150.0	-60.0	-90.0	-142.2	-110.4	-174.0	-93.6

Present Worth Cost for Year 0, Case 1

PW Cost Eq: $114.0 + 90.0(P/F_{15,1}) + 142.2(P/F_{15,2}) + 110.4(P/F_{15,3})$

(0.8696, 0.7561, .6575)

$+ 174.0(P/F_{15,4}) + 93.6(P/F_{15,5})$

(0.5718, 0.4972)

Present Worth Cost, Case 1:　$518.4
Present Worth Cost, Case 2:　$554.4
Present Worth Cost, Case 3:　$464.4

10-5 Solution Continued:

New Machine Cash Flow Calculations

Year		0		1	2	3	4	5
Case #	1	2	3					
Revenue								140.0
-Oper Cost				-88.0	-221.0	-108.0	-274.0	-140.0
-Deprec	-65.7	-65.7	-65.7	-112.7	-80.5	-57.5	-41.0	-41.0
-Write-off								-61.6
Taxable Inc	-65.7	-65.7	-65.7	-200.7	-301.5	-165.5	-315.0	-102.6
-Tax @ 40%	26.3	26.3	26.3	80.3	120.6	66.2	126.0	+41.0
Net Income	-39.4	-39.4	-39.4	-120.4	-180.9	-99.3	-189.0	-61.6
+Deprec	65.7	65.7	65.7	112.7	80.5	57.5	41.0	41.0
+Write-off								61.6
-Cap Costs	-460.0	-496.0	-406.0					
Cash Flow	-433.7	-469.7	-379.7	-7.7	-100.4	-41.8	-148.0	41.0

Present Worth Cost for Year 0, Case 1:

$$\text{PW Cost Eq: } 433.7 + 7.7\,\overset{0.8696}{(P/F_{15,1})} + 100.4\,\overset{0.7561}{(P/F_{15,2})} + 41.8\,\overset{0.6575}{(P/F_{15,3})}$$

$$+ 148.0\,\overset{0.5718}{(P/F_{15,4})} - 41.0\,\overset{0.4972}{(P/F_{15,5})}$$

Present Worth Cost, Case 1: $608.0
Present Worth Cost, Case 2: $644.8
Present Worth Cost, Case 3: $554.8

Case B)

If the total productive capacity of the new D9L can be utilized, the Case 1 present worth cost of the new machine would drop to $608/1.3 = $467.7 which makes the New Machine preferable to the Old Machine, Case 1 present worth cost of $518.4.

Break-even cost per unit of service analysis is only valid for Case 1 actual after-tax year 0 costs.

Old Machine Break-even Cost Per Unit of Service Equals:

PW Cost "Old" / PW Production(1-tax rate)

$$518,400 \,/\, [2,000\,\overset{3.352}{(P/A_{15,5})}(1-0.4)] = \$128.88 \,/\, \text{unit}$$

New Machine Break-even Cost Per Unit of Service Equals:

$$608,000 \,/\, [2,600\,\overset{3.352}{(P/A_{15,5})}(1-0.4)] = \$116.27 \,/\, \text{unit}$$

Select the New Machine with the minimum cost per unit.

10-6 Solution: *Lease vs Purchase Analysis, All Values in Dollars*

Case A) Expense Economics

```
            OC=18        OC=36        OC=36        OC=18
Lease       ─────────────────────────────────────────── L=0
            0            1            2            3

            C=100          -            -            -
Purchase    ─────────────────────────────────────────── L=30
            0            1            2            3

            OC=-18
Purchase    C =100       OC=-36       OC=-36       OC=-18
-Lease      ─────────────────────────────────────────── L=30
            0            1            2            3
```

Remember that a negative incremental operating cost is equivalent to positive savings or revenue. Also, do not net incremental capital cost of 100 against the incremental operating cost of -18 in year 0. They are treated differently for tax purposes.

Incremental Analysis, Purchase - Lease Cash Flows

Year	0	1	2	3	
Savings/Salvage	18,000	36,000	36,000	48,000	*includes salvage.*
-Depreciation	-20,000	-32,000	-19,200	-11,520	
-Deprec/Write-off				-17,280	
Taxable Income	-2,000	4,000	16,800	19,200	
-Tax @ 40%	800	-1,600	-6,720	-7,680	
Net Income	-1,200	2,400	10,080	11,520	
+Deprec/Write-off	20,000	32,000	19,200	28,800	
-Capital Costs	-100,000				
ATCF	-81,200	34,400	29,280	40,320	

PW Eq: $0 = -81,200 + 34,400(P/F_{i,1}) + 29,280(P/F_{i,2}) + 40,320(P/F_{i,3})$

       i = DCFROR = 13.1% < 15%, *reject purchase*

NPV $= -81,200 + 34,400(P/F_{15,1}) + 29,280(P/F_{15,2}) + 40,320(P/F_{15,3})$

     = -2,636 < 0, *reject purchase*

10-6 Solution, Case A Continued:

PW Cost of Leasing Cash Flows

Year	0	1	2	3
Revenue	-	-	-	-
-Lease Costs	-18,000	-36,000	-36,000	-18,000
Taxable Income	-18,000	-36,000	-36,000	-18,000
-Tax @ 40%	7,200	14,400	14,400	7,200
Net Income	-10,800	-21,600	-21,600	-10,800
-Capital Costs	-	-	-	-
ATCF	-10,800	-21,600	-21,600	-10,800

PW Cost = $-10,800 - 21,600(P/A_{15,2}) - 10,800(P/F_{15,3}) = -\$53,016$

PW Cost of Purchasing Cash Flows

Year	0	1	2	3
Revenue	-	-	-	30,000
-Depreciation	-20,000	-32,000	-19,200	-11,520
-Deprec/Write-off	-	-	-	-17,280
Taxable Income	-20,000	-32,000	-19,200	1,200
-Tax @ 40%	8,000	12,800	7,680	-480
Net Income	-12,000	-19,200	-11,520	720
+Deprec/Write-off	20,000	32,000	19,200	28,800
-Capital Costs	-100,000			
ATCF	-92,000	12,800	7,680	29,520

PW Cost = $-92,000 + 12,800(P/F_{15,1}) + 7,680(P/F_{15,2}) + 29,520(P/F_{15,3})$

$= -\$55,652$ Reject Purchase, Select leasing
   with the lowest present worth cost.

10-6 *Solution, Case A Continued:*

Alternate Methodology to get Incremental Cash Flows

Below are the after-tax cash flows for the cost of purchasing and leasing. By looking at the difference in these two streams, it is possible to avoid incorrectly mixing different types of before-tax dollars (i.e. capital costs vs. operating expenditures).

Purchase ATCF	-92,000	12,800	7,680	29,520
- Lease ATCF	-10,800	-21,600	-21,600	-10,800
Incremental Purch-Lease ATCF	-81,200	34,400	29,280	40,320

Incremental NPV

$$= -81,200 + 34,400(P/F_{15,1}) + 29,280(P/F_{15,2}) + 40,320(P/F_{15,3})$$

$$= -2,636 < 0 \text{ } so \text{ } reject \text{ } purchase$$

or, Incremental NPV = PW Cost of Purchase - PW Cost of Leasing

$$= -55,652 - -53,016 = -2,636$$

i = Incremental DCFROR = 13.1% < 15%, *reject purchase*

Case B) *Uniform Annual Equivalent Revenue Required (UAERR) is based on the alternative sign convention. In this case, the present worth costs are treated as positive values as follows:*

UAERR = Annual Cost / (1-tax rate)

$$\text{UAERR}_{Lease} = \$53,016 \overset{0.43798}{(A/P_{15,3})} / (1-.4) = \$23,220 / (1-.4) = \$38,700$$

$$\text{UAERR}_{Purch} = \$55,652 \overset{0.43798}{(A/P_{15,3})} / (1-.4) = \$24,375 / (1-.4) = \$40,624$$

10-6 *Solution Continued:*

Case C) Stand Alone Economics

Leasing Cash Flows

Year	0	1	2	3
Revenue				
-Lease Costs	-18,000	-36,000	-36,000	-18,000
-Loss Forward		-18,000	-54,000	-90,000
Taxable Income	-18,000	-54,000	-90,000	-108,000
-Tax @ 40%	0	0	0	43,200
Net Income	-18,000	-54,000	-90,000	-64,800
+Loss Forward		18,000	54,000	90,000
-Capital Costs				
ATCF	-18,000	-36,000	-36,000	25,200

PW Cost = -18,000 - 36,000(P/A$_{15,2}$) + 25,200(P/F$_{15,3}$) = -59,956

Purchase Cash Flows

Year	0	1	2	3
Revenue				30,000
-Depreciation	-20,000	-32,000	-19,200	-11,520
-Deprec/Write-off				-17,280
-Loss Forward		-20,000	-52,000	-71,200
Taxable Income	-20,000	-52,000	-71,200	-70,000
-Tax @ 40%	0	0	0	28,000
Net Income	-20,000	-52,000	-71,200	-42,000
+Deprec/Write-off	20,000	32,000	19,200	28,800
+Loss Forward		20,000	52,000	71,200
-Capital Costs	-100,000			
ATCF	-100,000	0	0	58,000

PW Cost = -100,000 + 58,000(P/F$_{15,3}$) = -61,864

Select Leasing with the least negative present worth cost.

Carrying losses forward versus expensing against other income has little effect on lease versus purchase analysis because cumulative tax deductions are similar for both and the life is short.

10-7 Solution: *All Values in Thousands of Dollars*

Old	-144*	-360	-390	-420	
	0	1	2	3	0

New	-1,000	-120	-160	-200	
	0	1	2	3	240

*Opportunity Cost = 240 - 96(tax) = 144 *for 3 Old Machines*

Cash Flows for Keeping the 3 Old Machine

Year	0	1	2	3
Revenue		–	–	–
-Operating Costs		-360	-390	-420
Taxable Income		-360	-390	-420
-Tax @ 40%		144	156	168
Net Income		-216	-234	-252
-Capital Costs	-144			
Cash Flow	-144	-216	-234	-252

$$0.8696 \quad 0.7561 \quad 0.6575 \quad 0.43798$$

$AC_{Old} = [-144-216(P/F_{15,1})-234(P/F_{15,2})-252(P/F_{15,3})](A/P_{15,3}) = -295.4$

UAERR = 295.4/(1-0.4) = 492.33 *for 3 Old Machines, 164.1 per Machine.*

Cash Flows for Purchasing 2 New Machines

Year	0	1	2	3
Revenue	–	–	–	250
-Operating Costs	–	-120	-160	-200
-Deprec/Write-off	-200	-320	-192	-288
Taxable Income	-200	-440	-352	-238
-Tax @ 40%	80	176	141	95
Net Income	-120	-264	-211	-143
+Depreciation	200	320	192	288
-Capital Costs	-1,000	–	–	–
Cash Flow	-920	56	-19	145

$$0.8696 \quad 0.7561 \quad 0.6575 \quad 0.43798$$

$AC_{New} = [-920 + 56(P/F_{15,1}) - 19(P/F_{15,2}) + 145(P/F_{15,3})](A/P_{15,3}) = -346$

UAERR$_{New}$ = 346/(1-.4) = 576.67 *for 2 New Machines, or 288.3 per Machine. Replacement of the Old Machines is not indicated to be economically desirable with either annual cost or UAERR analysis.*

10-8 Solution: *All Values in Thousands of Dollars*

Purchase vs Leasing a Plant
Assume other income exists against which to use deductions in any year.

		Rev/yr=800		800	800	
	C=1,000	OC/yr =200		200	200	
Purchase						L=400
	0	1		9	10	

		Rev/yr=800		800	800	
	OC=200	OC/yr=400		400	200	
Lease						L=0
	0	1		9	10	

	C=1,000					
Purchase	OC=-200	OC/yr=-200		-200	0	
- Lease						L=400
	0	1		9	10	

Purchase Plant Cash Flows

Year	0	1-9	10	Salv
Revenue		800	800	400
-Oper Costs		-200	-200	
-Deprec	-50	-100	-50	
Taxable Inc	-50	500	550	400
-Tax @ 40%	20	-200	-220	-160
Net Income	-30	300	330	240
+Deprec	50	100	50	
-Cap Cost	-1,000			
Cash Flow	-980	400	380	240

620

Lease Plant Cash Flows

Year	0	1-9	10
Revenue		800	800
-Oper Costs	-200	-400	-200
-Deprec			
Taxable Inc	-200	400	600
-Tax @ 40%	80	-160	-240
Net Income	-120	240	360
+Depreciation			
-Capital Costs			
Cash Flow	-120	240	360

Purchase PW EQ:

$$0 = -980+400(P/A_{i},9)+620(P/F_{i},10)$$

i = DCFROR = 39.7%
NPV @ 10% = +$1,563

Lease PW Eq:

$$0=-120+240(P/A_{i},9)+360(P/F_{i},10)$$

i = DCFROR = 200%
NPV @ 10% = +$1,401

Mutually exclusive alternative analysis requires incremental analysis.
Incremental Analysis, Purchase - Lease Cash Flows

-860	+160	+160	+260
0	1	9	10

DCFROR = 14% > 10%, *so purchase,* NPV = +162 > 0, *so purchase also*

10-8 *Solution Continued:*

Leave the revenues out of this analysis since they are projected to be the same whether purchase or lease is selected.

Cash Flows for Purchase of New Plant for Cost Analysis

Year	0	1-9	10	Salv
Revenue	-	-	-	400
-Operating Costs		-200	-200	-
-Depreciation	-50	-100	-50	-
Taxable Income	-50	-300	-250	400
-Tax @ 40%	20	120	100	-160
Net Income	-30	-180	-150	240
+Depreciation	50	100	50	-
-Capital Costs -1,000				
ATCF	-980	-80	-100	240
			140	

$$\text{PW Cost @ 10\%} = -980 - 80(P/A_{10,9}) + 140(P/F_{10,10}) = -1,387$$

$$\text{AW Cost @ 10\%} = -1,386.75(A/P_{10,10}) = -226$$

Cash Flows for Leasing Plant for Cost Analysis

Year	0	1-9	10
Revenue	-	-	-
-Oper Costs	-200	-400	-200
Taxable Income	-200	-400	-200
-Tax @ 40%	80	160	80
Net Income	-120	-240	-120
ATCF	-120	-240	-120

$$\text{PW Cost @ 10\%} = -120 - 240(P/A_{10,9}) - 120(P/F_{10,10}) = -1,548$$

$$\text{AW Cost @ 10\%} = -1,548.43(A/P_{10,10}) = -252$$

Select Purchase to minimize both present worth and annual worth cost.

The same economic conclusion to purchase has been reached with all techniques of analysis.

10-9 Solution: *All Values in Dollars*

Standard Cost of Service for a bulldozer

Let "X" equal the Before Tax Standard Cost Per Hour necessary to receive a 15% DCFROR on invested capital. Revenues are separated from costs for illustration and sensitivity analysis purposes. You may also obtain the same solutions by combining both into one cash flow calculation and solving for the standard cost of service/hr X. That solution is left to the reader.

Cash Flows for Break-even Revenues

Year	0	1	2	3	4	5
Revenue		4,000X	4,000X	3,000X	2,000X	2,000X
Taxable Income		4,000X	4,000X	3,000X	2,000X	2,000X
-Tax @ 40%		-1,600X	-1,600X	-1,200X	-800X	-800X
Cash Flow		2,400X	2,400X	1,800X	1,200X	1,800X

$$PW \text{ of Revenues} = (2,400X)P/F_{15,1} + (2,400X)(P/F_{15,2}) + (1,800X)(P/F_{15,3})$$
$$+ (1,200X)(P/F_{15,4}) + (1,200X)(P/F_{15,5}) = 6,368X$$

Cash Flows for Cost of Service

Year	0	1	2	3	4	5
Salvage Revenue		-	-	-	-	136,298
-Oper Costs		-27,948	-125,364	-100,441	-150,384	-45,499
-Deprec	-69,512	-119,164	-85,117	-60,798	-43,452	-43,403
-Deprec Write-off		-	-	-	-	-65,154
Taxable Inc	-69,512	-147,112	-210,481	-161,239	-193,836	-17,758
-Tax @ 40%	27,805	58,845	84,192	64,496	77,534	7,103
Net Income	-41,707	-88,267	-126,289	-96,743	-116,302	-10,655
+Deprec	69,512	119,164	85,117	60,798	43,452	43,403
+Deprec Write-off		-	-	-	-	65,154
-Cap. Cost	-486,585	-	-	-	-	-
Cash Flow	-458,780	30,897	-41,172	-35,945	-72,850	97,902

$$PW \text{ Cost} = -458,780 + 30,897(P/F_{15,1}) - 41,172(P/F_{15,2}) - 35,945(P/F_{15,3})$$
$$- 72,850(P/F_{15,4}) + 97,902(P/F_{15,5}) = -479,657$$

10-9 *Solution Continued:*

By setting present worth revenues equal to present worth costs we can determine the break-even standard cost of service per hour X, as follows:

Break-even Standard Cost of Service Per Hour:

$0 = -479,657 + X(6,368 \text{ hours})$,   therefore, $X = \$75.32$ per hour

Standard Cost of Service for a Bulldozer

For the alternate hours per year, calculate the after-tax discounted revenues and again, set equal to the present worth cost to determine X. Before-tax hours of service are 3,000 hours per year, therefore, the discounted after-tax revenues (cash flow) may be expressed as:

$$1,800X(P/A_{15,5}) = 6,034X$$

Break-even Standard Cost of Service *is equal to:*

$479,657 = X(6,034 \text{ hours})$ therefore, $X = \$79.46$ per hour

It becomes apparent that the faster equipment hours of operation, or production, occur over asset life, the more cost competitive equipment becomes. This happens because equipment productivity is related to product revenue generation and the faster revenues are generated, the better the economics of projects become.

10-10 Solution: *Values in Thousands of Dollars*

C=Capital Cost,   OC=Operating Cost, LP=Lease Payment,   L=Salvage

```
              -200
              -18              -39              -45              -24
Purchase     ━━━━━━━━━━━━━━━━━━━━━━━━━━━━━━━━━━━━━━━━━━━━━━━━━━━━━━━   50
               0                1                2                3


              -36              -72              -72              -36
              -18              -39              -45              -24
Lease        ━━━━━━━━━━━━━━━━━━━━━━━━━━━━━━━━━━━━━━━━━━━━━━━━━━━━━━━
               0                1                2                3
```

Purchase Cash Flows (Cost Analysis)

Year	Time 0	1	2	3	Salvage
Revenue					50.00
-Operating Costs	-18.00	-39.00	-45.00	-24.00	
-Depreciation	-40.00	-64.00	-38.40	-23.04	-34.56
Taxable Income	-58.00	-103.00	-83.40	-47.04	15.44
-Tax Due @ 40%	23.20	41.20	33.36	18.82	-6.18
Net Income	-34.80	-61.80	-50.04	-28.22	9.26
+Depreciation	40.00	64.00	38.40	23.04	34.56
-Capital Costs	-200.00				
ATCF	-194.80	2.20	-11.64	-5.18	43.82

$$38.64$$

Present Worth Cost @ 15% = -176

10-10 *Solution Continued*:

Leasing Cash Flows (Cost Analysis)

Year	0	1	2	3
-Operating Costs	-18.00	-39.00	-45.00	-24.00
-Lease Payments	-36.00	-72.00	-72.00	-36.00
Taxable Income	-54.00	-111.00	-117.00	-60.00
-Tax Due @ 40%	21.60	44.40	46.80	24.00
Net Income	-32.40	-66.60	-70.20	-36.00
Cash Flow	-32.40	-66.60	-70.20	-36.00

Present Worth Cost @ 15% = -167

Selecting the alternative with the least present worth cost suggests that leasing is the economic choice.

Incremental Analysis (Purchase-Lease), Before-tax Diagram, S = Savings

Capital Cost	-200			
Lease Pymt Savings	36	72	72	36
Salvage	-	-	-	50
Year	0	1	2	3

Incremental Cash Flows

Year	0	1	2	3	Salvage
Savings	36.00	72.00	72.00	36.00	50.00
-Depreciation	-40.00	-64.00	-38.40	-23.04	-34.56
Taxable Income	-4.00	8.00	33.60	12.96	15.44
-Tax Due @ 40%	1.60	-3.20	-13.44	-5.18	-6.18
Net Income	-2.40	4.80	20.16	7.78	9.26
+Depreciation	40.00	64.00	38.40	23.04	34.56
-Capital Costs	-200.00				
Cash Flow	-162.40	68.80	58.56	30.82	43.82

74.64

Incremental NPV @ 15% = -$9 < 0   *reject purchase*

Incremental DCFROR   = 11.6% < 15%   *reject purchase*

10-10 Solution: *Continued*

Monthly Analysis, Lease vs Purchase

```
        C=200
        OC=3.0   OC=3.0    OC=3.0   OC=3.5    OC=3.5    OC=4.0    OC=4.0    -
Purchase ────────────────────────────────────────────────────────────────── L=50
        0       1 ..... 11         12 ..... 23         24 ..... 35      36


        LP=6.0  LP=6.0   LP=6.0   LP=6.0   LP=6.0    LP=6.0    LP=6.0
        OC=3.0  OC=3.0   OC=3.0   OC=3.5   OC=3.5    OC=4.0    OC=4.0    -
Lease   ────────────────────────────────────────────────────────────────── L=0
        0       1 ..... 11         12 ..... 23         24 ..... 35      36
```

Purchase Cash Flow Calculations, Monthly Periods

Year 0 depreciation is spread over months 0 to 5, Year 1 depreciation is spread uniformly over months 6 to 17, Year 2 depreciation spread uniformly over months 18 to 29 and year 3 depreciation is spread over months 30 to 35.

Month	0	1-5	6-11	12-17	18-23	24-29	30-35	36
Revenue								50.00
-Op Cost	-3.00	-3.00	-3.00	-3.50	-3.50	-4.00	-4.00	
-Deprec	-6.67	-6.67	-5.33	-5.33	-3.20	-3.20	-3.84	
-Write-off								-34.56
Taxable	-9.67	-9.67	-8.33	-8.83	-6.70	-7.20	-7.84	15.44
-Tax @ 40%	3.87	3.87	3.33	3.53	2.68	2.88	3.14	-6.18
Net Income	-5.80	-5.80	-5.00	-5.30	-4.02	-4.32	-4.70	9.26
+Deprec	6.67	6.67	5.33	5.33	3.20	3.20	3.84	
+Write-off								34.56
-Cap Cost	-200.00							
Cash Flow	-200.87	0.87	0.33	0.03	-0.82	-1.12	-0.86	43.82

Effective Annual Discount Rate, $E = 0.15 = (1+i)^{12} - 1$

Monthly Interest Rate, $i = 0.0117$ or 1.17%   *by trial and error*

PW Cost Purchase:

$= -200.87 + 0.87(P/A_{1.17\%,5}) + 0.33(P/A_{1.17\%,12})(P/F_{1.17\%,5}) \cdots = -178.2$

Note that the monthly period analysis present worth cost of $178.2 is very close to the annual period analysis present worth cost of $176.3 Use of equivalent monthly period and annual period discount rates in the two analyses together with proper timing of the costs in the annual analysis is the key to obtaining equivalent results.

10-10 Solution: *Continued*

Monthly Analysis, Lease vs Purchase

Lease Cash Flow Calculations, Monthly Periods

Month	0	1-5	6-11	12-17	18-23	24-29	30-35
-Op Cost	-3.00	-3.00	-3.00	-3.50	-3.50	-4.00	-4.00
-Lease Pmt	-6.00	-6.00	-6.00	-6.00	-6.00	-6.00	-6.00
Taxable Inc	-9.00	-9.00	-9.00	-9.50	-9.50	-10.00	-10.00
-Tax @ 40%	3.60	3.60	3.60	3.80	3.80	4.00	4.00
Net Income	-5.40	-5.40	-5.40	-5.70	-5.70	-6.00	-6.00
ATCF	-5.40	-5.40	-5.40	-5.70	-5.70	-6.00	-6.00

PW Cost Leasing:

$-5.40 - 5.40(P/A_{1.17\%,11}) - 5.70(P/A_{1.17\%,12})(P/F_{1.17\%,11})$

$- 6.00(P/A_{1.17\%,12})(P/F_{1.17\%,23}) = -167.8$

Selecting the alternative with the least present worth cost suggests that leasing is the economic choice, consistent with the annual period evaluation.

Incremental Purchase-Lease

ATCF	-195.47	6.27	5.73	5.73	4.88	4.88	5.14	43.82
Month	0	1-5	6-11	12-17	18-23	24-29	30-35	36

PW Eq: $0 = -195.47 + 6.27(P/A_{i\%,5}) + 5.73(P/A_{i\%,12})(P/F_{i\%,5})$

$\qquad + 4.88(P/A_{i\%,12})(P/F_{i\%,17}) + 5.14(P/A_{i\%,6})(P/F_{i\%,29})$

$\qquad + 36(P/F_{i\%,36})$

Incremental NPV @ 15% Annually *(1.17% per month)*$=-\$10.44 < 0$ *reject*

Incremental DCFROR per month = $0.88\% < i* = 1.17\%$

Nominal Rate DCFROR is calculated as follows:

12(0.88%) = 10.56% per year, compounded monthly.

To evaluate the incremental investment using annual DCFROR, the monthly DCFROR should be converted to the equivalent effective discrete annual DCFROR rate. The effective discrete annual rate is calculated as follows:

$E = (1+.0088)^{12}-1 = 0.1109$ or $11.09\% < i* = 15\%$, *reject purchase*

10-11 Solution: *Values in Thousands of Dollars*

Service Analysis

	−100	−200	−200	−100	
Capital	−1,000	−	−	−	
Intensive, "A"					300
	0	1	2	3	

	−275	−550	−550	−275	
Less Capital					0
Intensive, "B"					
	0	1	2	3	

	Savings= 175	350	350	175	
"A-B"	Capital=1,000	−	−	−	
Incremental					300
	0	1	2	3	

"A-B" Incremental Analysis

Year	0	1	2	3
Savings	175.0	350.0	350.0	475.0
−Depr/Write-off	−200.0	−320.0	−192.0	−288.0
Taxable Income	−25.0	30.0	158.0	187.0
−Tax @ 40%	10.0	−12.0	−63.2	−74.8
Net Income	−15.0	18.0	94.8	112.2
+Depr/Write-off	200.0	320.0	192.0	288.0
−Capital Cost	−1,000.0	−	−	−
Cash Flow	−815.0	338.0	286.8	400.2

PW Eq: $0 = -815 + 338(P/F_{i,1}) + 286.8(P/F_{i,2}) + 400.2(P/F_{i,3})$

Incremental DCFROR = 12% < i*=15% *so reject "A", select "B"*

Incremental NPV @ 15%:

$$\overset{0.8696}{} \quad \overset{0.7561}{} \quad \overset{0.6575}{}$$

$-815 + 338(P/F_{15,1}) + 286.8(P/F_{15,2}) + 400.2(P/F_{15,3})$

=−41.09 < 0   *reject "A"*

10-11 *Solution Continued:*

Cost Analyses

Alternative "A" (Capital Intensive)

Year	0	1	2	3
Revenue	-	-	-	300.0
-Operating Costs	-100.0	-200.0	-200.0	-100.0
-Deprec/Write-off	-200.0	-320.0	-192.0	-288.0
Taxable Income	-300.0	-520.0	-392.0	-88.0
-Tax @ 40%	+120.0	+208.0	+156.8	+35.2
Net Income	-180.0	-312.0	-235.2	-52.8
+Deprec/Write-off	200.0	320.0	192.0	288.0
-Capital Cost	-1,000.0	-	-	-
Cash Flow	-980.0	8.0	-43.2	235.2

$$\text{PW Cost @ 15\%: } -980 + 8\overset{0.8696}{(P/F_{15,1})} - 43.2\overset{0.7561}{(P/F_{15,2})} + 235.2\overset{0.6575}{(P/F_{15,3})}$$

$$= -851.06$$

$$\text{End-of-Period Equivalent AC: } -851.06\overset{0.43798}{(A/P_{15,3})} = -372.75$$

$$\text{Beginning-of-Period Equivalent AC: } -372.75\overset{0.8696}{(P/F_{15,1})} = -324.14$$

10-11 *Solution Continued:*

Alternative "B" (Less Capital Intensive)

Year	0	1	2	3
Revenue	-	-	-	-
-Operating Costs	-275	-550	-550	-275
Taxable Income	-275	-550	-550	-275
-Tax @ 40%	+110	+220	+220	+110
Net Income	-165	-330	-330	-165
-Capital Cost	-	-	-	-
Cash Flow	-165	-330	-330	-165

PW Cost @ 15%:

$$\underset{0.8696}{} \quad \underset{0.7561}{} \quad \underset{0.6575}{}$$

$$-165 - 330(P/F_{15,1}) - 330(P/F_{15,2}) - 165(P/F_{15,3}) = -809.97$$

-809.97 < -851.06, *so select less capital intensive "B"*

End-of-Period Equivalent AC:

$$\underset{0.43798}{}$$

$$-809.97(A/P_{15,3}) = -354.75 < -372.75, \quad \text{select "B"}$$

Beginning-of-Period Equivalent AC:

$$\underset{0.8696}{}$$

$$-354.75(P/F_{15,1}) = -308.49 < -324.14 \text{ select "B"}$$

In the above analyses, the less capital-intensive alternative "B" is preferred. However, alternative "B" may be treated as an option to lease the equipment. In this case, the problem becomes a lease vs. purchase analysis. Assume, then, that a hypothetical 6% minimum discount rate, that reflects the after-tax cost of borrowing funds to finance the purchase of the asset, is used. Many companies do this. In that case, purchasing seems preferable to leasing. But is it really?

Should the appropriate minimum discount rate be affected by whether the analysis is described as lease vs purchase, or as an old asset compared to a new asset, or as labor compared to automated equipment? It seems evident the answer is "no," unless unique borrowed money financing that does not affect other capital budgets is available for purchasing instead of leasing.

CHAPTER 11 PROBLEM SOLUTIONS

11-1 Solution: Land Acquisition Analysis, All Values in Dollars

CASE A, Cash Investment:

Before-Tax Cash Flow Diagram

C=60,000
```
———————————————————————————————————  L = 150,000
0              1  ......................  5
```

Tax on gain = (150,000-60,000)(.4 tax rate) = 36,000

After-Tax Cash Flow Diagram

CF=-60,000
```
———————————————————————————————————  CF = 114,000
0              1  ......................  5
```

PW Eq: 0 = 60,000 - 114,000$(P/F_{i,5})$,   i=DCFROR=13.7% by trial and error.

CASE B, Leveraged Investment:

Before-Tax Cash Flow Diagram

```
        Int= 5,000 Int=4,000 Int=3,000 Int=2,000 Int=1,000
  C=10,000  C=10,000  C=10,000  C=10,000  C=10,000  C=10,000
  ————————————————————————————————————————————— L = 150,000
     0        1        2        3        4        5
```

Every dollar of interest saves $0.40 in tax at a 40% effective tax rate.

After-Tax Cash Flow Diagram

```
        Int= 3,000 Int=2,400 Int=1,800 Int=1,200   Int=600
  C=10,000  C=10,000  C=10,000  C=10,000  C=10,000  C=10,000
  ————————————————————————————————————————————— CF = 114,000
     0        1        2        3        4        5
Net CF=-10,000  -13,000  -12,400  -11,800  -11,200  -10,600
```

Costs vary by a constant gradient of $600 for years 1 to 5.

PW Eq: 0 = -10,000 - [13,000 - 600$(A/G_{i,5})$]$(P/A_{i,5})$ + 114,000$(P/F_{i,5})$
        i = DCFROR = 19.9%

The after-tax cost of borrowed money is 10%(1-.4 tax rate) or 6.0% which is less than the cash investment DCFROR of 13.7% so borrowed money works for the investor and the leveraged investment DCFROR of 19.9% is greater than the cash investment DCFROR of 13.7%.

11-2 Solution: Develop vs Sell Now Leveraged Analysis

	$C_{Bldgs}=30$	Income/Yr =	65	70	75
$C_{Land}=1$ (Sunk)	$C_{Equip}= 5$	OpCost/Yr =	25	30	35

-2		0 (Now)	1	2	3

Leveraged Develop Cash Flows:

Year	0	1	2	3	3 Salv
Revenue		65.00	70.00	75.00	40.00
-Operating Costs		-25.00	-30.00	-35.00	
-Deprec/Writeoff		-1.63	-2.18	-1.83	-30.37*
-Interest		-3.60	-3.03	-2.40	
Taxable Income		34.77	34.79	35.77	9.63
-Tax @ 35%		-12.17	-12.18	-12.52	-3.37
Net Income		22.60	22.61	23.25	6.26
+Deprec/Writeoff		1.63	2.18	1.83	30.37*
-Principal		-4.72	-5.29	-19.99	
-Cap. Costs	-35.00				
+Borrowed $	30.00				
Cash Flow	-5.00	19.51	19.50	5.09	36.53

41.72

Sale Cash Flow:

Year	0
Sale Value	7.0
-Book Writeoff	-1.0
Taxable	6.0
-Tax (35%)	-2.1
Net Income	3.9
+Book Writeoff	1.0
Cash Flow	4.9

$NPV_{Sell} = 4.9$

*Includes land and equipment.

$$NPV @ 20\% = -5.00+19.51(P/F_{20,1})+19.50(P/F_{20,2})+41.72(P/F_{20,3}) = +\$48.94$$

with factors: 0.8333, 0.6944, 0.5787

DCFROR = 401%, "i" value that makes NPV equal to zero

Since these projects are mutually exclusive we select the project with the largest NPV which is the "Develop" alternative with an NPV of +48.7.

Depreciation Calculations

Yr 1	5(0.1429)	= 0.72
Yr 1	30(1/31.5)(11.5/12)	= 0.91
Yr 2	5(0.2449)	= 1.23
Yr 2	30(1/31.5)	= 0.95
Yr 3	5(0.1749)	= 0.88
Yr 3	30(1/31.5)	= 0.95
Yr 3	Writeoff on 5	= 2.18
Yr 3	Writeoff on 30	= 27.19
Yr 3	Land Writeoff	= 1.00

Mortgage Payment: $30(A/P_{12,5}) = 8.32$

Year	1	2	3
Principal	30.00	25.28	19.99
Interest	3.60	3.03	2.40
Princ. Pd	4.72	5.29	19.99

11-3 Solution: Petroleum Property Evaluation

Develop (Before-Tax) Time Diagram

```
                                    Rev=7.0
                       IDC=2.0       OC=1.2
                       Tang=1.5     IDC=2.0    Rev=11.0    Rev=9.0
 Acq=3.0 (Sunk)      Borrow=4.0    Tang=1.0     OC=2.5      OC=2.1
                                                                         L=6.5
 ─────────────────────────────────────────────────────────────────────────────
   -1                    0(Now)       1          2            3
```

Develop Cash Flows

Year	0	1	2	3	3 Salv
Revenue		7.00	11.00	9.00	6.50
-Royalties		-1.05	-1.65	-1.35	
Net Revenue		5.95	9.35	7.65	
-Oper Costs		-1.20	-2.50	-2.10	
-Intangible	-1.40	-1.40			
-Depreciation	-0.21	-0.51	-0.51	-0.36	
-Deprec Write-off					-0.91
-Amortization	-0.12	-0.24	-0.24	-0.24	-0.36
-Interest		-0.48	-0.40	-0.32	
Depletion		-0.30	-0.48	-0.42	-1.80
Taxable Inc	-1.73	1.82	5.22	4.21	3.43
-Tax @ 40%	0.69	-0.73	-2.09	-1.68	-1.37
Net Income	-1.04	1.09	3.13	2.53	2.06
+Depreciation	0.21	0.51	0.51	0.36	0.91
+Depletion		0.30	0.48	0.42	1.80
+Amortization	0.12	0.24	0.24	0.24	0.36
-Principal		-0.63	-0.71	-2.66	
-Cap. Costs	-2.10	-1.60			
+Borrowed	4.00				
Cash Flow	1.19	-0.09	3.65	0.89	5.13

Sell Cash Flow

Year	0
Sale Value	5.0
-Write-off	-3.0
Taxable Inc.	2.0
-Tax @ 40%	-0.8
Net Income	1.2
+Write-off	3.0
Cash Flow	4.2

$NPV_{Sell} = 4.2$

NPV_{Dev} @ 25% = 6.54 > 4.2, Select Develop

Since neither project has any negative cash flow upon which to properly calculate DCFROR, both alternatives offer infinite leveraged DCFROR's on total investment. Incremental DCFROR analysis is required to make a proper economic decision. The incremental analysis is on the next page.

Loan Payment Schedule:
$4(A/P_{12,5}) = 1.11$

	Princ Bal	Interest	Principal Paid
Yr 1	4.00	0.48	0.63
Yr 2	3.37	0.40	0.71
Yr 3	2.67	0.32	2.66

Cost Depletion Schedule:
Yr 1 3(0.10)   = 0.30
Yr 2 3(0.16)   = 0.48 or [0.16X/(X-0.1X)](3-0.3) = 0.48, etc.

11-3 *Solution Continued:*

Incremental DCFROR Analysis:

	1.19	-0.09	3.65	0.89	5.13
Cash Flow "Develop"					
	0	1	2	3	3+

	4.2	-	-	-	-
Cash Flow "Sell Now"					
	0	1	2	3	3+

	-3.01	-0.09	3.65	0.89	5.13
Incremental "Develop-Sell Now" Cash Flows					
	0	1	2	3	3+

6.02

Incremental PW Eq: $0 = -3.01 - 0.09(P/F_{i,1}) + 3.65(P/F_{i,2})$

$$+ 6.02(P/F_{i,3})$$

i = Incremental DCFROR = 56.4% > i^* of 25%, so accept development

Incremental NPV @ 25% = +2.3 > 0, so accept development

Or,

The same incremental NPV results from NPV_{Dev} - NPV_{Sell}:

Incremental NPV = 6.5 - 4.2 = 2.3

11-4 Solution: Silver Property, Values in Millions

Acq Cost =2.0   Rev=4.5   Rev=6.0   Rev=7.5
Equipment =3.0   OC =3.0   OC=3.37   OC=3.75
Borrowed $=4.0   Dev=1.5

                                                              Salv = 6.0
      0   1   2   3

Loan Amortization Schedule: Cost Depletion Schedule:
4.0(A/P$_{10,10}$) = 0.65   Yr 1   2(0.3/3)   = 0.2
                                               Yr 2   (2-0.2)(0.3/2.7)   = 0.2
                                               Yr 3   (1.8-0.71)(0.3/2.4) = 0.14

Year   Interest   Principal
  1   4(0.1)   =0.4   0.65-0.4 =0.25
  2   3.75(0.1)=0.37   0.65-0.37=0.28
  3   3.47(0.1)=0.35   3.47

Cash Flows:

Year	0	1	2	3	3 Salv
Revenue		4.50	6.00	7.50	6.00
-Operating Costs		-3.00	-3.38	-3.75	
-Development		-1.05			
-Depreciation		-0.43	-0.73	-0.52	
-Deprec Writeoff					-1.32
-Amortization		-0.05	-0.09	-0.09	-0.22
-Interest		-0.40	-0.37	-0.35	
Before Depletion		-0.43	1.43	2.79	4.46
-50% Limit		0	-0.71	1.39	
-Percent Depl (15%)		0.68	0.90	-1.13	
-Cost Depletion		-0.20	0.20	0.14	
Taxable Income		-0.63	0.72	1.66	4.46
-Tax @ 40%		0.25	-0.29	-0.67	-1.78
Net Income		-0.38	0.43	1.00	2.68
+Depreciation		0.43	0.73	0.52	1.32
+Depletion		0.20	0.71	1.13	
+Amortization		0.05	0.09	0.09	0.22
-Principal		-0.25	-0.28	-3.47	
-Capital Costs	-5.00	-0.45*			
+Borrowed	4.00				
Cash Flow	-1.00	-0.40	1.68	-0.73	4.22

PW Eq: $0 = -1.00-0.40(P/F_{i,1})+1.68(P/F_{i,2})-0.73(P/F_{i,3})+4.22(P/F_{i,3})$

       i = Leveraged DCFROR = 73.25%

This is the "i" value that makes NPV for this leveraged investment NPV
equal to zero.

11-5 Solution: Land Acquisition Analysis

	Escalated $ Sale Price =	X
Borrowed $ = 160,000	Interest =	16,000
Cost of Land = 200,000	Loan Principal Payment =	160,000

$$
\underset{0}{\rule{0pt}{0pt}} \qquad\qquad\qquad\qquad\qquad\qquad\qquad \underset{1\ \text{year}}{\rule{0pt}{0pt}}
$$

Year	0	1
Escalated $ Sale Revenue		X
-Interest		-16,000
-Book Value (Initial Cost)		-200,000
Taxable Gain		X-216,000
-Tax @ 34%		-.34X+ 73,440
Net Income		.66X-142,560
+Book Value		+200,000
-Capital Cost	-200,000	
+Borrowed $	160,000	-160,000
Cash Flow	-40,000	.66X-102,560

For a 30% constant dollar DCFROR and 10% inflation per year, the equivalent escalated dollar DCFROR is calculated as follows:

$$i = (1+0.10)(1+0.30) - 1$$

$$= 0.430 \text{ or } 43.0\%$$

$$
\overset{0.6993}{\rule{0pt}{0pt}}
$$
PW Eq: $0 = -40,000 + (0.66X-102,560)(P/F_{43\%,1})$

$$40,000 = 0.46X - 71,720$$

X = \$242,870 = the escalated dollar sale price to give a 30% constant dollar DCFROR on leveraged equity investment.

11-6 Solution: Rental Machinery Analysis,
            All Values in Thousands of Dollars

Working Capital =	10	Rev/yr =	150	180	210	
Deprec Equip.	= 150	OC/yr =	50	70	90	
						Salv = 50
	0		1	2	3	3 Including WC Return

Escalated Dollar Cash Flow Calculations

Year	0	1	2	3	3 Salv
Revenue		150.00	180.00	210.00	50.00
-Oper Costs		-50.00	-70.00	-90.00	
-Depreciation	-21.43	-36.73	-26.24	-18.74	-46.86
-Interest		-12.00	-8.00	-4.00	
-Writeoffs					-10.00
Taxable Income	-21.43	51.27	75.76	97.26	-6.86
-Tax @ 40%	8.57	-20.51	-30.30	-38.90	2.74
Net Income	-12.86	30.76	45.46	58.35	-4.12
+Depreciation	21.43	36.73	26.24	18.74	46.86
-Principal		-40.00	-40.00	-40.00	
+Writeoffs					10.00
-Capital Costs	-160.00				
+Borrowed $	120.00				
Cash Flow	-31.43	27.49	31.70	37.10	52.74

                                                        89.84

Leveraged Escalated Dollar PW Eq:

$0 = -31.43 + 27.49(P/F_{i,1}) + 31.7(P/F_{i,2}) + 89.84(P/F_{i,3})$

i = Leveraged Escalated \$ DCFROR = 104.8%

NPV @ 20% = +\$65.48

Constant Dollar Equivalent Cash Flows:

Year 0	Year 1	Year 2	Year 3
-31.43	$27.49(P/F_{10,1})=24.99$	$31.7(P/F_{10,2})=26.2$	$89.84(P/F_{10,3})=67.5$

Leveraged Constant Dollar PW Eq:

$0 = -31.43 + 24.99(P/F_{i',1}) + 26.2(P/F_{i',2}) + 67.5(P/F_{i',3})$

i' = Leveraged Constant \$ DCFROR = 86.2%

Using Equation 5-1 we can check the results:

$(1+i) = (1+f)(1+i')$, $(1 + 1.048) = (1.1)(1.862) = 2.048$, so equivalent.

11-7 Solution: Depreciable Investment Analysis (in Thousands of Dollars)

```
Deprec Equip  = 100
Development   =  10      Revenues/yr = 150              150
Work Capital  =  30      Op Costs/yr = 118             118   WC Return
                                                       ────   = 30
                        0                 1 ............... 5
```

Cash Investment Analysis:

Year	0	1	2	3	4	5	5 Salv
Revenue		150.0	150.0	150.0	150.0	150.0	30.0
-Oper Costs		-118.0	-118.0	-118.0	-118.0	-118.0	
-Development	-10.0						
-Depreciation	-10.0	-20.0	-20.0	-20.0	-20.0	-10.0	
-Writeoffs							-30.0
Taxable Income	-20.0	12.0	12.0	12.0	12.0	22.0	
-Tax @ 40%	8.0	-4.8	-4.8	-4.8	-4.8	-8.8	
Net Income	-12.0	7.2	7.2	7.2	7.2	13.2	
+Depreciation	10.0	20.0	20.0	20.0	20.0	10.0	
+Writeoffs							30.0
-Capital Costs	-130.0						
Cash Flow	-132.0	27.2	27.2	27.2	27.2	23.2	30.0

$$53.2$$

Cash PW Eq: $0 = -132 + 27.2(P/A_{i,4}) + 53.2(P/F_{i,5})$
           i = Cash Investment DCFROR = 6.5%

Leveraged Investment Cash Flows:

Year	0	1	2	3	4	5	5 Salv
Revenue		150.0	150.0	150.0	150.0	150.0	30.0
-Oper Costs		-118.0	-118.0	-118.0	-118.0	-118.0	
-Development	-10.0						
-Depreciation	-10.0	-20.0	-20.0	-20.0	-20.0	-10.0	
-Interest		-12.0	-9.6	-7.2	-4.8	-2.4	
-Writeoffs							-30.0
Taxable Income	-20.0	0.0	2.4	4.8	7.2	19.6	0.0
-Tax @ 40%	8.0	0.0	-1.0	-1.9	-2.9	-7.8	0.0
Net Income	-12.0	0.0	1.4	2.9	4.3	11.8	
+Depreciation	10.0	20.0	20.0	20.0	20.0	10.0	
-Principal		-20.0	-20.0	-20.0	-20.0	-20.0	
+Writeoffs							30.0
-Capital Costs	-130.0						
+Borrowed $	100.0						
Cash Flow	-32.0	0.0	1.4	2.9	4.3	1.8	30.0

$$31.8$$

11-7 *Solution Continued:*   Depreciable Investment Analysis,
                              In Thousands of Dollars

Lev. PW Eq: $0 = -32.0+1.4(P/F_{i,2})+2.9(P/F_{i,3})+4.3(P/F_{i,4})+31.8(P/F_{i,5})$

i = Leveraged Investment DCFROR = 5.2%

Results for leveraged analysis are less attractive because the after-tax
cost of borrowed money (7.2%) exceeds the project cash investment
DCFROR, hence leverage works against the investor.

11-8 Solution: Leveraged Evaluation of Problem 10-10

Purchase Cash Flows (Cost Analysis)

Year	Time 0	1	2	3	Salvage
Revenue					50
-Operating Costs	-18	-39	-45	-24	
-Interest Payment		-15	-10	-5	
-Depreciation	-40	-64	-38	-23	-35
Taxable Income	-58	-118	-93	-52	15
-Tax @ 40%	23	47	37	21	-6
Net Income	-35	-71	-56	-31	9
+Depreciation	40	64	38	23	35
-Princ. Paid		-50	-50	-50	
+Loan Income	150				
-Capital Costs	-200				
Cash Flow	-45	-57	-68	-58	44

Present Worth Cost @ 15% = $154.8
Present Worth Cost @ 25% = $141.3

Leasing Cash Flows (Cost Analysis)

Year	Time 0	1	2	3
-Operating Costs	-18.00	-39.00	-45.00	-24.00
-Lease Payments	-36.00	-72.00	-72.00	-36.00
Taxable Income	-54.00	-111.00	-117.00	-60.00
-Tax Due @ 40%	21.60	44.40	46.80	24.00
Net Income	-32.40	-66.60	-70.20	-36.00
Cash Flow	-32.40	-66.60	-70.20	-36.00

Present Worth Cost @ 15% = $167.1
Present Worth Cost @ 25% = $149.0

Selecting the alternative with the least present worth cost suggests
that purchasing the equipment is now the economic choice. This was not
the choice in evaluating the alternatives from a 100% cash equity
analysis.

11-9 Solution:

Uniform mortgage payments over 3 years, at 12% annual interest:

$500,000 (A/P_{12,3}) = $208,175$

	Year 1	Year 2	Year 3
Before-Tax Interest	60,000	42,219	23,304
Principal Payment	148,175	165,955	185,870

Leveraged Cash Flows:

Year	0	1	2	3
Cash Investment CF	-800,000	400,000	500,000	550,000
-Loan Principal Pmt.	-	-148,175	-165,955	-185,870
-After-Tax Interest*	-	-36,000	-25,331	-13,382
+Borrowed Dollars	+500,000	-	-	-
Leveraged CF	-300,000	215,825	308,714	350,748

*After-Tax Interest = (1-tax rate)(interest)

A) PW Eq: $0 = -300,000+215,825(P/F_{i,1})+308,714(P/F_{i,2})+350,748(P/F_{i,3})$

NPV @ 72% = -$1,238
NPV @ 70% = $5,169

i = Leveraged DCFROR = $70\%+(72\%-70\%)(5,169-0)/(5,169+1,238) = 71.61\%$

B) Calculate the NPV at i* = 25%

$NPV = -300,000+215,825(P/F_{25,1})+308,714(P/F_{25,2})+350,748(P/F_{25,3})$

$= +\$249,820$

Let the acquisition cost in year 0 = X

X/3 is the annual amortization deduction

(X/3)(0.4) = 0.133X = tax savings per year

$$X - 0.133X(P/A_{25,3}) = 249,820$$
$$\phantom{X - 0.133X(P/A_{25,3}) = 2}^{1.952}$$

X = $337,419 = acquisition cost to give a 25% DCFROR*

AUXILIARY PROBLEMS

1. You have been asked to evaluate whether it is economically better to use a submersible centrifugal pump system or a down-hole positive displacement rod pump system to lift crude oil 4,000 feet in a well with an estimated producing life of 12 years. The submersible pump system's initial installed cost is $100,000 including tubing, wiring, and surface gear while the installed rod pump's cost, including sucker rods and surface gear, is $135,000. It is estimated that the submersible pump will need to be replaced every 3 years with a similar refurbished used pump for a cost of $35,000 at year 3, $45,000 at year 6 and $55,000 at year 9. Year 12 salvage value of the submersible pump is $50,000. The rod pump is estimated to need replacing every 4 years for costs of $8,000 at year 4, and $12,000 at year 8. Due to corrosion, the salvage value of the rod pump system at year 12 is estimated to be 0. The minimum ROR is 15%. Use present worth cost analysis to determine which pumping system is economically better. Verify your conclusion with ROR analysis.

2.

		I=100	I=250	I=375	I=500	I=500	L=100 I=400
C=100		C=500	C=100	C=125	C=150	C=150	C=200
0	1		2	3	4	5	6

A project has costs and revenues as shown on the diagram in thousands of dollars. The investor's minimum rate of return is 15%, calculate the ROR, NPV, PVR and Growth ROR for the project using a 6-year evaluation life.

3. A loader is being considered to tram coal from a stockpile to a coal load-out facility. The cost of the machine is estimated at $900,000 with an estimated salvage value of $225,000 at the end of year 7. Operating costs are estimated to be $200,000 per year with major repairs of $150,000 and $100,000 required at the end of the 3rd and 5th years respectively. Given the required tram distance, it is estimated the machine can move 2,400 tons of coal per day, 250 days per year. For a desired minimum rate of return of 12%, calculate the present and annual cost of operating this machine over the next 7 years and calculate the break-even cost per ton of coal being trammed.

4. Rank these non-mutually exclusive alternatives for a 20% opportunity cost of capital. Values are given in thousands of dollars.

		I=100	I=150				
A)	C=100	C=200	C=250	I=300	I=300	I=300	I=300
	0	1	2	3	4	5	6

			I=200				
B)	–	C=300	C=150	I=250	I=250	I=250	
	0	1	2	3	4	5	

C)	C=200	I=170	C=200	I=350	I=350	I=350	C=100
	0	1	2	3	4	5	6

5. A manager is trying to evaluate the economics of purchasing or leasing a natural gas processing facility. It may be purchased and installed on company land for $1,000,000 or leased for $250,000 per year with beginning of year lease payments. With either alternative, the annual revenue to the plant for natural gas liquids is expected to be $1,500,000 with annual operating costs of $800,000. The life of the plant is estimated at 8 years. If purchased, the net salvage value of the plant at the end of year 8 is estimated at $150,000. For a 15% minimum rate of return, determine whether the manager should purchase or lease the processing facility.

6. Evaluate the economic potential of purchasing a gold property now (time 0) for a $2 million mineral rights acquisition cost. Mining equipment costs of $3 million will be incurred at year 0. Mineral development costs of $1 million will be incurred at year 1. Production is expected to start in year 1 with 150,000 tons of gold ore. Production in years 2, 3, and 4 is estimated at 250,000 tons per year. It is estimated that the gold ore reserves will be depleted at the end of year 4. Reclamation costs (treated as operating expenses) of $0.5 million will be incurred at year 5. Equipment will be sold at year 5 for $1 million. All gold ore is estimated to contain 0.1 ounce of gold per ton of ore, and metallurgical recovery is estimated at 90%. The price of gold is forecast to be $300 per ounce in year 1, escalating 15% in year 2, 20% in year 3, and 10% in year 4. Operating costs are estimated at $20 per ton of ore produced in year 1, escalating 8% per year thereafter. Make before-tax ROR, NPV, PVR and Growth ROR analyses for a minimum ROR of 15%.

7. Consideration is currently being given to determine whether a dozer should be purchased or leased for necessary service over the next 5 years. The time 0 purchase price for the dozer is $750,000. Maintenance costs are estimated to be $50,000 at time 0, $100,000 at year 1, with that value increasing by 10% per year at years 2, 3, and 4, and $70,000 at year 5. Major repairs of $180,000 at the end of year 2, and $160,000 at the end of year 4 are also expected. The salvage value is estimated at $50,000 at the end of year 5. Alternately, the machine may be leased for $82.50 per hour. It is assumed the machine will operate 18 hours per day, 26 days per month, 12 months per year. An $82.50 per hour lease rate applies for the first 3 years, and is expected to increase by 10% to $90.75 per hour for years 4 and 5. The hourly lease rate includes all maintenance and repair costs. Allocate the value of the lease payments for the first 6 months to year 0. Allocate months 7 through 18 lease payments to year 1, and so forth, with months 43 through 54 allocated to year 4. Allocate the final six months of payments (55 through 60) to month 60 to best account for the time value of money. Assume the before-tax minimum rate of return is 20%. Calculate the present value (NPV) to determine which of these two alternatives is the best economic choice. What is the lease cost per hour that would make leasing break-even with purchasing?

8. Make the same analyses asked for in Auxiliary Problem #7 on an after-tax basis. Assume that if you purchase, the machine will be depreciated over 7 years using modified ACRS depreciation with the half-year convention, beginning in year 1. Expense all maintenance and repair costs in the year incurred assuming other income exists to utilize all deductions in the year they are realized. Write-off the remaining book value at the end of year 5. If the machine is leased, assume it is an operating lease so all lease payments will be 100% deductible in the year they are realized. The effective income tax rate is estimated to be 38%. Assume the after-tax minimum DCFROR is 20%. Calculate the after-tax present worth costs for each alternative and the incremental after-tax NPV to determine which of these two alternatives is the economic choice. Determine the lease cost per hour that would make leasing break-even with purchasing.

9. Development of a natural gas property is projected to involve production, costs and prices as follows with costs expressed in thousands of dollars and production and price in units as noted.
    Mcf = thousand cubic feet, MMcf=million cubic feet and M$=thousands of dollars.

Year	0	1	2	3	4
Production, MMcf/Yr		300	700	500	150
Price, $/Mcf		2.00	2.25	2.50	2.75
Royalties, % of Revenues		15%	15%	15%	15%
Operating Cost, M$		60	70	80	90
Intangible Well Cost, M$	600	300			
Tangible Well Cost, M$		400			
Tangible Pipeline Cost, M$		200			
Mineral Acquisition Cost, M$	100				

A) Calculate the annual before-tax cash flow, and then calculate ROR, NPV, PVR and Growth ROR for a 15% minimum ROR. Assume the investor has a 100% working interest in the property and that salvage value is 0.
B) Assume this project is in an area requiring a $600,000 reclamation cost at the end of year 5. Calculate a valid project ROR.

10. A mutually exclusive alternative variation of the development described in Auxiliary Problem #9A is to delay the start of development until 4 years from now (time 0) to take advantage of sharply escalating natural gas prices expected to occur 4 to 8 years from now. The 4-year development delay would make the start of new development time 0 equal to year 4 in Problem #9A. Assume the mineral rights acquisition cost is incurred at time 0 and all other costs given in Problem #9A will escalate 5% per year over the 4-year delay period. Assume that year 5 to 8 production rates for the delayed project will be the same as in years 1 to 4 in Problem #9A. The natural gas selling price of $2.75 per Mcf in year 4 of Problem #9A is estimated to escalate 20% per year over the following 4 years. Is it better to develop now for the development scenario described in Problem #9A or delay the development for 4 years as described in this problem statement? Use the analysis method of your choice for a minimum ROR of 15%.

11. Two used machines can be acquired for $60,000 per machine to provide necessary service for the next 2 years. The salvage of these machines is estimated at $20,000 per machine at the end of year 2 when the old machines will be replaced with one new machine capable of providing the same total service. The new machine would cost $350,000 at the end of year 2 and is anticipated to yield a salvage value of $170,000 at the end of year 4. Operating costs associated with the used machines are estimated at $60,000 per machine at year 1 and $70,000 per machine at year 2. Operating costs with a new machine purchased at year 2 are estimated to be $80,000 at year 3 and $85,000 at year 4. Instead of buying the old machines and replacing them at year 2, a new machine providing the necessary service can be purchased today (time 0) for a cost of $300,000. Service with either the old or new machines is needed for the next 4 years; therefore, a 4-year evaluation life should be used. It is estimated that a new machine purchased at time 0 will yield a salvage value of $80,000 at year 4. Operating costs with a new machine purchased now (time 0) are estimated at $75,000 at year 1, $80,000 at year 2, $85,000 at year 3, and $90,000 at year 4. Assuming a minimum discount rate of 15%, use a present worth cost analysis of each alternative to determine the least cost approach for providing the necessary service. Then, determine the 4 equal end-of-year revenues at years 1 through 4 for each alternative that would cover the cost of service and yield a 15% ROR.

12. Two mutually exclusive alternatives exist to invest $100,000 as shown on the following time diagrams.

A) -100,000   -   - . . . . . . -   627,500

       0   1   2 6   7

B) -100,000   44,190   44,190 44,190

       0   1   2 7

Assuming a minimum ROR of 15%, determine the economically better choice using:

A) ROR analysis
B) NPV analysis
C) PVR analysis
D) Growth ROR analysis
E) Future worth profit analysis

13. Investment of $100,000 at time zero is projected to generate increasing annual production that gives today's dollar before-tax cash flow (BTCF) of $30,000 in year 1, $40,000 in year 2, and $50,000 in year 3. Year 3 salvage value is projected to be $40,000. All values are end of period values. The BTCF and salvage are projected to escalate 8% in year 1, 6% in year 2, and 4% in year 3. Calculate the escalated dollar ROR and NPV for a minimum escalated dollar ROR of 20%. Then calculate the equivalent constant dollar project ROR and NPV, assuming inflation will be 8% in year 1, 10% in year 2, and 12% in year 3.

14. A chemical company wants you to analyze whether it is better economically to sell patent rights to a new chemical process for $300,000 cash now (time 0) or whether it would be better to keep the patent rights and develop them using one of two development scenarios for which projected costs and incomes are given on the following time diagrams. All dollar values are in thousands of dollars.

A) C=700   I=100   I=420   I=420
             C=300   C=200 . . . . . . C=200

       0   1   2 9

B) C=500   I=670   I=670   I=670
             C=800   OC=250 . . . . . OC=250

       0   1   2 9

Use ROR analysis to determine whether it is better to sell, or develop with the A or B scenario, assuming a minimum ROR of 15%. Verify your results with NPV and PVR analyses. If the minimum ROR is raised to 25%, use any valid analysis to determine the economic choice.

15. Consider a cost of $16 million for an ore conveyor system at time 0. Operating costs are estimated at $2.5 million in year 1 increasing by an arithmetic gradient of $300,000 per year in each year after year 1 for an estimated 15-year mine life. Two major repairs costing $4 million and $6 million are expected at the end of evaluation years 5 and 10. Salvage value is estimated to be $7 million in evaluation year 15. The alternative to the conveyor system is to use 7 new haul trucks with a 170-ton capacity and a cost of $800,000 per truck at time 0. The haul trucks would have a 5-year life and salvage values of $100,000 each. Operating costs per truck are estimated to be $400,000 in year 1 increasing by an arithmetic gradient of $60,000 per truck year through year 5. In 5 years, the 7 trucks would be replaced with new trucks costing an estimated $1,400,000 per truck with expected salvage values in year 10 of $150,000 per truck. Operating costs per truck are estimated at $550,000 in year 6 increasing by an arithmetic gradient of $70,000 per truck for evaluation years 7 through 10. At the end of year 10, the 7 trucks would be replaced again with new trucks costing $2,300,000 per truck with an estimated salvage value of $200,000 per truck 5 years later in evaluation year 15. Operating costs per truck are estimated at $700,000 in year 11 and to increase by an arithmetic gradient of $80,000 per truck for evaluation years 12 through 15. Evaluate the economics of using the ore conveyor system as an economic alternative to the haul trucks. Use PW Cost analysis for a 15-year life and a minimum rate of return of 15%.

16. Production of crude oil from a 10,000-foot deep north sea well, with L-80 carbon steel 5 inch tubing, requires down-hole injection of chemicals to control tubing corrosion due to high temperatures, pressures and corrosive chlorides in the crude oil. It is proposed to replace the L-80 carbon steel tubing, which cost $8.50 per foot 1 year ago, with 13% chrome stainless steel tubing costing $30 per foot. Ten thousand feet of tubing is needed and installation costs are estimated at $80,000. Annual cost savings in chemicals, labor and chemical injection equipment are projected to be $100,000 in year 1 following the installation of the new tubing with savings escalating 7% per year in succeeding years. Using NPV for a 15% minimum ROR, a 6-year evaluation life, and a salvage value of 0 in year 6, determine the economic desirability of replacing the steel tubing. Assume the existing L-80 carbon steel tubing has no salvage value at time 0. What breakeven life will cause the 13% chrome tubing replacement investment to yield a 15% ROR?

17. An existing mineral operation is expected to generate annual before-tax cash flow (revenue − operating costs) of $100 million per year at each of years 1, 2, 3, and 4. Being considered, is the purchase of the mineral rights in an adjacent property for $40 million now (time 0) with the expectation that $50 million would be spent on development and equipment at year 1, and another $55 million at year 2. This expansion would make the total project revenue minus operating costs $100 million at year 1 (same as present scenario), $140 million at year 2, $150 million at year 3, $160 million at year 4, and $65 million in each of years 5 through 10. Equipment will need to be repaired or replaced for an expected cost of $65 million at the end of year 6 with a salvage value at the end of year 10 of $40 million. Make before-tax NPV analysis to determine whether the project expansion is economically justifiable, given a minimum ROR of 15%. Verify your NPV conclusion using before-tax ROR and PVR analyses.

PRESENT:	−	100	100	100	100	0	0	0	0	0	0
	0	1	2	3	4	5	6	7	8	9	10

EXPAND:	-40	100	140	150	160	65	65	65	65	65	65
		-50	-55				-65				40
	0	1	2	3	4	5	6	7	8	9	10

18. A mineral property is producing at a rate that will generate $5 million in annual net revenue (revenue minus operating costs) during the next year (assume end of year 1). Escalation of operating costs is expected to be offset by sales escalation in future years, so that annual end-of-year net revenue will remain constant at $5 million each year until mineral reserves are depleted. At the current production rate, mineral reserves will be depleted 10 years from now. Increase of the production rate is being considered by incurring a $2 million equipment and development cost now (time 0) and a $4 million equipment and development cost a year from now (year 1). These expansion costs would permit increasing mineral production to give projected total net revenues of $6 million at year 1 and $8 million per year at years 2 through 8 when reserves will be depleted at the increased production rate. Use NPV analysis to evaluate the economic desirability of the expansion investments for a minimum ROR of 20%. Verify your results using ROR analysis and PVR analysis.

```
PRESENT: -      I=5    I=5  . . . . . . . . . . . .  I=5   I=5   I=5
         ─────────────────────────────────────────────────────────
          0      1      2   . . . . . . . . . . . .   8     9    10
                I=6
EXPAND:  C=2    C=4    I=8  . . . . . . . . . . .  I=8    0     0
         ─────────────────────────────────────────────────────────
          0      1      2   . . . . . . . . . . . .   8     9    10
```

19. A chemical company has done research in recent years that has resulted in a new process patent. To acquire the patent rights, an outside investor has offered to pay $2 million now and another $4 million in 2 equal deferred payments of $2 million each 4 and 5 years from now. The investor has an excellent credit rating and sufficient assets so that the offer seems financially solid. The company estimates that internal development of a new plant to implement the patent rights would cost $0.5 million now and $4 million a year from now to generate net income (revenue minus operating costs) of $1 million a year from now and $2 million per year 2 and 3 years from now. If the plant is developed internally, it is projected that it would be sold for $6 million 3 years from now. Use ROR analysis to determine if the economics favor internal development or selling, assuming other opportunities exist to invest capital at 15%. Determine the single lump sum sale value that, received now, would make the economics of selling and developing equivalent.

20. A deep water-flood project has been on line for 2 years. Engineering calculations indicate that the producing wells are each capable of 750 barrels of fluid per day (BFPD), but problems with the existing artificial lift system has limited production to 400 BFPD per well. The project engineer has to decide whether to (1) reduce the injection rates to match the artificial lift capabilities, or (2) maintain injection and modify the artificial lift equipment to lift larger volumes of fluid (750 BFPD). Production for each alternative is listed in the following table.

YEAR	REDUCED INJECTION Production (M Bbl)	MODIFIED LIFT Production (M Bbl)
1	1200	1500
2	1300	1700
3	1500	2200
4	1700	2150
5	1400	1700
6	1300	1500
7	1200	1300
8	1100	750
9	1000	350
10	750	100
11	400	0

20. Continued...

The time 0 cost of the upgraded artificial lift facility is estimated at $7 million, with operating costs of $1.5 million more per year relative to the present operation. Working interest is 100%, the net revenue interest is 80%, and oil price per barrel is $24. Assume escalation of incremental operating expenses exactly offsets escalation of incremental revenues. Determine whether it is economically preferable to reduce the injection rates or to redesign and modify the lift system if the minimum acceptable before-tax ROR is 15%.

21. A mining company is evaluating whether it is economically desirable to pay $5 million now for a partially developed gold mine if another $3 million must be spent a year from now for further development with a 70% probability of success. If successful, another $4 million must be spent 2 years from now with a 90% probability of this final investment giving a profitable producing gold mine that will generate profits of $4 million per year for 20 years of production starting 3 years from now. Assume a washout of income and operating cost escalation. Salvage value is estimated at 0 at the end of the project. If the project fails at years 1 or 2, assume net abandonment costs and salvage value will be 0. Assuming an escalated dollar minimum ROR of 20%, determine whether the project is economical.

22. A coal mining project has been on line for 2 years. Engineering mine plan calculations indicate that the present mine production can be increased to the accelerated coal mining production schedule shown below, by changing the mine plan and acquiring additional new equipment. The project engineer has to decide whether to (1) maintain current production rates, or (2) accelerate production by purchasing the additional mining equipment necessary to increase coal production.

YEAR	PRESENT PRODUCTION (Thousand Tons)	ACCELERATED PRODUCTION (Thousand Tons)
1	1200	1500
2	1300	1700
3	1500	2200
4	1700	2150
5	1400	1700
6	1300	1500
7	1200	1300
8	1100	750
9	1000	350
10	750	100
11	400	0

The time 0 cost of the accelerated coal mining production equipment is estimated at $7 million with operating costs of $1.5 million more a year relative to the current operation. Working interest is 100%, net revenue after royalties is 80%, and coal price per ton is $24.00. Assume escalation of incremental operating expenses exactly offsets escalation of incremental revenues. Is it economically desirable to maintain present coal mining production rates or to accelerate production? The minimum acceptable before-tax ROR is 15%.

23. BTCFs are in dollars.

A)	0	1	2	9
Revenue	–	8,000	8,500 → gradient = +500/yr	–
Costs	-25,000	–	–	

B)	0	1	2	10
Revenue	–	8,000	18,000	18,000
Costs	-12,000	-15,000	-10,000	-10,000

C)	0	1	2	3	11
Revenue	–	18,000	19,000	22,000	22,000
Oper Costs	–	-10,000	-10,000	-10,000	-10,000
Cap Costs	-20,000	–	-21,000	–	–

If alternatives A, B, and C are mutually exclusive, which alternative, if any, would be the economic choice is the minimum acceptable ROR is 20%? If alternatives A, B, and C are non-mutually exclusive, rank them in order of economic desirability using PVR.

24. A prospect consists of two parallel structures (referred to as "A" and "B") on opposite sides of a fault. Both structures are long and narrow and must be drilled separately. Structure A has two potentially productive zones, while structure B has only one potentially productive zone. The total area considered is 6,400 acres, 65% in structure A and 35% in structure B. Zone 1 has a geologic chance factor (probability of success) of 9% in structure A, and 25% in structure B. Zone 2, found only in structure A, has a geologic chance factor of 5% and is 500 feet deeper than zone 1. Assume development can only occur in the following cases:

   • All zones are productive.
   • Zone 2 of structure A and zone 1 of structure B are both productive.
   • Zones 1 and 2 of structure A are productive.

Draw a decision tree for this problem and label each branch with the appropriate probability of occurrence.

25. The acquisition of mineral rights at time 0 will cost $200,000 with expected exploration drilling costs at time 0 of $800,000 with a 20% probability of success. Exploration drilling failure will require incurring a $50,000 year 1 abandonment cost. If logs from the exploration well indicate success, well completion, producing equipment, tank battery and pipeline costs of $700,000 will be incurred at year 1 with an estimated 100% probability of successfully bringing the well into production. Year 1 operating profit (revenue minus operating expenses) of $300,000, and year 2 through 10 operating profit of $400,000 per year are projected over the well producing life. Make a big assumption and assume that declining production is offset by increased selling prices of crude oil and natural gas. If the exploration well is successful, two development wells will be drilled simultaneously at year 1 for an estimated cost of $600,000 per well with an 80% probability of success. Development drilling failure will require a $50,000 per well year 2 abandonment cost. Successful wells will be completed at year 2 for an estimated cost of $500,000 per well. Year 2 development well projected net revenues are $300,000 per well, and $500,000 per well per year in years 3 through 11. Make expected NPV and expected PVR analysis, assuming a minimum ROR of 15%.

26. A gold project is currently under consideration. It is estimated that $1,000,000 would be spent on defining reserves and acquiring the rights and necessary permits for the property at time 0. The acquisition cost would be followed by an investment of $5,000,000 in mine development, $7,000,000 in mine equipment, and $2,000,000 in working capital for spare parts, product inventories, etc. All three costs (development, equipment, and working capital) are allocated at the end of year 1. Working capital is assumed liquidated at the end of year 8 when the project is terminated. Revenue is treated as regular income at year 8.

    The property is expected to generate 6,000 tons of ore per day, 150 days per year, starting in year 2. Mining is limited to 150 days per year due to weather considerations. The ore is expected to have and average grade of 0.05 ounces of gold per ton with an anticipated recovery rate of 0.85. Assume the average selling price of gold is $330 per ounce per year, and operating costs are $210 per ounce per year. Escalation of price and operating costs each year is a washout, meaning the before-tax profits are constant each year at $120 per ounce ($330/oz minus $210/oz). In acquiring the property, the company has agreed to pay a 6% royalty on net profits (gross revenue minus operating costs) until the project pays out. After payout, the royalty changes to 30% of net profits for the remaining life of the project. Payout of the cumulative, undiscounted time 0 and year 1 capital costs of $15,000,000 is based on undiscounted net profits minus the 6% royalty.

    Calculate the ROR, NPV, and PVR for the mine development investor and also for the royalty recipient, assuming the before-tax, escalated dollar minimum ROR is 15%. Determine the before-tax dollar amount that could be invested in reclamation costs at year 9 that would give the development investor a 15% ROR.

27. Make the analysis asked for in Auxiliary Problem #26 on an after-tax basis. Assume the time 0 $1,000,000 acquisition cost will be deducted for tax purposes by cost depletion. The $7,000,000 year 1 equipment cost will be depreciated by 7year MACRS depreciation starting in year 1 with the half-year convention. Of the year 1 mining development cost of $5,000,000, 70% will be expensed at year 1 with the remaining 30% amortized over 60 months with a full 12-month deduction at year 1. Assume an effective income tax rate of 40%.

    Calculate the DCFROR, NPV, and PVR for the mine development investor and for the royalty recipient, assuming the before-tax escalated dollar minimum ROR is 15%. Determine the before-tax dollar amount that could be invested in reclamation costs at year 9 that would give the development investor a 15% after-tax DCFROR. Assume the cost would be 100% deductible at year 9. Neglecting the reclamation cost and prior to incurring costs at time 0, determine the before-tax acquisition cost (at time 0) that would give the development investor a 15% after-tax DCFROR.

28. An investor paid $100,000 for a machine today (time 0) that is estimated to have a 70% probability of successfully producing 5,000 product units per year for each of the next 3 years, at which time the machine is estimated to be obsolete with a salvage value of 0. Product price (the unknown, X, yet to be calculated) is estimated to be $X per unit in year 1 escalated dollars and to increase 10% per year in year 2 and 6% in year 3. Total operating costs are estimated at $8,000 in year 1 escalated dollars and to increase by 15% in year 2 and 8% in year 3. The annual inflation rate is estimated at 7%. Determine the year 1, 2, and 3 escalated dollar product selling price necessary for the investor to receive a 12% annually compounded constant dollar expected DCFROR on invested dollars. Use MACRS depreciation rates for a 5-year life, starting depreciation at time 0 with the half-year convention. Write-off the remaining book value at the end of year 3. Assume other taxable income exists to use time 0 negative taxable income against. Assume a 40% income tax rate. If the project fails, assume a zero net after-tax cash flow is realized in year 1 (30% of the time). This assumes that after-tax equipment dismantlement costs will exactly offset tax write-off and salvage value benefits and simplifies the problem.

29. A non-mineral project with the following cash investment after-tax cash flow stream has been analyzed.

-800,000		+400,000	+500,000	+500,000
0		1	2	3

Convert the cash investment cash flow to leveraged cash flow assuming $500,000 is borrowed at time 0 for 12% interest per year with the loan paid off in three uniform and equal mortgage payments at years 1, 2, and 3. Assume a 40% effective ordinary income tax rate.

A) Calculate the leveraged project DCFROR.
B) Determine the amount that could be paid at time 0 to acquire the rights to develop the leveraged project and realize a 25% leveraged DCFROR on equity dollars. Assume the acquisition cost is amortizable over three years (in each of years 1, 2, and 3).

30. A proposed project has today's dollar costs and revenues as follows:

C=200	Rev=300 OC=100	Rev=300 OC=100
0	1	2

For cases A through D, assume an escalated dollar i* of 12.0%:

A) Calculate the project escalated dollar NPV at time zero for revenue escalation of 5.0% in year 1 and 6.0% in year 2, and cost escalation of 8.0% in year 1 and 10.0% in year 2.
B) Calculate the project constant dollar NPV assuming 7.0% inflation per year and escalation of costs and revenue will be as defined in Part A.
C) Calculate the project escalated dollar NPV assuming today's dollar values equal escalated dollar values. State the explicit cost and revenue escalation assumption built into this analysis.
D) Calculate the project constant dollar NPV, assuming today's dollar values equal constant dollar values. Use the same 7.0% annual inflation rate. State the explicit cost and revenue escalation assumption built into this analysis.

31. You are to determine the investment DCFROR that an investor who pays $400,000 for an office building at time 0 would realize on equity investment based on the following data. Of the acquisition cost, 90% will be for the building that goes into service in the first month of year 1, (business buildings are real property and, therefore, depreciable straight line over 39 years). 10% of the acquisition is for land, which is deductible only against the terminal sale value estimated at $500,000 at the end of year 2. Any sale gain would be taxed as ordinary income. $320,000 of the acquisition cost will be borrowed at time 0 at 10% annual interest with the loan paid off over 5 years with uniform and equal mortgage payments. Assume unpaid loan principal will be paid off at the end of year 2 when the property is sold. Revenues are projected to be $80,000 in year 1 and $85,000 in year 2. Operating costs are estimated at $30,000 in year 1 and $35,000 in year 2. The effective ordinary income tax rate is 30% and other income exists against which to use deductions in any year negative taxable income exists.

    A) Calculate the leveraged investment DCFROR.
    B) Determine the maximum investment price that could be paid to give the investor a 15% leveraged DCFROR on his equity-invested dollars assuming the investment is 10% land and 90% building.
    C) Calculate the cash investment DCFROR that corresponds to the leveraged DCFROR calculated in part A for the $400,000 investment price. Determine the maximum investment price that would yield the investor a 15% cash equity investment DCFROR, assuming 10% for land and 90% for office building.

32. A project manager is evaluating whether it is economical to develop a project requiring expenditures at time 0 of $20,000 for land, $30,000 for inventory working capital, $80,000 for a business building, $240,000 for equipment and $60,000 for vehicles. Starting in year 1 he estimates that production will generate annual end-of-year escalated revenue of $500,000 with escalated operating costs of $300,000. In the following years, it is estimated that operating costs and revenue will both escalate at 10% per year. At the end of year 4, it is expected that all the assets and working capital can be sold for an escalated terminal value of $600,000. Use straight-line depreciation over 39 years for the building cost starting in year 1, assuming 12 months of service in year 1. Use MACRS depreciation for a 7-year life for the equipment cost starting in year 1 with the half-year convention and for a 5-year life for the vehicle cost starting in year 1 with the half-year convention. Assume the terminal value gain is taxed as ordinary income. Write-off the entire remaining tax book values at the end of year 4.

    Determine the investment DCFROR, assuming a 40% effective income tax rate. For an after-tax escalated dollar minimum ROR of 15%, determine the NPV and PVR.

33. A corporation has requested that you evaluate the economic potential of purchasing a gold property now (time 0) for a $2 million mineral rights acquisition cost. Mining equipment costs of $3 million will be incurred at time 0. The equipment will be placed into service at time 0 when depreciation starts. Use modified ACRS 7-year life depreciation with the half-year convention at time 0. Write-off the remaining book value at year 5. Mineral development costs of $1.5 million will be incurred at month 1 of year 1. Production is projected to start in year 1 with the mining of 150,000 tons of gold ore, with uniform production of 250,000 tons of gold ore per year in each of years 2, 3, and 4. It is expected that gold ore reserves will be depleted at the end of year 4. Reclamation costs, treated as operating expenses, estimated at $0.5 million in escalated dollars will be incurred at year 5 along with a projected $1 million in escalated dollars from equipment salvage value. All gold ore is estimated to contain 0.1 ounce of gold per ton of ore, and metallurgical recovery is estimated at 90%. Gold prices are estimated at $300 per ounce in year 1 and to escalate 15% in year 2, 20% in year 3, and 10% in year 4. Operating costs are estimated at $20 per ton of ore produced in year 1 and to escalate 8% per year. Assume other income exists against which to use negative taxable income in any year and an effective income tax rate is 40%.

A) Calculate the cash investment DCFROR and NPV for a minimum escalated dollar DCFROR of 15%.

B) Consider it likely that, after acquiring the property and before spending money on development and equipment, the company can generate a cash offer of $5 million for the property with the execution of the sale agreement and cash payment at year 1. Is it economically better for the company to sell or keep and develop the property?

C) Determine the sale value at year 1 that makes the economics of selling break-even with development for the sale assumptions of part B.

D) If development is partially financed with $5 million borrowed at 10% annual interest at time 0, to be paid off with 4 equal mortgage payments at years 1 through 4, calculate the leveraged investment DCFROR and NPV for a leveraged minimum escalated dollar DCFROR of 15%.

E) Determine the sale value at year 1 that makes the economics of selling break-even with development using borrowed money for the sale assumptions of part B.

34. A pipeline to transport natural gas from a new gas well to an existing trunk line is estimated to cost $200,000 at time 0 with escalated dollar operating costs estimated at $9,000 per year at each of production years 1 through 4. The gas well is expected to be shut-in at the end of year 4 and that the pipeline's salvage value will be 0. The projected natural gas production to be handled by the pipeline is as follows where "MMcf" = million cubic feet:

Year	0	1	2	3	4
Average Annual Production (MMcf)	-	2,000	1,500	1,000	500

The pipeline cost of $200,000 is to be depreciated over a 7-year life using MACRS depreciation, starting in year 1 with the half-year convention. A write-off on remaining book value would be taken at year 4. Assume an effective income tax rate of 40%. Calculate the uniform transportation price per Mcf (thousand cubic feet) of natural gas transported that would give the pipeline investor:

A) A 15% escalated dollar DCFROR on invested capital.
B) A 15% constant dollar DCFROR on invested capital for inflation of 8% per year over the project life.

35. A conveyor to transport coal (or mineral concentrate) from a loading point to a shipping facility is estimated to cost $200,000 at time 0 with escalated dollar operating costs estimated at $9,000 per year at each of production years 1 through 4. The use of the conveyor is expected to terminate at the end of year 4 and that the conveyor's salvage value will be 0. The projected coal (or mineral concentrate) production to be handled by the conveyor is as follows where "M tons" = thousand tons:

Year	0	1	2	3	4
Average Annual Production (M tons)	-	2,000	1,500	1,000	500

The conveyor cost of $200,000 is to be depreciated over a 7-year life using MACRS depreciation, starting in year 1 with the half-year convention. A write-off on remaining book value would be taken at year 4. Assume an effective income tax rate of 40%. Calculate the uniform transportation price per ton of coal (or mineral concentrate) transported that would give the investor:

A) A 15% escalated dollar DCFROR on invested capital.
B) A 15% constant dollar DCFROR on invested capital for inflation of 8% per year over the project life.

36. An investment opportunity has projected costs and revenues as shown on the diagram in thousands of dollars.

C=450	I=200 C=300	I=250 C=450	I=575 C=225	I=600 C=150	I=600 C=150	I=600 C=250
0	1	2	3	4	5	6

The investor's minimum rate of return is 12%, calculate the project before-tax cash flow (BTCF) and then determine the ROR, NPV, PVR and Growth ROR for the project using the 6-year evaluation life. Then develop the cumulative cash position diagram to illustrate the meaning of the rate of return result. Finally, develop the cumulative NPV diagram and indicate the project maximum capital exposure, discounted payback and NPV on your diagram.

37. Rank these non-mutually exclusive alternatives if other opportunities exist to earn a before-tax minimum rate of return of 10%. Values are in thousands of dollars.

A)

-300	-200	100 -250	550 -300	600	600	600
0	1	2	3	4	5	6

B)

-	-500	-150	350	450	550
0	1	2	3	4	5

C)

-200	150	-500	600	600
0	1	2	3	4

38. A production facility is currently utilizing carbon steel tubing. The current process requires injection of chemicals to control tubing corrosion due to high temperatures and pressures and corrosive chlorides in the product. It is proposed to replace the carbon steel that cost $12 per foot 1 year ago, with chrome stainless steel tubing that would cost $38 per foot today, (time zero). 20,000 feet of tubing would be required and installation costs are estimated to total $100,000 (also at time zero).

Annual cost savings in chemicals, labor and chemical injection equipment are projected to be $250,000 in year 1 following the installation of the new tubing with savings escalating 7% per year in succeeding years. Use a 6-year evaluation life with a salvage value of zero at the end of year 6. Assume a 15% minimum ROR. Use NPV and ROR analyses to determine if installation of the chrome tubing is economically desirable. Assume the existing carbon steel tubing has no salvage value today, at time 0.

39. An existing operation is producing annual before-tax cash flows (BTCF) of $125 million per year (assume end-of-year values) expected to be realized over the next 4 years (years 1-4). However, if environmental improvements are not made, the property will have to be shut down in year 5. Assume the cash flow from year five will be used to cover all shutdown costs in that period (therefore zero cash flow would be realized in year 5 and beyond).

An alternative to a plant shutdown is to make the necessary environmental improvements to the property. These improvements would include expenditures of $50 million now (time zero) with the expectation that $125 million would be spent in year 1 and another $95 million cost incurred at the end of year 2. In addition to maintaining the existing cash flow, these expenditures would extend the life of the plant and increase the cash flow from operations to the separate figures identified on the "upgrade" diagram below. An equipment repair/replace expenditure of $75 million has been charged to the project at the end of year 6. Terminal value is estimated to total $50 million at year 10.

Values in millions;

BTCF Current	0	125	125	125	125	0	0	0	0	0	0
	0	1	2	3	4	5	6	7	8	9	10

		0	125	140	160	175	75	75	75	75	75	75
		-50	-125	-95				-75				50
BTCF Upgrade		-50	0	45	160	175	75	0	75	75	75	125
		0	1	2	3	4	5	6	7	8	9	10

Use NPV analysis to determine if the upgrade is economically justifiable. The investor's minimum rate of return is 15%. Verify your NPV analysis conclusion using ROR and PVR. Remember that these later techniques require an incremental analysis when evaluating mutually exclusive alternatives.

40. Suppose you want to acquire a computer for use during the next three years. After identifying the machine, you are now considering whether it is economically better to purchase the unit with cash or to make beginning of month lease payments over the next 36 months (months 0-35). Sales tax is 7.0% and shipping charges amount to $125 for either alternative. If you purchase the machine, the cost today is $3,400 and salvage is negligible.

If you choose to lease, the payment is $115 per month, beginning today. Neglect any option to purchase upon termination of the lease as the machine will likely be worthless after three years. Your minimum rate of return is a nominal 12.0% compounded monthly. Use a 35 month-life and present a nominal rate of return analysis to determine which alternative is economically preferred. This is for personal use so no tax effects are relevant.

41. A commercial airline has a decision that has to be made concerning replacement of an air duct associated with an SF6 engine. The original design of the air duct allows for the duct itself to loosen, which can result in severe vibrations that have required unscheduled engine repairs (UER's). The cost of an unscheduled repair is estimated at $1,500,000 in today's dollars. This cost is based on anticipated flight cancellations, diversions and related duct and engine repairs. Such costs will escalate 7.0% in future years.

A new duct has been designed and a schedule for replacing the existing units with the new design is being proposed. The total fleet cost of duct replacement is estimated in today's dollars (shown below). These costs will actually escalate 7.0% per year. Due to the scheduled installation over two years, the company can expect to incur a total of three unscheduled engine repairs due to the severe vibration problem. Allocate two of the anticipated UER's to the end of year 1 with the remaining failure expected to occur at time zero.

Installation should result in savings, or avoidance of 2 unscheduled engine repairs per year beginning in year 2. How many years of savings will be required for the company to get a 12.0% return on the investments? Be sure to account for all escalation in this analysis and calculate the breakeven life on a cumulative and discounted basis.

Summary data in today's dollars:

Year	Installation Cost	UER Costs	Annual Savings
0	-1,500,000	-1,500,000	-
1	-1,500,000	-3,000,000	-
2	-500,000	-	3,000,000
3	-	-	3,000,000
4	-	-	3,000,000
5	-	-	3,000,000
6	-	-	3,000,000
?	Breakeven life n = ?		

42. Two used engines that are not currently utilized in a commercial airline's fleet are leased periodically by the airline for average annual income totaling $400,000 for both engines. Average annual operating costs to maintain both engines total $100,000 per year. These numbers are believed to be attainable for the next 2 years, after which, a total modification cost of $250,000 for both engines will be required (assume an end of year 2 cost). Depreciate the $250,000 modification cost straight line over 5 years starting in year 3 since it is assumed to extend the life of the engines. This modification will allow the engines to generate total lease income of $500,000 per year for the next 3 years (3, 4 & 5). Assume the same total operating costs of $100,000 in each of those years. To simplify the analysis, assume the engines would be scrapped at the end of year 5 as spare parts for a total value of $200,000. The current historical book value of the engines is a combined $500,000. The book value has three remaining years of depreciation amounting to $200,000 per year for the next 2 years (1 & 2) and $100,000 in year 3.

The effective tax rate is 40% and other income is assumed to exist against which to use deductions. The after-tax minimum rate of return is 12.0%.

The company is considering selling the engines for $1,200,000 today. From an economic viewpoint, would you recommend selling or keeping the engines and leasing them for the next 5 years?

43. A commercial airline needs to develop a maintenance program for equipment utilizing a new destination site. The company has to make a decision of either; outsourcing the necessary maintenance to a competitor with maintenance facilities already in place, or, develop their own on-site program. The anticipated end of year one cost of the outsource approach would be $8,500,000, increasing to $9,000,000 in year 2 and $9,500,000 in years 3, 4 and 5.

If they choose to develop, the initial outlay would total $12,500,000 in equipment and spare parts inventory costs. The assumed salvage value is $6,500,000 after five years inclusive of all equipment and inventory returns. Operating costs would be $5,000,000 in year 1, $5,500,000 in year two and $6,500,000 in each of years 3, 4 and 5. The investor's minimum rate of return is 10.0%. Use present worth cost analysis to determine which alternative is economically preferred and support those cost findings with an incremental NPV analysis.

The 2 five-year programs can be summarized on the following diagrams;
All values are in (000's).

Outsource, BTCF	0	-8,500	-9,000	-9,500	-9,500	-9,500
Year	0	1	2	3	4	5
Develop, BTCF	-12,500	-5,000	-5,500	-6,500	-6,500	0
Year	0	1	2	3	4	5

44. A venture capitalist is considering investing in the following project. From an economic viewpoint, would you recommend it? This business would require expenditures at time 0 of $320,000 for land, $300,000 for inventory working capital, $1,800,000 for a business building, $3,000,000 for equipment and $360,000 for vehicles. Starting in year 1 it is estimated that production will generate annual end-of-year escalated revenue of $5,000,000 with escalated operating costs of $2,000,000. In the following years, it is estimated that revenues will escalate at 12% per year while operating costs will escalate 8% per year. At the end of year 4, it is expected that all the assets and working capital can be sold for an escalated terminal value of $6,000,000. Use straight-line depreciation over 39 years for the building cost starting in year 1, neglect the impact from the mid-month convention in year 1. Also, use straight-line depreciation for a 7-year life for the equipment cost starting in year 1 and straight-line depreciation for a 5-year life for the vehicles also starting in year 1 (assume the half-year convention is relevant for both the 7 and 5 year property in year 1). Assume the sale value gain is taxed as ordinary income. Write-off the remaining tax-book values at the end of year 4.

Determine the investment DCFROR, assuming a 40% effective income tax rate. For an after-tax escalated dollar minimum ROR of 15%, also determine the NPV and PVR.

45. Your company is currently considering an acceleration program to enhance the timing of production and quantity of reserves from an existing lease. The before-tax cash flows for the two alternatives are summarized below.

Current	-	3,600	2,800	2,200	1,640	1,120	600
	0	1	2	3	4	5	6

Proposed	-2,940	7,000	4,600	2,400	400	0	0
	0	1	2	3	4	5	6

The investor's before-tax minimum rate of return is 12.0%. Use rate of return analysis to evaluate the economics of this acceleration program and support those findings with NPV analysis.

46. Two used machines can be rebuilt for $50,000 per machine to provide necessary service for the next 2 years. The current value of each machine is $10,000 which relates to an opportunity cost if the machines are kept, or sale cash to help pay for the new alternative. Only one of these approaches should be considered in your solution. The salvage of these machines is estimated at $30,000 per machine at the end of year 2 when the old machines will be replaced with one new machine capable of providing the same total service. The new machine would cost $340,000 at the end of year 2 and is anticipated to yield a salvage value of $200,000 at the end of year 4. Operating costs associated with the used machines are estimated at $50,000 per machine at year 1 and $60,000 per machine at year 2. Operating costs with a new machine purchased at year 2 are estimated to be $80,000 at year 3 and $85,000 at year 4.

Instead of rebuilding the old machines and replacing them at year 2, a new machine providing the necessary service can be purchased today (time 0) for a cost of $300,000. Service with either the old or new machines is needed for the next 4 years; therefore, a 4-year evaluation life should be used. It is estimated that a new machine purchased at time 0 will yield a salvage value of $80,000 at year 4. Operating costs with a new machine purchased now (time 0) are estimated at $75,000 at year 1, $80,000 at year 2, $85,000 at year 3, and $90,000 at year 4. Assuming a minimum discount rate of 15%, use net present value analysis and determine the economically preferred approach for providing the necessary service.

47. Suppose you wanted to borrow $200,000 to apply towards the purchase of a home. You have found terms that include a 30-year annual percentage rate (APR) of 7.0% compounded monthly. But the loan includes 2.5 points, which will be paid out of the loan amount at closing. (A point is equal to 1% of the loan value).

A) Calculate the monthly mortgage payment.
B) How much interest is paid on the 2nd month's payment?
C) How much principal is paid on the 2nd month's payment?
D) What is the effective interest rate, or effective cost of borrowing from this lender?

Case D recognizes the cost of points, and asks you to express the cost in terms of the effective compound interest really being paid. You must recognize that you will not have $200,000 to apply against the purchase, (due to the points), but will have to pay back $200,000 in principal payments plus the accrued interest. Note that the term "effective interest," as used here is different than in savings account examples related to the development and application of text Equation 2-9.

NOTES ON D,D&A CALCULATIONS

MACRS Depreciation Table 7-3, p. 347

Year	3	5	7	10
1	.3333	.2000	.1429	.1000
2	.4445	.3200	.2449	.1800
3	.1481	.1920	.1749	.1440
4	.0741	.1152	.1249	.1152
5		.1152	.0893	.0922
6		.0576	.0892	.0737
7			.0893	.0655
8			.0446	.0655
9				.0656
10				.0655
11				.0328

Regular Corporation, Mining Project
- Expense 70% of Development & Exploration, p. 331-2.
- Amortize 30% of Dev. & Explor. Over 60 Months, p. 331-2.
- Take Larger of Percentage or Cost Depletion, p.350.
Use Table 7-4, & 50% Limit on Percentage Depln, p. 353-4.

Integrated Petroleum Company Project
- Expense 70% of Intangible Drilling Costs, p. 332-3.
- Amortize 30% of IDC's Over 60 Months, p. 333.
- Only Take Cost Depletion, p. 350.

Non-Integrated Petroleum Company Project
- Expense 100% of Intangible Drilling Costs, p. 332-3.
- Take Larger of Percentage or Cost Depletion
  On First 1,000 Bbls/Day of Production, Table 7-4, p. 350.
- 100% Limit Applies to Qualifying Percentage Depletion
- Cost Depletion Only on Prod. Above 1,000 Bbl/Day

Cost Depletion, Pg 350.

Percentage Depletion Rates in Table 7-5, Pg 354.

Cost Depletion, Pg. 350.

$$\frac{\text{Units Removed \& Sold Each Yr.}}{\text{Total Reserves @ Beginning of Yr.}} \;(\text{Adjusted Basis})(\quad) = \text{Cost Depletion}$$

"Adjusted Basis" is reduced each year for "actual" depletion taken in preceding year.

SUMMARY WORKSHEET FOR CASH FLOW CALCULATIONS

PROBLEM #	Time 0	1	2	3	4	5	6	7
Year								
Production								
Selling Price $/Unit								
Gross Revenue								
- Royalties								
Net Revenue								
- Research / Develop / IDC's								
- Operating Expense								
- Depreciation								
- Amortization								
- Writeoff's on D, D & A								
Taxable Income Before Depl.								
- Limit (50% or 100%)								
- Percentage Depletion								
- Cost Depletion								
- Loss Forward								
Taxable Income								
- Tax @ ___ %								
+Tax Credits (If Applic.)								
= Net Income								
+ Depreciation Deduction								
+ Amortization Deduction								
+ Depletion Deduction								
+ Writeoff's on D, D & A								
+ Loss Forward Deduction								
Capital Costs:								
- Depreciable Equip. Costs								
- Amortizable Costs								
- Mineral Rts. Acq. Costs								
- Land (Surface Rts)								
- Working Capital								
- Other								
= Cash Flow								
x(P/F 12%, n)	1.0000	.8929	.7972	.7118	.6355	.5674	.5066	.4523
= PW Cash Flow								
= Cum. CF (Yearly NPV)								

Table 7-4, Text Pg 353, (Not Applicable for Integrated Producer's & Independents Over 1,000 Bbls/Day)

Percentage Depletion →
50% / 100% Limit on
Percentage Depletion → Take Smaller → Take Larger as Allowed Depletion
(Apply Table 7-4 Each Year)

Cost Depletion → Cost Depletion

SUMMARY WORKSHEET FOR CASH FLOW CALCULATIONS

PROBLEM #							
Year	Time 0	1	2	3	4	5	6	7
Production								
Selling Price $/Unit								
Gross Revenue								
- Royalties								
Net Revenue								
- Operating Expense								
- Research / Develop / IDC's								
- Depreciation								
- Amortization								
- Writeoffs on D, D & A								
Taxable Income Before Depl.								
- Limit (50% or 100%)								
- Percentage Depletion								
- Cost Depletion								
- Loss Forward								
Taxable Income								
- Tax @ %								
+Tax Credits (If Applic.)								
= Net Income								
+ Depreciation Deduction								
+ Amortization Deduction								
+ Depletion Deduction								
+ Writeoffs on D, D & A								
+ Loss Forward Deduction								
- Capital Costs:								
- Depreciable Equip. Costs								
- Amortizable Costs								
- Mineral Rts. Acq. Costs								
- Land (Surface Rts)								
- Working Capital								
- Other								
= Cash Flow								
x(P/F 12%, n)	1.0000	.8929	.7972	.7118	.6355	.5674	.5066	.4523
= PW Cash Flow								
= Cum. CF (Yearly NPV)								

NOTES ON D,D&A CALCULATIONS

MACRS Depreciation Table 7-3, p. 347

Year	3	5	7	10
1	.3333	.2000	.1429	.1000
2	.4445	.3200	.2449	.1800
3	.1481	.1920	.1749	.1440
4	.0741	.1152	.1249	.1152
5		.1152	.0893	.0922
6		.0576	.0892	.0737
7			.0893	.0655
8			.0446	.0655
9				.0656
10				.0655
11				.0328

Regular Corporation, Mining Project
- Expense 70% of Development & Exploration, p. 331-2.
- Amortize 30% of Dev. & Explor. Over 60 Months, p. 331-2.
- Take Larger of Percentage or Cost Depletion, p.350.
- Use Table 7-4, & 50% Limit on Percentage Depln, p. 353-4.

Integrated Petroleum Company Project
- Expense 70% of Intangible Drilling Costs, p. 332-3.
- Amortize 30% of IDC's Over 60 Months, p. 333.
- Only Take Cost Depletion, p. 350.

Non-Integrated Petroleum Company Project
- Expense 100% of Intangible Drilling Costs, p. 332-3.
- Take Larger of Percentage or Cost Depletion
  On First 1,000 Bbls/Day of Production, Table 7-4, p. 350.
- 100% Limit Applies to Qualifying Percentage Depletion
- Cost Depletion Only on Prod. Above 1,000 Bbl/Day

Cost Depletion, Pg 350.

$$\frac{\text{Units Removed \& Sold Each Yr.}}{\text{Total Reserves @ Beginning of Yr.}} \times (\text{Adjusted Basis}) = \text{Cost Depletion}$$

"Adjusted Basis" is reduced each year for "actual" depletion taken in preceding year.

Percentage Depletion Rates in Table 7-5, Pg 354.

SUMMARY WORKSHEET FOR CASH FLOW CALCULATIONS

PROBLEM # _____

Year	Time 0	1	2	3	4	5	6	7
Production								
Selling Price $/Unit								
Gross Revenue								
- Royalties								
Net Revenue								
- Research / Develop / IDC's								
= Net Income								
- Tax @ ___ %								
Taxable Income								
- Loss Forward								
- Cost Depletion								
- Percentage Depletion								
- Limit (50% or 100%)								
Taxable Income Before Depl.								
- Writeoff's on D, D & A								
- Amortization								
- Depreciation								
- Operating Expense								
Net Revenue								
- Research / Develop / IDC's								
= Net Income								
+ Tax Credits (If Applic.)								
= Net Income								
+ Depreciation Deduction								
+ Amortization Deduction								
+ Depletion Deduction								
+ Writeoff's on D, D & A								
+ Loss Forward Deduction								
- Capital Costs:								
- Depreciable Equip. Costs								
- Amortizable Costs								
- Mineral Rts. Acq. Costs								
- Land (Surface Rts)								
- Working Capital								
- Other								
= Cash Flow								
x(P/F 12%, n)	1.0000	.8929	.7972	.7118	.6355	.5674	.5066	.4523
= PW Cash Flow								
= Cum. CF (Yearly NPV)								

Table 7-4, Text Pg 353, (Not Applicable for Integrated Producer's & Independents Over 1,000 Bbls/Day)

Percentage Depletion

50% / 100% Limit on Percentage Depletion

→ Take Smaller →

Cost Depletion →

→ Take Larger as Allowed Depletion (Apply Table 7-4 Each Year)

SUMMARY WORKSHEET FOR CASH FLOW CALCULATIONS

PROBLEM #							
Year	Time 0	1	2	3	4	5	6	7
Production							
Selling Price $/Unit							
Gross Revenue							
- Royalties							
Net Revenue							
- Research / Develop / IDC's							
- Operating Expense							
- Depreciation							
- Amortization							
- Writeoff's on D, D & A							
Taxable Income Before Depl.							
- Limit (50% or 100%)							
- Percentage Depletion							
- Cost Depletion							
- Loss Forward							
Taxable Income							
- Tax @ %							
+Tax Credits (If Applic.)							
= Net Income							
+ Depreciation Deduction							
+ Amortization Deduction							
+ Depletion Deduction							
+ Writeoff's on D, D & A							
+ Loss Forward Deduction							
- Capital Costs:							
- Depreciable Equip. Costs							
- Amortizable Costs							
- Mineral Rts. Acq. Costs							
- Land (Surface Rts)							
- Working Capital							
- Other							
= Cash Flow							
x(P/F 12%, n)	1.0000	.8929	.7972	.7118	.6355	.5674	.5066	.4523
= PW Cash Flow							
= Cum. CF (Yearly NPV)							

MACRS Depreciation Table 7-3, p. 347

Year	3	5	7	10
1	.3333	.2000	.1429	.1000
2	.4445	.3200	.2449	.1800
3	.1481	.1920	.1749	.1440
4	.0741	.1152	.1249	.1152
5		.1152	.0893	.0922
6		.0576	.0892	.0737
7			.0893	.0655
8			.0446	.0655
9				.0656
10				.0655
11				.0328

Regular Corporation, Mining Project
- Expense 70% of Development & Exploration, p. 331-2.
- Amortize 30% of Dev. & Explor Over 60 Months, p. 331-2.
- Take Larger of Percentage or Cost Depletion, p.350.
- Use Table 7-4, & 50% Limit on Percentage Depln, p. 353-4.

Integrated Petroleum Company Project
- Expense 70% of Intangible Drilling Costs, p. 332-3.
- Amortize 30% of IDC's Over 60 Months, p. 333.
- Only Take Cost Depletion, p. 350.

Non-Integrated Petroleum Company Project
- Expense 100% of Intangible Drilling Costs, p. 332-3.
- Take Larger of Percentage or Cost Depletion
  On First 1,000 Bbls/Day of Production, Table 7-4, p. 350.
- 100% Limit Applies to Qualifying Percentage Depletion
- Cost Depletion Only on Prod. Above 1,000 Bbl/Day

Cost Depletion, Pg 350.

Percentage Depletion Rates in Table 7-5, Pg 354.

$$\frac{\text{Units Removed \& Sold Each Yr.}}{\text{Total Reserves @ Beginning of Yr}} = \text{Cost Depletion}$$

(Adjusted Basis)( )

"Adjusted Basis" is reduced each year for "actual" depletion taken in preceding year.

Table 7-4, Text Pg 353, (Not Applicable for Integrated Producer's & Independents Over 1,000 Bbls/Day)

Percentage Depletion ⟶ Take Smaller
50% / 100% Limit on
Percentage Depletion

Cost Depletion ⟶ Take Larger as Allowed Depletion
(Apply Table 7-4 Each Year)

SUMMARY WORKSHEET FOR CASH FLOW CALCULATIONS

PROBLEM # ___

Year	Time 0	1	2	3	4	5	6	7
Production								
Selling Price $/Unit								
Gross Revenue								
- Royalties								
Net Revenue								
- Research / Develop / IDC's								
- Operating Expense								
- Depreciation								
- Amortization								
- Writeoff's on D, D & A								
Taxable Income Before Depl.								
- Percentage Depletion								
- Cost Depletion								
- Loss Forward								
Taxable Income								
- Tax @ ___ %								
+ Tax Credits (If Applic.)								
= Net Income								
+ Depreciation Deduction								
+ Amortization Deduction								
+ Depletion Deduction								
+ Writeoff's on D, D & A								
+ Loss Forward Deduction								
- Capital Costs:								
- Depreciable Equip. Costs								
- Amortizable Costs								
- Mineral Rts. Acq. Costs								
- Land (Surface Rts)								
- Working Capital								
- Other								
= Cash Flow								
x (P/F 12%, n)	1.0000	.8929	.7972	.7118	.6355	.5674	.5066	.4523
= PW Cash Flow								
= Cum. CF (Yearly NPV)								

- Limit (50% or 100%)